Hannah   2013
- from Mom
        I started
this book and
Hannah would love
this! So here is your
copy.

Starting from Scratch

Starting from Scratch
Memoirs of a Wandering Cook

Patty Kirk

THOMAS NELSON
Since 1798

NASHVILLE   DALLAS   MEXICO CITY   RIO DE JANEIRO   BEIJING

Published in Nashville, Tennessee, by Thomas Nelson. Thomas Nelson is a registered trademark of Thomas Nelson, Inc.

Thomas Nelson, Inc. titles may be purchased in bulk for educational, business, fund-raising, or sales promotional use. For information, please e-mail SpecialMarkets@ThomasNelson.com.

Scripture quotations marked NIV are from HOLY BIBLE: NEW INTERNATIONAL VERSION®. © 1973, 1978, 1984 by International Bible Society. Used by permission of Zondervan Publishing House. All rights reserved.

Scripture quotations marked KJV are from KING JAMES VERSION.

In some cases, names and details have been changed or left out entirely to make people or events less recognizable.

Library of Congress Cataloging-in-Publication Data

Kirk, Patty.
    Starting from scratch : memoirs of a wandering cook / Patty Kirk.
      p. cm.
    Includes index.
    ISBN 978-0-7852-2047-3
    1. Cookery. 2. Food writing. 3. Kirk, Patty. I. Title.
TX652.K466 2007
641.5—dc22   2007038626

Printed in the United States of America

07 08 09 10 11 QW 5 4 3 2 1

Dedication

L ong ago, back when women owned no land, enjoyed little formal education, and seldom looked for employment beyond the boundaries of the family plot, tutelage in how to cook was often a daughter's sole inheritance. Later, women joined the literate and enlarged their daughters' birthright with recipes scribbled on scraps of paper or in diaries or in the margins of the family cookbook. Nowadays, most women, like me, have jobs and other interests outside the kitchen, and we assume our daughters will, too. Ever fewer of us find time or energy to cook daily meals, much less to teach our children to cook. Families subsist increasingly on food prepared by factories and mercenaries. Cooking has become a hobby of the elite, and the ordinary cooks of the past, our mothers' mothers and their mothers before them, are gradually fading from memory. As a result, not only our children but culture itself is losing an irretrievable legacy: the art and praxis of daily nourishment.

I dedicate these food stories and recipes to my daughters, Charlotte and Lulu. Although they, like many of their generation, did not learn to cook at my side, they were nevertheless nourished from childhood at my table, from birth at my breast, from the very first moments of life—as they explained to me once when they were little—from the same blood that pulses through my veins and capillaries and animates my fingers and nose and tongue. Lest you think me proud of these acts of provision, let me stress that they are God's miracles, not mine. He created in our very bodies the capacity not only to create other beings like us but to provide them with perfect food, just as he created and provides for us—all marvels for which I can never be sufficiently grateful.

This book represents, above all, my attempt at thanks for our abundant provision, through no merit of our own, at God's hand. For Charlotte and Lulu, I hope the book will serve as something like an inheritance, one I wish I had from their grandmother, who died before they were born, and from *her* mother and all the mothers before them: namely, the tangible vestige of those forgotten cooks' shared presence in us as we stir and sniff and taste a meal into existence and place it before the ones we love.

Contents

1

Good Food, Finally

Shortly before my mother's death after a long struggle with a brain tumor, my sister Sharon brought her home from the nursing home where she had been living for some months. The increasing dementia of her last years and the nursing home's monotonous routine had dulled her. She had stopped responding to the nurses' jokes and requests, stopped paying attention to what was going on around her, stopped eating with any enthusiasm, stopped talking. The nurses no longer strapped her into her wheelchair every morning but frequently left her empty-eyed in bed. They told my sister that, in the end, Mom would become unable to swallow. When that happened, they said, she'd have to be fed through a tube, if at all. Her overall sensory lethargy made it clear that such a time was approaching.

On the evening of our mother's return to Sharon's house, where she had lived for years before the sojourn at the nursing home, Sharon made tacos for dinner. It was complicated food for an invalid: the fried corn tortillas precariously filled and hard to swallow. Just for form's sake—and perhaps remembering that tacos had been one of our mother's favorite foods throughout our childhood—Sharon raised one to Mom's mouth. She bit, looked around her as if waking up in a familiar room after a terrifying dream, chewed, and then pronounced her first words in many weeks: "Good food, finally."

I wasn't there at the time. I wouldn't arrive on the scene until a few months later to hear the story and, as my other siblings trickled in from other cities and states, to watch our mother die. Nevertheless, those words, that moment, those tacos, resonate in me as though I had experienced them firsthand. As though I had heard them. As though I had said them myself. In my mind, I crack the chewy-crisp tortilla with my own teeth with the same astonishment and delight that jolted my mom's almost mute tongue into words of gratitude.

It seems fitting to me that we eat and speak with the same organ, that we both enjoy food and communicate with the same assemblage of muscles and membranes and bones. The mouth was made for acts of appreciation, I think. To taste God's gifts. To give back thanks.

My mother's words of candid appreciation of my sister's cooking unconsciously mimic God's own words of approval in the first days, when we're told again and again, "And God saw that it was good" and even "very good." But my mother's words were also wistful, calling to notice at once the bland institutional food of the nursing home in her present experience and the distant memory of foods she had loved in an irretrievable past—before the nursing home, before the brain tumor, before my sister and I were born perhaps—back when sensory pleasures were things to be pursued, not merely happened upon, when they were so likely to be encountered that they often went unappreciated. Perhaps, in a reverie of gratitude for the crack of the tortilla and the tang of tomato and peppers, my mother's tongue was summoning the other corn dishes she had loved in her receding past: the tamale pies she had concocted for my father in the early years of their marriage, the Fritos corn chips to which she was addicted in her teenage years, the cornbread with lima beans and chow chow she ate at her own mother's table as a child.

In my mother's words, distilled, I hear the longings of my own lost past: my fading childhood, the blind flights of my later years, and the stirrings of my struggles to return home. I see myself in the kitchens of my memory: teaching myself to cook as a child, gleaning everything I could of cookery unknown to me from my parents' and grandparents' and friends' families, cooking with friends in college, working in restaurants in my years abroad, eating alone, cooking for my new husband and my countrified mother-in-law, for my demanding daughters. I see the recipes I have accumulated over the years, some my own, others given to me. Scraps of paper in piles on shelves or spilling out of folders. Cryptic scribblings in the margins of my cookbooks. A plastic box of yellowed index cards that represents one of my many failed attempts to organize the good food of my life into something accessible, repeatable, eternal.

The language of food commands a complex rhetoric. What we cook and eat is, after all, an expression of who we are, what we value, how we live. In all cultures, the meals we prepare express and comment upon our emotions. We eat to celebrate good fortune as well as to assuage misery. We cook special meals to commemorate important life events: belonging, leaving, joining, mourning. In the extremes of loneliness and longing, we remember the foods of our past lives, just as the fleeing Israelites yearned for the cucumbers and onions they had eaten as slaves in Egypt. In pain, in loss, in terror, these memories comfort us.

I have a cookbook written by women in the Terezin ghetto during the last years of the Second World War, a compilation of recipes for elaborate dishes whose ingredients were long since unavailable to the ghetto's starving inmates, recipes representing a prosperity and leisure these women would never recover, if they survived at all, and most of them didn't. Recipes frequently *are* our loved ones' survival: not merely voices from the past but tastes, smells, and textures that outlast the grave.

In fact, as anthropologist Arjun Appadurai concludes in an article on cookbooks in contemporary India, "cookbooks appear to belong to the literature of exile, of nostalgia and loss." Our recipes represent our often unsuccessful attempts to relive the past, to recover lost comforts or reclaim a forgotten heritage. We take them with us into foreign lands. We pass them on to our friends and children. We share them with strangers. The foods of our pasts are the most elemental artifacts of who we are: who our parents and friends and lovers were and are, where we have been and where we ended up, what we treasure, what we disdain, what fuels our endeavors, what comforts, what sustains. So powerful is food as an expression of the self that we even orchestrate favorite meals for those we execute. We want to honor at least that much of the worst criminal. Good food. Finally.

Somewhere in our hearts, we all hunger for what good food represents. Comfort. Succor. Abundance. We long for the first fruits of God's love for his creation: literally fruit, his gift of all the seed-bearing plants and trees. Like the Israelites in the desert, we study the horizon for evidence of his abiding provision to his children. We long not only to enjoy this food ourselves but to proffer it to one another, to mimic and complete God's most essential creative act—provision—in the baking and sharing of our daily bread. In my mother's wistful words, I hear a latent challenge that it's up to me, the family cook, as a child and now, to pass on what I have learned of provision to my children and my children's children and thereby to model and encourage the only godly habit I seem capable of practicing without considerable effort: appreciation. Good food. Finally.

TACOS THE WAY MY FAMILY MADE THEM

Use three times as many tortillas as you have people eating.

Heat about 1/4 inch oil in a skillet. Slip a tortilla into the hot oil. When the edges are beginning to appear cooked but the tortilla is still flexible, turn it over with tongs and fold it in half, using the tongs to keep it slightly open. After one side of the folded tortilla browns and hardens, turn it over and fry the other side. Drain the fried tortilla open side down in a baking pan lined with paper towels while you fry the remaining tortillas. When tortillas have all been fried, remove the paper towel and arrange the taco shells open side up in the baking pan. Fill each taco about 1/3 full with meat filling (Recipe follows.) and grated Monterey Jack or cheddar cheese. Keep the tacos warm in a 250° oven until serving, which should be soon. The cheese should melt but not harden.

At the table, each person fills his or her own tacos with some or all of the following, set out in pretty bowls:

shredded lettuce (It was always iceberg lettuce when I was a child, but now I coarsely chop the leaf lettuce that I use in salads.)

chopped tomatoes

chopped sweet onion (I have had numerous Central and South American students complain that the food item they miss the most from back home is the onion, which is milder and more flavorful than the yellow onions we eat. Although this dish is more Californian than it is genuinely Mexican, I still recommend that you buy the sweetest onions you can get—Vidalias, Texas Sweet, or almost any Mexican variety. They may cost more, but they're worth it.)

chopped green pepper

sour cream

fresh salsa (Salsa wasn't known in my childhood but is indispensable nowadays.)

Meat Filling

Sauté about one pound of ground beef (enough for 12 tacos) until it goes from pink to grey. Add 1 to 2 tablespoons chili powder per pound and salt to taste.

Salsa

I usually make lots of salsa—enough to fill a large mixing bowl. Store any leftovers in the refrigerator to use in omelets; on leftover Mexican food; with chips; or, with the addition of a chopped cucumber and vinegar and sugar to taste, as gazpacho.

Chop:

> **some good-looking fresh tomatoes**—I like to mix sandwich-style with plums.
> **green chile peppers**—ancho, jalapeño, serrano, and/or others that smell
>   intriguing
> **a good smelling bell pepper**
> **a sweet white onion**
> **a few green onions**
> **a big handful of well washed cilantro**
> **a smashed garlic clove**

Mix everything together in a big pretty bowl as you chop. Do *not* use a food processor. It will make the mixture too mushy and will also create tiny, white air bubbles that dull the deep reds and greens of the salsa to a less appealing pink with light green specks. Add salt to taste. Let the salsa sit out for a while on the counter (not in the refrigerator) to let the juices run. If the resulting salsa is not juicy enough to suit you, add a little more salt and/or some cut-up canned tomatoes or a big spoonful of prepared salsa from a jar.

An Imaginary Ancient Israeli Salad

Here's what I imagine those Israelites were thinking about when they longed for cucumbers and onions: the simplest and most refreshing salad in the world that I, too, might fantasize about after a long sojourn in the desert. Make it in summer, when the vegetables come from local fields, not hothouses, and buy sweet onions, such as Vidalias. Or, better yet, use cucumbers and onions from your own garden.

Wash a cucumber; then peel off some or most of the skin, especially if it looks waxy, but leave little slivers of peel for color. Cut off the bitter stem end to the point at which you can see the sections of seeds. Cut along these sections to make three long spears. Slice the spears into thickish triangles into a bowl. (For me it's important to use a clear glass bowl for this dish.)

Peel a sweet onion. Then, using a paring knife, chip it into the bowl in irregular curved pieces somewhat smaller than the cucumber triangles.

Salt the cucumbers and onions and add a little chopped dill or mint, if you have some fresh. Or, instead of the herbs, use a little coarsely ground pepper. Add buttermilk, sour cream, or heavy cream and stir. I usually use sour, Bulgarian-style buttermilk these days, but as a child cooking for my family I used sour cream, and in Germany I made this salad with heavy cream and a pinch of sugar with the salt. Serve immediately.

2

Sucking on Steak

When I was a baby, my parents stuck a long strip of rare steak in my mouth. I sucked and gummed it white and bloodless. After they wrestled it from my fist, they gave me another strip and another, and it became a tradition that defined me, my first food obsession. Blood.

Of course, I don't remember any of this. I know it only from stories. And my parents didn't tell the rest of it, the setting and the parts about themselves. But I can piece it together from similar meals later in my childhood. My dad had grilled the steak on our little hibachi. It was probably sirloin, my dad's favorite. As the family got bigger, we ate chuck, which was cheaper. He had marinated the meat the day before in vinegar and oil seasoned with mashed garlic, Worcestershire, Tabasco, and whatever herbs and spices were on hand. I watched him cook while I sat in my mother's lap out on the patio. In my imagination, the iron patio furniture scraped on the dimpled concrete, and, when my dad went in to make the salad, the sliding glass door rumbled open and closed, exposing for a moment another inner world than the one I was sitting astride.

Somewhere behind the glass, my father whistled to himself and whacked the head of iceberg lettuce on the Formica counter to loosen the stem so he could gouge it out. Then he hacked about half of the gutted head of lettuce into chunks and scooped them from the chopping block into our big green Tupperware bowl, a multipurpose vessel with a grid-like, snap-on lid that I would later find perfect for collecting grasshoppers, mixing a cake batter, or bathing a small dog. My dad added to the lettuce chopped up onion, celery, cucumber, and whatever other vegetable was in the refrigerator. Except, probably, tomatoes, because I hate tomatoes in salads, and I don't know where else I could have gotten this

7

attitude from. Then my father came back out on the patio, chomping on the salted iceberg stem.

"The best part of the lettuce," he would tell my siblings and me every time he made salad as we were growing up. Sometimes he would pare off a celadon-green slice for one or the other of us so that we would know that what he said was true. It had a clean, vaguely astringent taste. Like hose water on the first hot day of summer.

My parents drank martinis. My mom held me tightly across the middle, facing outward, on her lap. She wore a dress with big flowers, tight across the belly already with my next sister, the third of what would be a total of six children in thirteen years. My older sister Sharon played in the sprinklers or at the pretend wishing well out in the front yard, returning every once in a while to be told not to get too near the hibachi. "It's hot!"

Before we sat down at the kitchen table to eat, my mom changed my diaper and sloshed together a bottle of Dr. Spock's famous formula of watered down evaporated milk and Karo syrup. My dad meanwhile dressed the salad with cider vinegar, salt, pepper, and just a dribble of oil. Sour salad, we called it in our family, the side dish of almost every meal. Nowadays I tear up loose salad greens instead of chopping head lettuce—iceberg makes me burp—and I take care to toss the vegetables with the oil first to make the dressing stick, but my dad just swished it all together however he happened to grab the ingredients.

With his bare hands he danced two huge baked potatoes off the cookie sheet in the oven, back and forth to the counter, and onto plates. Sharon would eat part of my mom's potato. Then we sat down at the chrome-rimmed kitchen table to eat, my parents first intoning the blessing:

> Bless us, oh Lord, for these Thy gifts, which we are about to receive, through Thy bounty, through Christ, our Lord, amen.

I'm sure my sister, like me in the years that followed, joined our parents in prayer, casting forth the jumble of words without really understanding their meaning beyond that their cadence in our mouths was a prerequisite to picking up a fork or dipping the serving spoon into a bowl on the table.

Sharon drank reconstituted skim milk, I had my formula, and my parents had a second martini. I was too young, then, to beg for one of their olives to savor the junipery tang of gin trapped in the coils of what in those days was a genuine piece of pimiento and not that chopped and formed red stuff that's in olives now. Tension from that second martini might build—triggered by my fussiness or Sharon spilling her milk or my mother complaining of being tired or telling the story of how one of our Southern California neighbors was looking down on an Arkie like her. Maybe she had gone by the house next door that morning to visit and the neighbor had yelled from inside, without opening the door, "I'm busy doing things," and my mom had taken it personally.

But meanwhile, before my parents' voices tightened into impatience and the laps and toys and rhythms of evening coalesced into bedtime, I alternately sucked the sweet formula and gummed the soft, slightly salty nub of meat, sensually the closest I would ever get to a wet warm human nipple, and I believed myself in heaven.

MY DAD'S GRILLED, MARINATED STEAK

Buy any big cheap cut of steak: chuck, sirloin, flank, etc. Pick the fattiest one you can find. Don't use expensive cuts for this recipe. Really good steaks should be grilled unadulterated by marinades and seasonings.

Put the steak in a gallon-size, ziplock bag with the following marinade:

About a cup of vinegar—cider, wine, balsamic, or a mixture

1/4 cup oil—olive oil, plain vegetable oil, or a mixture

1/4 cup soy sauce (In my childhood, my dad didn't use soy sauce, but he does now. I like it with or without.)

A good couple of dashes of Worcestershire sauce

A good dash of Tabasco sauce

A mixture of dried herbs such as rosemary, basil, thyme, oregano, etc.
One way to do this might be to use some from every jar of green herbs that you have. Alternately, use mostly a green herb that you especially like—such as dried basil—and a little of something else—say, sage—to complicate the flavor somewhat. Crumble the herbs as you add them to the bag. Of course, use fresh herbs, if you have them, in which case crush and tear them with your fingers.

A few garlic cloves smashed with the flat of a knife blade. Mash hard. This makes you look professional to anyone who happens to be in the kitchen and breaks the cloves up enough to release the juice. Go ahead and leave the papery skins on. They won't make it past the grilling. (Nowadays my dad uses garlic salt and onion salt. Old age has, in other words, set in. You can follow his lead if you want—or use a big scoop of that chopped up garlic that comes in jars, which Dad also buys these days. In truth, it doesn't matter. You can throw any sour or salty or savory thing you want into this marinade, and it will come out great.)

Salt and pepper

Zip the bag closed, squeezing out as much air as you can, and leave the bag on the counter all afternoon or in the refrigerator overnight or even as long as a couple of days. Don't be finicky about the raw meat sitting around that long. The vinegar sort of cooks it—at least, that's what they say of ceviche, the marinated raw fish dishes of Central America. Indeed, the surface of the marinated beef gets grayish, as though cooked. The longer you marinate it, the more deeply the flavors penetrate.

Grill the steak, sopping wet from the bag, directly over the coals. Just plop it on the hot grill. When the juices start to run on the top side and the edges are getting burnt, flip the steak over and grill the other side. A hibachi is great because the coals are so close to the meat that it gets black on the outside before the middle gets too done. You want it quite pink. To test doneness, press on the steak with your finger every minute or so after you turn it over. At first your finger will make a deep dent in the meat, but as the meat approaches that ideal place between red and pink, it will begin to resist pressure slightly. The more done it gets, the more it will resist. It's better to err on the side of raw for this dish. Expect the juices to be red and flavorful. If, after you've taken the meat off the grill and begun slicing, you find that it is too bloody for your taste—and do taste it to find out!—then plop the steak back on the grill just a tiny bit longer on each side.

Slice the steak on the slant into thin thin slices with a sharp butcher knife. Do it on a platter or something that will catch the juices, which will keep the meat wet and warm until it's eaten up. The juices can be drizzled on the baked potato you should be eating with this meal.

Caveat: Do NOT cook this meat too long. Cheap meats are too tough when grilled well-done. In my family, we like our meat black on the outside and close to raw in the middle. Even if you're in the habit of cooking your meat more than that, grill this marinated meat a bit rarer than you usually eat it. Diners who must have well-cooked meat—fools, according to my dad, for whom a restaurant's worst cuts of meat are destined—can eat the outermost edges. Even my Oklahoma husband, who used to raise cattle and grew up finding even the suggestion of undercooked beef repulsive, likes marinated steak grilled to a juicy, pink medium. Something about all that vinegar makes the juices not seem like blood to him, I guess.

THE RIGHT WAY TO DRESS A SALAD

I learned this method at a restaurant in Italy, where they routinely toss salads at the table. IMPORTANT: Begin just as you are about to sit down to eat.

Wash the greens and dry them thoroughly. I use a salad spinner nowadays, but as a child cook I used to put the wet lettuce in a towel and then go outside and swing it upward in a circle to centrifuge the water out.

Sprinkle a *tiny* bit of good-tasting oil over the greens. (I buy the greenest virgin olive oil I can find in the largest glass jar that costs the least—often a store brand—and I use it for everything except frying, which I don't do much of anyway. Do NOT use tons of oil, as most salad dressing recipes do. A tablespoon or so should be enough for a huge salad that will feed a whole family.) Toss lightly, with a big slotted spoon, until all the leaves glisten.

Sprinkle with crunchy sea salt and cracked pepper. You may also sprinkle on a tiny bit of sugar—no more than a teaspoon for a big salad—if you like your salad a little sweet. Sprinkle with a small amount of cider or wine vinegar. Balsamic vinegar is good, too, but reduce or eliminate the sugar if you use it. Serve and eat immediately.

BAKED POTATOES THE WAY I LIKE THEM

Use any kind of potatoes. There is no such thing as a "baking potato." All are good, and, like beans, they all taste different. I like everything from mealy Idaho russets to redskins to the sweet yellow ones. Try any variety they have at the store. Here is a thing to splurge on at your natural foods market. Get the little skinny Russian fingerlings and those peculiar purple-fleshed ones. Mmm.

Bake one potato per person plus a couple extra to eat the next day: cold, sliced, spread with sour cream and sprinkled with salt and pepper—one of my daughters' favorite snacks and a great appetizer when guests are ranging around the kitchen getting on your nerves right before a meal. Be sure to select potatoes that are about the same size, so they'll all be done at the same time.

Scrub the potatoes really well, as you will eat the skins, which, in addition to tasting good and providing textural contrast, contain all the potato's vitamins, according to my mom. Use the point of a knife to get every speck of dirt out of the eyes. Wipe the potatoes with a towel and then let them dry completely. This is an important step. Butter won't stick to wet potatoes.

Grease the potatoes with soft butter. Use your hands to do this. Make your children do it, if you can't stand to have butter on your hands. (NEVER wrap baked potatoes in foil, which just steams them. For a good baked potato, the skin needs to get a little crusty.)

Roll the buttered potatoes in coarse salt, put them on a baking sheet, and prick them all over with a knife point so they won't blow up in the oven. (I didn't prick them once because I didn't believe my dad when he said they'd blow up. Sure enough, one did. What a mess.) Then place the potatoes directly onto a baking sheet.

Bake at 375° or higher. The hotter the temperature, the crustier they get on the outside. They're done when you can dent them with your thumb, anywhere from 30 minutes to an hour, depending on their size and shape. Serve.

To eat, slice twice to make a cross, then press your thumbs and forefingers into the four resulting corners to smash the whole potato. Add butter and/or sour cream or plain yogurt. Sprinkle with salt, pepper, and chopped chives or green onion tops. Eat with a knife and fork so that you can get part of the crusty skin with each bite of soft white middle and toppings.

3

My Mother's Cooking

My mother was born in Joy, a tiny Ozark town—population forty these days but probably a few more back then—on a high hill called Joy Mountain near Searcy, Arkansas. The only baby story I know about her is that, as a relative at a funeral put it, "She was bad to bite." Evidently she had to be disciplined throughout her childhood for biting other children or anyone else who got in her way. She told few stories from her childhood, all of them rather puny and sour, as they seem to me now. But as children, my sisters and brothers and I begged for them, just as my own children do mine. We hungered for them, for the flavor of her life before we knew her. Stories are like food, I think, satisfying deep inner urges for identity and truth.

"Tell us about the red coat you had when you were little," we pleaded, not because we didn't have clothes much finer, but because we wanted to taste the exotic poverty of our mother's experience, to us like some fetid foreign spice. We wanted to share with the unknown child she once was the sweetness of her pride in having something that wasn't handed down from distant cousins or donated by charities, something that wasn't merely necessary but pretty, something that she really liked.

Her father was an alcoholic who abandoned his two children when they were toddlers, and her mother brought home man after man before she finally, when my mom was in her early teens, settled on the one I knew as Grandpa, her fifth or sixth husband. Among some yellowed marriage licenses a relative sent me after my grandmother's death, there is a letter in my mother's loopy adolescent hand, written on my illiterate grandmother's behalf, begging this man, a stranger, to come to where they were living. The hesitant cursive and spelling errors of my mother's letter reveal a person I never knew—even though, having begun my life inside of her, I should have known her better than I knew any other person in the world. She wrote lightly, in pencil, on a single page of lined notebook paper, and she folded the letter up small in an envelope now blotched and darkened like an old person's skin. Here is a fragile, partial version of who she was—a tiny, hopeful, hopeless voice cowering beneath the shrieks and threats and confident statements about how to be that I later believed were my mother:

Dear Albert,

I guess you're very suprised to hear from me. I don't know whether you will be very glad tho. Mother and her husband don't live together any more so when you want to you can come and see us. Are you married yet?

Mother had me to write and tell you this so when you get ready to come write and tell us and we will meet you at the Bus Station.

A month later, they were married by a justice of the peace, and they stayed together for the rest of their lives. I can hardly imagine the contours of the life—the illiteracy, the serial marriages, the poverty, the enmeshed interdependence, the despair that for the bereft wins out, always wins out, over decorum—that would have occasioned this secondhand plea from a fourteen-year-old.

They lived hard, especially before Grandpa came along. That much my mother told us. They moved around a lot, my grandmother working in factories and cleaning houses and picking vegetables. Some summers the whole family worked in the fields—my mom, her younger brother, and their mother. They picked green beans and cotton. My mom was once sent home from grade school with lice, and her mother shaved off all her hair and scrubbed her bald scalp with gasoline before she sent her back to class. At fifteen, my mom's brother lied about his age in order to join the army and fight in the Korean War, returning not long after, having been shot—between the legs. These were the kinds of stories my siblings and I liked to hear.

My mother did well in school and always liked it, especially her math classes. When she got to high school, her mother wanted her to quit school to work full-time. They needed the money. Grandma herself had quit school in the second grade and, at fifteen or so, married a widower much older. If I strain, I can almost hear her telling my mother the stories of that life. But my grandmother probably kept as mum about her past as my mother did about hers. I do know that once, in a fit of rage over how much time her teenage daughter spent studying, my grandmother got hold of my mom's high school textbooks and burned every one of them. When, as a child, I went to visit my grandparents in the house they bought for three hundred dollars, I imagined Grandma burning those books out in their yard in the blackened oil drum my grandparents used for burning trash, although the barrel in which my grandmother burned my mom's books surely didn't exist in those days. In any case, my grandparents' trash barrel operated as an icon of my mother's childhood, in my mind. Greasy. Blackened along the rim. Filled with deep orange flames that descended into the barrel and disappeared as the contents of the can burned, until nothing remained but an oily, black smoke that stuck to your hair and your skin and that you could still smell even after you showered and changed your clothes.

My mom fought her way to a diploma, despite her mother's objections, and then through two years of college. With an A.A. in engineering, she pursued a brief career with the Air Force that ended when she discovered she was pregnant. Eventually, with my toddling sister to provide for, she took a job in California as a low-level engineer and met my father. Somehow she got rid of her Arkansas accent for the most part, slipping into it only with certain words—like *pin*, *pen*, and *pan*, which for her were phonologically identical—and when she sang along with Hank Williams on the radio.

"Ah cain't hep it if Ah'm steel in love with you!" she wailed as she ironed or sewed our clothes or scrubbed the toilets with her bare hands.

She never lost her reputation as an Arkansas wildcat, as she was called in those years. She was loud and impulsive, had big breasts and black hair, and wore dark red lipstick. She was part Choctaw—"somewhere way back," she told us—and she was proud of that.

"You've got a little Indian in you," she was always telling us. I imagined it as a tiny Indian person who lived inside of me. A wild and foreign part of me that I could never really know. Someone caught up in ancient Indian activities we learned about in grade school: trapping raccoons and cooking them, weaving baskets, pounding leached acorns into bread. Someone silent and industrious and wise. Someone who knew all the stories my mother never told.

My mother never really learned to cook. The poverty of her childhood and the temporary housing they lived in when they worked in the fields was how she explained it.

"Mama never had time to teach me," she said. "And sometimes, there was nothing to cook but green beans, and, after picking them all day, you didn't want to eat them."

They ate, she said, mostly fried baloney sandwiches, fried potatoes, fried cabbage. As a child, she may have made herself a childhood delicacy called "bread, butter, and sugar" that my grandmother made for my siblings and me when she visited: gritty sandwiches of margarine and sugar on a single slice of white bread, folded over. I know that, as a treat, my mother and her best friend Fanny would share a bag of Fritos corn chips, to which she gave a pet name, Tippie-Toes. "I just lovvvvvve those Tippie-Toes," she'd sing out whenever we saw the yellow bags on the grocery store shelf. Sometimes she would buy us all a bag to share, but that was rare. Even in Southern California, living in a ritzy neighborhood and married to an aeronautical engineer, she remained frugal.

I figure my mother must also have grown up eating the foods my grandmother cooked whenever I visited her and Grandpa in Arkansas as a child. Biscuits and gravy. Poke greens boiled or fried with eggs. Fried okra or squash or eggplant or green tomatoes. Chicken and dumplings. Brown beans and chow chow. Catfish or chicken pieces or fatback breaded and then deep-fried out in the yard. Poor people food.

When I visited, my grandparents always fried fish over an open fire down by the catalpa tree from which we had gathered the fat, brilliant green catalpa worms we used as bait. Grandpa made the fire, while Grandma coated the fish with yellow cornmeal seasoned with salt and pepper and then poured about two inches of oil into a metal frypan with a long handle and almost perpendicular sides. Grandpa must have had some sort of tripod to put the pan on, but I don't remember that. They used no other spices than salt and pepper in any of their cooking—that I remember. Just fatty meats and starches and garden vegetables, these last also breaded and fried or else boiled beyond recognition as plant matter and then seasoned with sugar, salt, and bacon grease.

Simple, tasty, bad-for-you foods. Every relative or friend of theirs—ours—that I ever met suffered from diabetes or colon cancer or ended up in the hospital with peritonitis. It was my mother's firm belief—one of the many I have inherited—that digestive diseases are caused by bad eating. Here are her theories. Not enough water—urinary infections. Too many fatty, starchy foods low in fiber constipate a person, and if a person's bowels don't move, then nasty bad fecal matter festers in the lower bowel and in the little dead end of the appendix, causing colon troubles or appendicitis, often both. Eating too much sugar causes your insulin to go all out of whack—voilà, le diabète. Food, according to my mother, was as likely to blight as to sustain.

It could be due to these preoccupations that my mother rarely cooked the foods of her childhood when I was growing up, much less taught me how to cook them.

No one did, that I remember. But somehow I know how to cook them anyway. Must be in my blood. Or maybe it's that little Indian in me, guiding my hand and informing my palate from babyhood. My grandmother's cuisine was the same food my Oklahoma husband grew up with—fried meats, unseasoned starches, long-boiled vegetables—and he's way more Cherokee than I am Choctaw. And as far as I can tell from considerable research, the so-called Five Civilized Tribes— who, after all, were all from the South—cooked pretty much the same foods.

The dishes I do remember my mom cooking were the 1960s standards nation-wide. She baked meatloaf topped with sweetened ketchup and hotdogs rolled up in canned biscuit dough and called Pigs-in-the-Blanket. She made tamale pie by a recipe very close to the one in the *Joy of Cooking* cookbook of that time except that, for some reason, she added to the meat and vegetables under the cornmeal topping canned tamales, which back then came wrapped in paper inside the can and swimming in jellied red grease. She made Chicken à la King and chipped beef, both served over toast, and she fried pork chops dark brown, then layered them with thinly sliced potatoes and diluted mushroom soup and baked them in the oven.

Desserts were a rarity, in my early years. If we had one at all, it was usually Jell-O salad: green or yellow Jell-O embedded with canned fruit cocktail, which had gritty white chunks of pear that made us children gag. On really special occasions— when there were guests—we had pie.

Pie making, to my mom, was the mark of one's success as a housewife. Although I have no memory of her making a pie herself, I'm sure she did, and she saw to it that I and even my non-cooking sisters knew how to make one by the time we were ten or twelve. Double crust fruit pies. Blueberry pie topped with sweetened sour cream. Dutch apple pie thick with crumbs. She was more interested in our dexterity with the pie dough than with what went inside, and, to please her, we made pies with fancy crimped rims and woven lattice crusts. But she was impressed, too, by the culinary tenacity of a friend of hers, who was incapable of rolling out pie dough but who, determined to make pies anyway, just mixed up the dough and then pressed it bit by bit into the pie plate with her fingers.

"And you know, it tasted just the same, and no one ever knew the difference!" my mother crooned.

My mother was adamant about the nutritional commandments of the day: Meals had to include a protein, a yellow vegetable, a green vegetable, and a starch. We ate vegetables and salad as part of every dinner and had to drink a gigantic glass each of milk and orange juice every day to ward off colds, build strong bones, and "keep us regular." She taught us to scrape off the white underside of navel orange skins with our teeth because she had read that's where most of the vitamins were, and she wouldn't hear of peeling other fruits—apples and peaches and pears—as our friends' mothers did.

"The peel is the most nutritious part!" she told us.

Choice was never at issue in our family. My siblings and I ate what our parents put before us: a cuisine governed not only by the current rules for healthy eating but by my mother's parsimonious shopping habits and a certain wacky impulse to combine contrasting flavors and textures that I have inherited and passed on to my girls. A typical after school snack for us kids—the only snacking allowed in our household—was celery with peanut butter or pickley tuna salad on crackers. Never chips or soda pop or homemade cookies. She combined what was cheap and nutritious, however weird, and we ate it.

One day my siblings and I all came home with one of the stomach viruses we called the flu back then, and our snack for that day was a hunk of Jack cheese with a glass of thick apricot nectar. None of us felt like eating anything, especially what our mother offered us that afternoon out on the patio table, but she made us, and we all threw it back up throughout the afternoon. I remember, in that blessed moment of relief that always follows vomiting, staring down at the puddle of orange and white chunks on the cement and tasting the delicious exhilaration of revenge.

As my siblings and I grew up, the food of the day increasingly involved more assembly than actual cooking, and my mother was good at that. For cocktail or bridge parties—in those days the primary forms of adult entertainment among my parents' acquaintances—my mom served Chex Mix or ruffled potato chips with California Dip. Or, if she was feeling fancy, chicken livers rolled-up in bacon and called rumaki or some other delicacy high in calories and fat and salt to counter-balance all the alcohol in the cocktails so that the guests could successfully weave their ways home.

I always volunteered to help my mother with the hors d'oeuvres, which my dad called horses' ovaries. She gladly let me stir the soup mix into the sour cream or massage the Worcestershire sauce and melted butter into the cereal mixture—being careful not to spill or drip—or wrap the bacon around a slippery lobe of chicken liver and a sliver of water chestnut and then spear it all together with a toothpick.

And, because I was present when these delicacies were being assembled, I also got to taste them, on the sly, at every phase of their making. Cooks know an elemental joy, I think, foreign to mere eaters. I relished the salty milk solids from the melted butter and the strange dry-wetness of the water chestnuts in their metallic water. I licked little mounds of dry Lipton Onion Soup mix from the palm of my hand and sucked tastes of Worcestershire sauce straight from the plastic-tipped bottle. I scraped the liver drippings—coagulated knobs of black-ened blood—from the bottom of the broiler pan. And my mother, setting out ashtrays and dishes of bridge mix, either didn't notice my unhygienic doings or else, frantic before her party, didn't care.

Mostly, though, my mother isn't there at all in the kitchens of my memory. That couldn't be true—she must have cooked, and I know we ate—but that's how I remember it. When he was not at work, my dad cooked. And later, when I was nine or ten, my parents surrendered the kitchen to me.

Green Beans

In my travels to Arkansas, Switzerland, Germany, and back to Oklahoma, I was intrigued to find virtually the same delicious, overcooked green beans everywhere I went.

Arkansas-Style Green Beans

Snip or break off just the very ends of the beans. I recommend cutting off only the stem end and leaving the little, curved tail, but if you must cut off both ends, be sure you cut only enough to get rid of whatever offends you and never so much that the bean is no longer bean-shaped but truncated and flat-ended. If your beans have a tough thread down one side, zip it off with the stem end as you go.

Sauté a chopped onion in bacon grease—I use olive oil these days—until it begins to turn translucent. Add the beans and sauté a few minutes. Add enough water—or broth, if you have it—to come about halfway up the beans in the pot. Cook the beans a long time, until they lose all their brightness and turn the gray-green color of army blankets. You can't overcook them. Beans cooked this way are by nature overcooked. Salt to taste. Serve them with a sliced sweet onion, such as Vidalia or Texas Sweet. They go with almost any country meal.

Oklahoma-Style Green Beans

Leave out the onions and the sautéing. My mother-in-law adds bacon grease and sugar to the water for seasoning and makes them really salty. They're good that way, especially when she makes mashed potatoes to go with them, the sweetened gray-green brine serving as a sort of gravy. She also serves them with wedges of sweet onion.

Swiss or German-Style Green Beans

Add some winter savory along with the sautéed onions and beans. The German word for winter savory is *Bohnenkraut*, or bean herb. As far as I know, this is the only dish in which anyone uses *Bohnenkraut*, but Germans find it is so essential to green beans that green grocers in Germany give you a few sprigs of it for free when you buy green beans in the market. In the States, I have only ever found winter savory in health food stores that sell dried herbs and spices in bulk. I can't honestly say it tastes a whole lot different from thyme, but the leaves are bigger. Any herb you like—such as thyme, marjoram, or oregano—would probably be a good substitute.

FRIED BALONEY SANDWICH

Use only all-beef bologna for this sandwich, as it's the only kind with enough fat to fry itself the way it needs to.

Put several thickish slices of bologna in a fry pan. Cut once into each slice, from edge to center, to keep it from bowing up as it cooks. Fry on one side till the edges are brown; then turn and fry on the other. Put the fried slices on white bread spread with bright yellow American mustard. Voilà! The high cuisine of mother's childhood.

GRAVY

Gravy is simply a little fat cooked with an equal amount of flour, to which a liquid is added. The keys for success are (1) to use more liquid than you want gravy and then let it cook down to the desired thickness; and (2) to use a whisk to avoid lumps.

For meat gravies, use the drippings from a roast or the fat left in the pan after searing or frying chops, sausage, or other meat. Pour off some of the grease if it looks like too much, but keep as much of the dark, flavorful crumbs as possible. For a darker gravy, cook the roux until it turns light or even dark brown, whisking all the while, before you add any liquid. For the liquid, except when I am making sausage gravy, I use broth or the boiling water from cooking potatoes, but my mother-in-law, in the manner of the South, generally uses milk. Salt enthusiastically. I sometimes use a bouillon cube or two—beef for dark meats, chicken for light ones—instead of salt. The basic procedure here, by the way, is the same for béchamel sauce (French for white sauce). To make white sauce, start with butter instead of drippings, and use milk instead of broth or water, hold back on the salt, and add a little nutmeg.

Sausage Gravy

For about a cup and a half of gravy—enough for four—leave about three table-spoons of grease in the skillet after frying sausage (or bacon or ham) and whisk in enough flour to make a paste about the consistency and smoothness of yogurt. Scrape the paste, called a *roux*, around a minute or two over a medium flame so that the brown scrapings become part of the roux as it cooks. Whisk in slightly more than 11/2 cups of milk and cook it down, stirring with the whisk, until it's the consistency you like. The longer it cooks, the thicker it gets. I make sausage gravy somewhat thin, since it thickens as it cools. Season with salt and a good amount of pepper. Serve over biscuits. (See page 224 for a biscuit recipe.)

(You can add some crumbled up sausage to the gravy, if you like how that looks. I don't. In the military, I'm told, they serve this gravy with sausage chunks over toast and affectionately call it S.O.S., *Shit-on-a-Shingle*. Enough said. It looks and tastes great without the meat, though, especially over biscuits instead of toast. I avoid gravies over toast. Too much like the Chicken à la King that I hated as a child.)

Poke

Poke—also known as pokeweed or poke salad (salat, or sallet)—grows wild in every part of the United States in which I've ever lived: California, Oklahoma, Arkansas, Connecticut, Boston, and New Orleans. It grows taller than a person and has broad lanceolate—leaf-shaped—leaves, which are bright deep green and sometimes mottled. In late summer, poke has beautiful, deep purple berries, which are shaped like tiny Turkish cushions and yield a brilliant magenta dye. The berries are clustered along a bright pink stem and dangle enticingly from the ends of the branches, but don't eat them. They are poisonous. Eat only the upper, more tender leaves and stems, preferably from young plants. Poke cooks down, so gather a lot. I typically gather in late spring and break off the top of each plant I come to—ten leaves or so—leaving the rest of the plant standing. In no time it will grow more stems and leaves that branch out from where you broke it. Every recipe you read will say to parboil poke first and drain off the cooking water before you cook or sauté it further—either to get rid of some sort of poison or else to lessen poke's strong flavor, I'm not sure. I don't do this, and neither does my mother-in-law; we've never gotten sick or died from eating poke, and we like its taste.

Plain Old Boiled Poke

Boil young leaves in a little salted water as you would spinach or mustard greens. Cook them until they have lost their bright green color.

Poke and Eggs

Boil some poke in a little salted water until it is tender but still green, drain the leaves well, and squeeze out as much liquid as you can. Chop them coarsely and sauté them in oil or bacon grease a few minutes. When they have sizzled out their wetness, add some eggs that you have stirred together with a fork. Sprinkle with salt and pepper as they scramble.

Poke Greens, Boiled the Way My Mother-in-Law Does It

Wash and pick through the greens. Add a little bacon grease, salt, and sugar for flavor and water to barely cover. Then, boil the pooey out of them. Expect to cook them an hour at least. My mother-in-law uses her pressure cooker. It's not, in other words, possible to overcook them. Serve with the hot yellow vinegar that you shake out of those long, skinny bottles of tiny peppers.

Fried Poke Stems

My mother-in-law fries poke stems the same way she does okra. Collect stems from the tops of young plants. Lower down and on older plants, the stems are too hollow and woody. Slice the soft stems into disks. Toss them in a bowl or plastic bag with cornmeal, salt, and pepper. Fry in shallow oil until crusty and brown. These taste like a cross between asparagus and fried okra.

CHICKEN AND DUMPLINGS

Cook chicken and dumplings when someone you love feels bad. It is about the most comforting food there is.

Broth

Put chicken in a lot of salted water—that is, several inches above the chicken. Bring it to a boil; then lower the temperature, cover, and cook on low until tender, about an hour. My mother-in-law uses a couple of boneless, skinless chicken breasts and pressure cooks them until they're very tender. When I cooked chicken and dumplings as a child for my family of eight, I used one whole cut-up chicken and left in all that good yellow fat from the skin, which made beautiful yellow circles on the surface of the dish. Now, though, I just use scraps from a chicken I have cut up for something else. As such, my chicken and dumplings are mostly just dumplings with specks of chicken here and there in a gravy-like broth.

Here's how I make the broth out of the trimmings: As I wrestle with the rest of the chicken I'm trying to cut up, I drop the scraps into a big pot of cold, salted water. I use the backs, skin, bones, and wing ends, throwing nothing away, not the smallest bone or bit of fat. (Understand here that I'm cooking one and a half meals at once—the chicken meal, whatever it is, and the broth for the chicken and dumplings we'll have a day or two later.) After the chicken scraps have boiled an hour or so, I let them cool in the pot on top of the stove until they are cool enough for me to pick through with my fingers to separate the edible bits of meat from the skin, fat, and bones. Sometimes I get caught up in the other things I'm cooking for that night, and I forget and leave the pot cooling on top of the stove until I'm doing the dishes after the meal, or even until the next morning. I don't worry at all about salmonella developing. I figure, it's cooked, it has salt in it, and I've been cooking chicken scraps this way my whole life and so far haven't gotten sick from it. Anyway, I pick out the meat, put it back in the broth, and stick the whole thing in the refrigerator until I'm ready to make the chicken and dumplings. The fat comes to the surface and hardens, so it is easy to remove before I heat up the broth to make chicken and dumplings: I just lift it off and give it to our dogs, along with the bones and skin.

Sometimes, though, I save the cooked pieces of skin to make a version of a treat a German friend—whose cooking is much informed by her Jewish heritage—once served me. I lay the pieces of skin out on a folded paper towel on a plate, cover them with another paper towel, and microwave them until the fat is all dried out and the bits of skin are brown and crispy. (My friend did it in the oven, minus the paper towels, but it takes a lot longer.) When they're done, I pry them loose from the towel or pan, salt them liberally, and give them—if I'm feeling affectionate—to the girls. If I'm not, I eat them all myself. These are called *Grieben* in German, kind of the German equivalent of pork skins. Germans cut up the skin and bits of fat of fowl—especially goose—and fry them till they're browned, then cool the resulting fat (*Schmalz*) together with the browned bits to make *Griebenschmalz*, which they spread on bread like butter and frequently eat in bars. Top it with sliced raw onion and it's *Griebenschmalz mit Musik* (*Griebenschmalz* with music, for reasons I will leave to your imagination).

Dumplings

The rest goes quick. About half an hour before you want to eat, bring the broth to a boil while you make the dumpling dough. To serve four, mix:

> **2 cups flour**
> **1 teaspoon each of salt and sugar**
> **1/2 teaspoon baking powder**
> **enough milk, buttermilk, or water to make a tough dough**

Knead the dough a second or two; then roll it out on the floured counter, some-what thicker than you would for pie dough—between 1/4 and 1/2 inch thick, maybe. Cut into strips about an inch wide and two or three inches long. I use a roller to cut them, but a long knife will do fine. Don't drag the knife through the dough, though, but instead cut straight down, as if cutting out biscuits.

Drop the dumpling strips into the boiling broth, a strip here, a strip there, trying not to overlap them too much if you can help it. Stir the pot when you get them all in the broth. Let dumplings cook about ten minutes or until the broth starts to thicken and the strips are chewy. Serve them with some sort of salad or slaw. My mother-in-law always serves chicken and dumplings with mashed potatoes, using the broth as a sort of gravy. She does this with her chicken and noodles, too. At my house, though, we eat chicken and dumplings all by itself, out of wide bowls, with spoons.

BEANS

We ate beans a lot during my childhood—it doesn't cost much to feed beans to a family of eight—and I still do to this day. Growing up, I made legumes for my family several times a week. Gigantic white lima beans with ham hocks. Split peas or lentils as soup, with ham, onions, carrots, and potatoes. Pinto beans with kielbasa. Cooked fresh (or canned) kidney or red beans added to ground beef and onions and chili powder to make chili. Nowadays, though, I like beans best just plain, with salt, and served with rice or cornbread, a cut-up sweet onion, and pickled hot peppers.

The basic recipe is the same as on any bag: Soak the beans overnight and boil them, partially covered, until done. (I often forget to soak them and end up having to cook them a long time—maybe two or three hours.) Add salt and, if you like, whatever else you think suits the sort of beans you're cooking: a cut-up onion, a bay leaf, a ham hock or ham bone, a scrap of bacon, a piece of polish sausage. All beans are good this way: pintos (known as "brown beans" in Oklahoma), red beans, kidney beans, garbanzo beans, black beans, navy beans, small baby limas, and the big white lima beans known as "butter beans" in the South. Other dried legumes—such as black-eyed peas, purple-hull peas, field peas, split peas, lentils, etc.—are also good this way.

MY GRANDMA'S CHOW CHOW

Grind in a sausage grinder in any amounts:

green tomatoes
cabbage
onions
peppers

Nowadays you might use a food processor, but be careful not to get the mixture too fine. Salt heavily and let sit in a bowl overnight. The next day, when the juice is visible, drain through a big cotton dish towel draped over a colander. Squeeze most of the salty juice out by twisting the towel up around the chopped vegetables; then put them in a big pot and just barely cover with cider vinegar. Add whole spices (mustard, black pepper, allspice, celery seed, cloves, a slice of a nutmeg, and a broken-up stick of cinnamon). If you like it somewhat sweet, you can add a little sugar—but no more than two or three tablespoons. My grandma's chow chow was sour, not sweet, unlike the chow chows I see in cookbooks. Bring the vegetables to a boil, cook them for about an hour, and then turn off the heat. While the chow chow is cooking, boil some jars and lids in water in another big pot. Fish a jar out of the hot water with tongs and use a one-cup measuring cup and a canning funnel to fill the hot jar with the hot chow chow. Wipe the rim clean with a wet cloth; then fish out a canning flat and lid, screw them on tightly, and turn the jar upside down. Repeat until you've used up all the chow chow. I liked making and looking at this relish more than eating it, to be honest. As a child, I especially liked how those black spices looked against the various pale greens of the vegetables through the glass of the jars in my grandma's pantry. My grandma typically served her chow chow with pinto beans or fried catfish.

FRIED STUFF

I hate frying things. I hate the way it makes my house and clothes and hair smell. I hate that it takes so much oil and that you typically end up with a lot of fishy or otherwise nasty oil that you have to somehow get rid of. Putting it down the garbage disposal always seemed wrongheaded to me when we had one growing up, and nowadays we don't have a garbage disposal, anyway. The culinary conservative in me thinks garbage disposals—and deep frying, for that matter— are morally wrong. My alternatives for disposing of oil—feeding it to the dogs, putting it in a jar in the trash, dumping it out in the fields beyond our house, etc.—all have their drawbacks. Usually I convince myself that I'll fry again and that it'll be soon enough and the food I'm frying will be close enough to the original thing I fried that it won't taste horrible. So, I put the jar of brown oil in the refrigerator to get rid of months later, when I do a major throwing-out. Luckily, the list of fried things that I like is short:

- *Beignets, made only by Café du Monde in New Orleans at about 3:00 a.m. and accompanied by several cups of their chicory coffee with boiled milk.*

- *Tempura—but not as much as I like sushi and Japanese stews, so I rarely order it in restaurants and have never made it.*

- *Popeyes spicy fried chicken breasts—another hangover from my graduate school days in New Orleans, when I made $315 a month and spent $200 in rent. Popeyes was my monthly treat. I bought a spicy breast and wing with dirty rice, slaw, and a biscuit. Nowadays I eat the same meal about once a year, usually on the road somewhere.*

- *My mother-in-law's yearly raised doughnuts, which she makes in July or August, in million-degree heat. Somehow I nevertheless manage to eat at least half a dozen.*

- *The fried catfish my grandparents used to make out of fish they had caught. Unfortunately, my grandparents both died some years ago, and I don't like farm-raised catfish, and I don't fish myself, so the only time I ever get to eat it is when someone who does fish brings me catfish.*

As you see, none of these items are dishes that I myself create.

My grandparents loved fried food, though. They fished at the Dardanelle River often enough to keep their freezer stocked with cat, bullhead, and buffalo fish. They only ever ate fish one way: mealed, seasoned with salt and pepper, and fried out in the yard. They also pan-fried all the vegetables they ate. And fried chicken was the pinnacle of my grandparents' cuisine. At my mother's staid California funeral, my grandmother was outraged because there was no fried chicken, and we had to go out and get a bucket of the fast-food kind to put out on the table to appease her. My grandpa was a big man and always sensationally overweight, probably close to four hundred pounds in his overalls, which he wore without a shirt. Near the end of his life, the doctor at the VA Hospital ordered him to eat more vegetables and fish and less fat. So, when my husband and I went to visit and Grandpa took us to an all-you-can-eat buffet, he dutifully loaded up on deep-fried breaded okra, fried green tomatoes, fried potatoes, and fried fish. Here are some of their recipes, plus a few modified versions of my mother's fried favorites that I serve to my family on occasion.

Fried Okra

Okra gets slimy if cooked wet. The cafeteria cooks at Tulane University stewed whole okra pods with whole canned tomatoes and onions, and I always put a little beige plastic dish of them on my tray, along with my usual grits and andouille, and I ate the slimy combination with tons of Tabasco sauce. Okra is pretty good that way. And in soups such as gumbo and my mother-in-law's red vegetable soup. They're also good raw, straight from the garden. If I have okra fresh and young from the garden, though, there's only one way to fix it, as far as I'm concerned: dusted with seasoned meal and fried. Every other way is a waste. Oh, and, by the way, never batter or "bread" it with layers of egg and meal or buy that frozen, batter-coated kind they serve in restaurants. All these methods squelch the taste and texture of the okra. A culinary scandal!

Fry okra as you would poke stems: tossed first in cornmeal seasoned with salt and pepper, then fried in shallow oil until good and dark. You'll need to use a fair amount of oil, as the porous disks of okra soak it up. Even though this dish is greasy and caloric and makes me feel sickish if I eat too much, as all fried food does, I do not feel guilty about eating fried okra. First off, it's hard to get enough. It's only available for a short season. More important, though, is that it's the most delicious Southern food I know of. I always eat too much and feel yucky afterwards, but it's worth it.

Note: Okra is originally from Africa. Apparently, slaves being transported wore the dried pods in their hair as a decoration and then planted the seeds throughout the South, where these transposed Africans soon became the arbiters of Southern cooking. Actually, even the food I know as Native American—the Five Civilized Tribes were all in the South and much influenced by the colonizing cultures—is hardly distinguishable from the slave recipes that we think of today as Southern cooking.

Fried Fatback

The quintessential fried food of my grandparents was one that they served often when I visited them as a child: fried salt pork, called fatback. This tastes exactly as it sounds: like the fatty edge of a breaded, fried pork chop that one normally cuts off and leaves on one's plate. Nevertheless, for posterity, here's the recipe.

Slice into 1/4 to 1/2 inch thick slabs:

salt pork soaked in water to remove salt: one slab for each person dining

Press fatback slices into a plate of meal or flour seasoned with salt and pepper. Fry in shallow oil or bacon grease until brown on both sides. Eat it with something sour—such as chow chow or a tart slaw or cucumbers and onions in seasoned vinegar and water—to cut the fat.

Fried Potatoes

These are very good, and you can get by with as little as a tablespoon of oil for four big potatoes—enough to feed four.

Cut potatoes, peeled or unpeeled, into short, rectangular chunks and fry in a little hot oil, stirring from time to time, until they are browned on the edges. Salt and pepper them and serve them with bright yellow American mustard and sliced sweet onion.

Fried Cabbage

Cut half a cabbage and an onion into large chunks and fry, stirring occasionally, in a little oil or bacon grease until browned on the edges. The chunks will fall apart into leaves and cook down into more manageable pieces as you fry them. They will also get sweet. Season with salt and pepper. Serve. Yum.

Pan-Fried Summer Vegetables, Southern-Style

My mother-in-law serves fried green tomatoes and squash with yellow mustard. I like to squeeze a lemon on pan-fried squash. My favorite vegetable cooked this way is pattypan squash—because of its name and because it is so pretty: pale pale white-green and flower-shaped, like something in a faded Japanese painting.

Slice into disks:

> **eggplant, green tomatoes, or any kind of summer squash—yellow,**
> **pattypan, or zucchini**

Dab the sliced vegetables onto a plate covered with flour seasoned with salt and pepper. Brown in small batches in hot shallow oil, first on one side, then on the other. Don't overlap them in the pan. Remove to a plate covered with a couple of paper towels to drain as you fry the rest. Serve on a fresh plate, preferably bright-colored, so they look pretty.

Pan-Fried Sliced Vegetables, Italian-Style

This is my daughters' favorite way to eat zucchini. I never seem to be able to cook enough zucchini this way to satisfy them.

Use any of the summer vegetables listed previously. (Except maybe green tomatoes, but why not try them this way?) Slice them either lengthwise or in strips. Fry as many as will fit flat in the pan in a little olive oil—I use as little as I can get away with, maybe a tablespoon and a half—until brown on the edges; then flip and brown them on the other side. When they are just about browned all over, add a few smashed cloves of garlic to the pan and a lot of chopped parsley. Turn the vegetables over in the pan, carefully, so that the cooked slices don't break apart but the garlic gets cooked. Serve.

Pie

The basic recipe for pie is simple. Once you get the hang of it, you can find recipes in cookbooks for all sorts of interesting fillings.

Dough

Makes enough for a two-crust pie.

Combine in a cup and set aside:

> **1/4 cup water**
> **several ice cubes**

Combine:

> **1 1/2 cups flour**
> **1/2 teaspoon salt**
> **1 tablespoon sugar**—optional

Using a food processor, if you have one, or a pastry blender—or, as I did as a child, two knives scraped against each other—cut in:

1/2 cup butter—until the mixture looks like very coarse corn meal

Drizzle water out of the ice cubes into the flour mixture and pulse your food processor or stir with a fork just until a dough forms. You won't use all the water. Your goal is a cold, firm, slightly crumbly dough.

Assembly

For a two-crust pie, roll out half a recipe of pie dough on your floured counter into a circle about an inch bigger than the pie pan turned upside down on the dough. Fold the dough circle carefully in half so that you can lift it lightly and quickly into one half of the pan. Unfold the dough. Trim it to drape over the edge about an inch or so all the way around. If you tear or mangle it in the process or if there's too little dough on one side and too much somewhere else, don't fret. Just mend it by pressing it together or cutting off a bit to patch a skimpy place. Fill. Roll the other dough half for the top crust—slashing it before folding, if you like how that looks or if your filling is juicy and likely to burst the pie open and leak all over if you don't. Fold the two edges under on top of the rim of the pie pan and crimp the turned under edges together either with a fork or with your thumbs and index fingers. If you are baking a juicy pie, put it on a cookie sheet, just in case it over-flows, for ease of cleaning. Bake at 350° until golden.

For a lattice-topped pie, follow the instructions for a two-crust pie for the bot-tom crust. For the top crust, slice the rolled out dough into narrow strips and lay half of them, with spaces between, on top of the filling. Fold back every other strip halfway, lay a strip over the ones lying flat; then lay the folded-over strips back down. Now fold back the strips you left flat before and lay a second strip across the ones lying flat. Repeat the weaving process until half the pie is latticed; then do the same to the other half.

For a one-crust, crumb-topped pie, make half a recipe of dough (or freeze half for another day) and top with a crumb topping from a cookbook. Most comprise close to equal parts flour (or oats, crushed graham crackers, etc.) and some sort of sugar, plus half that amount of butter, either melted or cut in.

Basic Fruit Filling

You can fill a pie with just about anything. For fruit pies, use sour fruit. For fruit like apples, pears, and peaches: peel, quarter, and slice them; sprinkle them with

lemon juice; and then toss with a little sugar and, if you like, flour and spice.
Cinnamon is nice; allspice is interesting. Flour and spice are really not necessary,
though, and complicate the flavor of the pie, so often I leave them out. Soft fruits
like cherries—fresh pitted or canned and drained or frozen—are best cooked first
with sugar and a tiny bit of water and then thickened with tapioca (amounts for
different fruits are recommended on the box) or a little cornstarch in water. If you
like, seasoned with a few drops of almond flavoring or lemon juice. Very soft fruits,
such as berries, need tapioca and sugar. Fruits are forgiving, and every pie teaches
you something, so just go with your impulses. The worst that can happen is that a
pie is too runny or too stiff, but neither problem is a disaster. Serve some vanilla
ice cream with it—or unsweetened whipped cream—and everyone will think it was
intentional, however it comes out.

RUMAKI

Even if you don't like chicken liver, you will like these. Nevertheless, I've known
people to leave out the livers altogether and just marinate water chestnuts, wrap
them in bacon, and broil them. In truth, even such castrated rumaki are tasty.

Marinate for several hours to a day:

1 pound chicken livers, trimmed of all fat and separated into two tidy lobes
1 small can of sliced water chestnuts, drained
2 tablespoons sherry
2 tablespoons soy sauce

Slice each liver almost in half, insert a slice of water chestnut into the cut, and fold
closed. Wrap the liver lobe in 1/2 slice of bacon and secure the roll with a wooden
toothpick. Set on a plate and repeat with the rest of the lobes of liver. Broil the rolls
with enough space between them to turn them, so the bacon gets crispy all over.

4

Eggs with Bacon and Onion

I am six. We are at Sequoia National Park. Redwood needles are everywhere. Underfoot like a sponge. In the morning air. Touching our faces in the dark, like ghosts from the forest, when we make our nightly trek to the campfire.

The campfire sends sparks zigging into the night. Like fireflies, all the grownups say, but I have never seen fireflies. We sing, "B-I-N-G-O, B-I-N-G-O, B-I-N-G-O, and Bingo is his name, oh!" My baby brother Larry says he wants a dog, and Daddy says we will get one when we get home, and Larry says he will name it Bingo.

My parents tell again and again a story from the other time we went to Sequoia, when I was little. It was with Grandpa when he used to be alive, but I don't remember him. I don't remember anything of the other trip to Sequoia at all, except somehow I do: a shape and my popsicle gone and Grandma running after me screaming, "Patreesher! Patreesher!" And Daddy saying it was only a popsicle. Now it is a better story, though, because the shape is a Grizzly Bear and I Could Have Been Killed. It was an orange popsicle. The best kind.

We go to a gift shop, and my father buys me a burl, although it is a waste of money. It is a giant redwood baby that will grow sprouts if you keep it in water. I beg and beg to have it, and Mommy says, "Honey just get it," and he gets it, growling when he pays. And then he gives it to me, and now I have it. It's in a plastic bag with the instructions on it about how much water it drinks and how often. We won't sprout it until we go home because it's too messy. It smells red, like Sequoia.

One night we go to Beetle Rock. It is a mountain, but Daddy says it is all made out of one rock and so it's called Beetle Rock. It smells like night. Like air. We lie on our backs to see the stars. There are so many stars there is almost no sky between them. Layers and layers of stars. Some stay where they are. Some fall.

Some rise. Some go to Canada—that's north. Some go home—that's south. They all move at the same time, in different directions, like fireflies.

It is our last night. Tomorrow we will get up early, and the car will be all packed up already, and that will be good. But now, we are hungry, and there is nothing in our little refrigerator. Mommy says, "There's eggs. That's not nothing." And Daddy and I look, and there are eggs and onions and bacon, and that's really not nothing.

Daddy makes a fire in our ring of stones and puts the big frying pan on top of the grill and then coaches me. First the bacon, because that will make the grease we need to cook the rest. While the bacon is frying, he helps me cut the onions. It is a bad knife, but it doesn't matter if they are even or not. We chip them into the hot grease. I do not cut off any of my fingers. When the onions get glassy and sweeter—Daddy fishes one out with a big spoon from the drawer so I can taste— and when the bacon has turned all brown, I crack the eggs into the pan, one by one. Daddy shows me how. One for each of us and two for the pot. No three, because that's how many there are left, and we don't want to have to take them with us. And I stir it all up with a fork. All together in one pan, not like breakfast, and the smell of the bacon and onions together is my favorite thing about Sequoia. It smells delicious, Mommy says, and she is right.

And then we eat it, and everyone likes it, even Baby Larry. My sisters fight to scrape at what's left in the frying pan, as if they are starving. I fight, too. But mostly I watch them all eat what I cooked. And listen to their voices. And smell the delicious smell disappearing into the redwoods. And I like cooking.

Eggs with Bacon and Onions

This may well be the most satisfying meal you will ever eat.

Brown bacon in a frying pan. Chip an onion unevenly into the hot grease with a paring knife and fry until glassy and sweet but still crisp. Crack eggs into the pan—one or two per person—and stir on and off until set. Eat for dinner, not breakfast, some time when everyone's very hungry and tired after some taxing exertion, like shoveling snow or raking leaves or swimming in a creek.

5

The History of California

I am a mouth learner. Others may learn better by hearing or touching or reading about an object of inquiry. I learn best when I taste it, chew it, eat it. And what I learn in this way, I never forget.

Out of my entire six years of elementary education, I remember not one grade distinctly and only one of my teachers: Mrs. Berry, who once called my mother in because of my atrocious handwriting and who read *The Hobbit* and the entire *Lord of the Rings* trilogy aloud to whichever fourth graders didn't want to go out to recess. As she read, I savored in my mind the hobbit diet of pan-fried mushrooms and streaky bacon and wondered what the elfin bread *lembas* tasted like.

But who taught me to add and subtract? And where did I develop the hunger for literary food that drove me to read and reread the culinary passages in all the books I loved as a child: *Green Eggs and Ham, Heidi,* and *The Five Little Peppers and How They Grew.* Robinson Crusoe, I read with particular interest, trapped and bred goats for meat and dried grapes to make raisins. But who pressed that engrossing story of his life, unabridged and so bizarrely refracted through Defoe's eighteenth century prose, into my eight-year-old hand? Who taught me to find salvation from fear and glimpses of heaven in its pages?

Some fourth or fifth or sixth grade teacher surely gave me the grasp of grammar I must have had to have excelled in seventh grade English with Mr. Bolduc, a cranky tyrant who once sailed our thick grammar book across the room at me for chewing gum. But I can't recall that forgotten teacher's pleasant face or encouraging words or hand upon my shoulder. What I do remember is inventing for Mr. Bolduc a horror-inspiring version of the contents of my family's actually pristine refrigerator: an imaginary chaos of upset bowls, sticky shelves, and jars overflowing with hardened and unrecognizable contents. I was amazed—and embarrassed—when Mr. Bolduc not only believed my lies but found my description convincing enough to read aloud to the class. But this memory is of the result, not the process, of an earlier education in composition that I have largely forgotten. I would have lost my entire schooling to my faulty memory, I think, were it not for that part of my brain that archives the researches of the tongue.

Tasting is the first way children undertake to study, and it is also, I would argue, the most comprehensive way of learning. How much more can you know about a bug than if you put it in your mouth? That it is alive is immediately clear. And a bug is not like a plant, which lies limp and has none of the same tastes or textures. A bug moves. Perhaps it has pinchers or sticky little feet that test your palate for a foothold. Parents forbid you to put bugs in your mouth. Your mother doesn't eat bugs. Not ever. Beetles taste a little like dirt, but when you bite down on them, they are crunchy and have a soft interior that tastes different from dirt—saltier, slightly sour. You would have to eat more than one bug to satisfy hunger. Different bugs have different flavors. Grasshoppers are tasty, but there is a tiny crawling bug that lives in California that I don't know the name of—exactly the color of my yellow-green Crayola crayon and about the size of a gnat—that's even better. Tart and clean-tasting, with a satisfying grit to it. I could go on for pages with what I knew about bugs before I ever learned about them in school.

The only subject I remember actually studying in elementary school was California, the place where I lived. We learned about the region's indigenous people—diverse tribes referred to in those days simply as "Indians"—who lived along the coasts and further inland. I learned that they fished and collected plants and berries and ground the long acorns of local oaks into flour. The black oak and the California live oak have the sweetest acorns, I learned, but even they are too tannic to eat as is. I tasted one to be sure. We read about how the Indians leached the bitter tannins out of the flour by soaking it in ocean water. Then they dried it and baked it into a bread that I have longed to taste since I was maybe seven years old. It sounded so nutty and wonderful. Acorn bread.

I was a tiny bit Indian myself. Perhaps my ancestors had eaten bread made of acorns, I speculated. If it weren't for my dad's Irish and German forebears and the rest of my mother's ancestors—a mishmash of Scottish and English and people my mother told me were no particular race at all, just poor—perhaps I would be eating acorn bread for breakfast every morning on some idyllic reservation on the coast. And picking raw crustaceans from their shells for lunch. Dining, as the sun sank into the sea beyond my grass-covered hut, on squirrel stew and dandelion greens.

After the Indians, in some forgotten social studies book, the explorers came up from Mexico, populating California with brash Europeans and introducing into the region the high cuisine of my youth: tacos, tostadas, guacamole, enchiladas. When I was a child, my siblings and I liked tacos so much that my parents had to make a couple dozen for a meal. My skinny sister Joanie and I had contests to see who could eat the most. We usually tied at five apiece.

The earliest explorer of California, another lost teacher must have taught my classmates and me, was Juan Rodríguez Cabrillo, a soldier and adventurer. In 1542, in a yearlong expedition of the California coast commissioned by the Spanish governor of Guatemala, he "discovered" our state, as we were taught to refer to the European conquest of the region where we lived.

It came at the end of a military career so eventful it reads like fiction. A page as a child, Cabrillo became first a crossbowman in Pánfilo de Nárvaez's bloody conquest of Cuba and later a captain in Hernán Cortés's unauthorized and even bloodier invasion of Mexico before going on to head his own expedition.

In researching these events as an adult, I learned that Cabrillo had played a particularly grisly role in the fall of the Aztec capital, the island city of Tenochtitlán, in the center of a salt lake that no longer exists in present day Mexico City. According to his most recent biographer, Cabrillo was charged with building thirteen small ships to ferry soldiers in and out of the city during Cortés's three-month siege, but his shipbuilders lacked the beef tallow usually used in combination with pitch to make the ships watertight. So, Cabrillo had ordered his men to use instead the fat of the local people they slaughtered.

Cabrillo's subsequent conquest of California was considerably more benign. Certainly, he and his men scuffled with the Indians and brought them deadly diseases. But, in all, the expedition was relatively peaceable in comparison to those of Nárvaez, Cortés, and another explorer carrying on an inland campaign of terror at the time, Francisco Vásquez de Coronado. Cabrillo and his three ships sailed almost without incident from the Baja Peninsula to the Russian River in present day Oakland, touching land only briefly here and there to scout for food, collect pearls, and claim dominion. Some of the native Californians he encountered apparently trusted him enough to approach him for protection against Coronado.

Everywhere Cabrillo and his little armada stopped, he performed for the locals a solemn ceremony: He tossed stones and water onto the ground, then read aloud from an official document—written in Latin and Spanish—that formally claimed that spot for Spain. Having claimed the region, he renamed it, usually ignoring whatever the locals had previously called the place and even its more enduring landmarks in favor of some reminder of his own ephemeral experience there. Today, the names read like postcards of his trip. A place where he sighted some canoes he called Canoe Village. Coming upon a sheltered beach encampment with lots of cooking fires, he called the area the Bay of Smokes. And a place where the locals took pity on him and his men and gave them food he called the Town of the Sardines.

In the end, Cabrillo's land-grabbing expedition cost him his life, though. According to contemporaneous accounts, he and some of his men stopped for water on one of the Channel Islands, where they had been welcomed before, and got into a fight with the people there. In the fray, Cabrillo broke a limb. He died some weeks later of gangrene.

Of course, we didn't study any of these "Explorers" as imperialists or aggressors but as something more akin to tourists among the corn-eating, cocoa-drinking Aztecs and Mayans, the ancient kin of the few Mexican-American students among us. We did learn a slightly more accurate term for such men, but only in Spanish, a language most of us didn't know. *Conquistador*. Conqueror. Subduer. Killer. We certainly never learned that Cabrillo and his men once—like characters in one of the horrific German fairy tales we knew only in tamed-down Disney versions—slaughtered our Mexican-American classmates' ancestors like livestock and then used their fat to build the very ships with which to destroy them.

Instead, we examined the tusk-like spiral seashells littering a beach named after Cabrillo not far from our school. On a field trip there, we peered into tide pools Cabrillo himself might have investigated looking for something to eat—an abalone maybe or a handful of sardines—if it were not for the fact that Cabrillo Beach was manmade: dredged up in 1929 to extend a breakwater from Los Angeles's southern edge into the stormy bay. San Pedro Bay, to be exact. The Bay of Smokes, for those of us in the know. And what I remember best about Cabrillo is this: a scrambled ostrich egg to which we were treated at the Cabrillo Maritime Museum—big enough to feed all twenty-something of us kids, plus our teacher and the museum curator who served it to us.

It remains a mystery of my education where this ostrich egg came from or what relevance it was intended to have to Cabrillo, or to that beach, or to California, for that matter. Ostriches came from Africa, I may have known even then, so maybe there was some African connection I missed. Something to do with Cabrillo's slaves, perhaps. According to his biographers, he had many slaves working his vast cattle ranchos and goldmines in Guatemala. These slaves, we know, were largely Guatemalans, but some may have been the West African slaves popular with the other Conquistadors. And we know that Cabrillo's first stop in the New World was Jamaica, which in the early sixteenth century was just beginning to support the growing European passions for sugar, rum, tobacco, cocoa, and coffee with what would become the brisk international commerce I at some point in my education learned to call the Slave Triangle.

Who knows who taught me that term? Or traced on the chalkboard jagged white lines, like barbed wire, connecting Europe, Africa, and the New World? All I actually remember of this lesson is that scrambled 1/24th of an ostrich egg, which in my memory was yellower and sharper-tasting and—how can I describe it?— eggier than our chicken eggs.

After Cabrillo's party left California, the Spanish explorers abandoned their new territory for a couple hundred years, and the next hero of California history we studied was Father Junípero Serra, an eighteenth century Franciscan priest of Mallorcan peasant stock now hailed as the father of the California wine industry. Father Juniper, as I privately referred to him, was a small, humble man by all accounts. Although lame from a bug bite that got infected early in his travels, he insisted on walking everywhere he went, even when his entourage rode. He limped thousands of miles up California's desert coastline, leaving in his wake a handful of converts and twenty-odd missions, each surrounded by voluptuous orchards, herds of fat cattle, and the vineyards that would someday engender the wines of Napa Valley.

I was fascinated with wine even as a child. I liked the foreignness of wine words, their oddly elliptical pronunciations—chablis, chenin blanc, bordeaux—so contrary to the spelling rules I had learned in school and so elegant-looking next to the American brand names I came to know wine by growing up: Inglenook, Paul Masson, Gallo. My favorite vineyard was the Christian Brothers Winery, founded by real monks—a whole monastery of Father Serras, I imagined, babbling in Latin and lifting wooden goblets to the heavens. Later, inspired as much by *The Grapes of Wrath* as by César Chávez and the United Farm Workers, I would boycott California wine along with many of my peers. But as a child, I loved wine—its lofty words and gestures as much as its taste—and the only wines I knew were the ones from California. Rosés and glittering yellows called "whites" and deep dark reds, all with screw-on lids instead of corks. Wines with absolutely no *terroir*, as the French call the elusive combination of land and climate and tradition that result in the highest quality. Wines that my parents drank when we had company or on holidays.

We were a family of true Californians, snug in our rancho, on our cul-de-sac, sailing the freeways in our boat-like cars. Like many Californians, both my parents were transplants from other states and socioeconomic groups: my dad the son of a New York lawyer, my mom a veritable Joad, the displaced daughter of a sometime migrant worker from Arkansas. We barbecued steak on a hibachi and ate tacos but had few direct encounters with anyone not like us. Occasionally, my mother would pack us kids up in the station wagon and travel—an endless voyage across the whole state, it seemed to me—to a Mexican market with muddy floors and brown beans in barrels and massive papayas that smelled like cheese. There we bought vegetables for almost nothing and always, for us all to share as a special treat, a greasy bag of salty, crunchy pork skins, a delight of my mother's childhood that we never had at any other time.

My father was never in on this treat. I suspect he would have disapproved of it, as he did the other bland, greasy foods—sausage gravy, cornbread, anything fried— of my mother's upbringing. He preferred what *he* knew: the crunchy sauerkraut and back-burner ragùs of the Brooklyn immigrant neighborhood he grew up in. I could never reconcile his open-mindedness about most foreign foods—which he indulges to this day—with his snobbishness about others. But, as he would later tell my sisters and me whenever we brought up the topic of racism, a favorite object of study in our teenage social studies classes, "Everyone is prejudiced against someone else, whether they want to admit it or not."

The blend of cultures in my parents' marriage typified our neighborhood: blurrily Caucasian, for the most part, but culturally inclusive as far as it went. The neighborhood embraced a range of Old World religions—Jewish, Protestant, Catholic, atheist, perhaps even Hindu or Buddhist—and a variety of ethnic backgrounds. The surnames were German, Jewish, Irish, English, Norwegian. A Japanese-American family lived at the bottom of our street. An Indian-American woman named Meena lived next door and once brought us a tray of crunchy triangular snack breads made of chick pea flour and a fiery green chutney to dip them in. Neutralized in our neighborhood by professional status and the economic equalizer of buying on credit, the various groups merged at regular cocktail, bridge, and block parties and eventually disappeared entirely into a racial group I came to think of as "Californian": culinarily-speaking the race-neutral opposite of "ethnic," a word that started appearing in grocery stores as I grew up.

Californian moms cooked what was emerging in the fifties and sixties as the standard American cuisine: back-of-the-box recipes with important-looking, capitalized names for international dishes unknown in any of the nations that populated this country throughout its history. Beef Wellington. Stroganoff. Duck "à la Orange," as my mom called it. German Potato Salad, a warm, bacony, sweet-sour mixture I never encountered in my years in Germany. Chili Con Carne and

Tamale Pie, dishes never eaten in Mexico. A tomatoey Gazpacho Junípero Serra would never have recognized.

Soon, we left Junípero behind for the Gold Rush, which brought to California not only gold-seekers from all over the world but the women who serviced them in every way—as launderers and hotelkeepers, wives and fellow miners, prostitutes and entertainers, and even muleteers, and victims of the inevitable rapes and murders. Surely we studied the Forty-Niners and their doings in some detail, but all I remember are those women who tagged along after them and threw together massive pots of hash or beans to earn back the men's gold. Later, intrigued, I studied them. Some of them profited nicely, like eighteen-year-old entrepreneur Mary Jane Caples, a Kentuckian who moved with her husband James to Placerville, California in 1849. As soon as they arrived, James got dysentery, an ailment common among the Forty-Niners, and was laid up for three months. Mary Jane had to make some money. She writes:

> . . . I concluded to make some pies and see if I could sell them to the miners for their lunches, as there were about one hundred men on the creek, doing their own cooking—there were plenty of dried apples and dried pealed peaches from Chili, pressed in the shape of cheese, to be had, so I bought fat salt pork and made lard, and my venture was a success. I sold fruit pies for one dollar and a quarter a piece, and mince pies for one dollar and fifty cents. I sometimes made and sold a hundred in a day, and not even a stove to bake them in, but had two small dutch ovens.

So much to learn here. Married young women were apparently free to do business on their own. Peaches and apples were grown in Chile and exported, dried, in big wheels. The Forty-Niners lunched on pies probably pretty much like the apple pies truckers stop for at gas stations these days, I imagine, and they cost about the same amount.

But, as with all real learning, there's so much more I want to know. How were those fruit wheels imported from faraway Chile? And where did the spices for the mincemeat come from? For the salt pork, were the pigs raised locally? What produce was being raised then, in what would soon become the major farming region of the United States? And above all, how does one bake pies in a Dutch oven over a camp fire?

Jo Ann Levy, another mercenary cook of the Gold Rush, reports having "no oven" and baking "all my pies and bread in a dutch oven," but I have trouble imagining this culinary feat. How do you "bake" anything in a pot over a fire? Doesn't it burn on the bottom of the pot? Did they elevate the pie above the bottom, on a trivet of some sort? Or could these cooks have meant *fried* pies, like the "mince turnovers" yet another Gold Rush cook, Mary Ballou, mentions in a letter to her son back in New Hampshire? The letter was posted from a place called "California Negrobar," a settlement of African-American gold-panners on the American River, where Ballou and her husband ran a boarding house. In addition to the turnovers, she made "Donuts," pies of all sorts, "Buiscuit," stuffed ham, baked chickens, "Indian jonny cake," and "coffee for the French people strong enough for any man to walk on that has Faith as Peter had." I'd so like to have these women's recipes.

The Gold Rush and the later construction of the transcontinental railroad also brought the ancestors of my Asian-American classmates—like Eddie Wong, one of my earliest crushes—and with them popular new foods like *chow mein* and *chop suey*. Such standard Chinese-American dishes are neglected these days in favor of Thai curries and Vietnamese noodles, but they were familiar in the culinary lingo of my childhood: the food of restaurants, of city people and their city ways, foods mocked in takey-outy jokes and the cartoons I watched on Saturday mornings.

But how did *I* know what these dishes were? We certainly never cooked *chow mein* or *chop suey* at home. And, in a family with six kids and only one income, we rarely went out for dinner or even ate the hot lunches at school, and we never brought food in. I wouldn't really even experience what we called Chinese food in this country until many years and places later, as an adult, at an odd little Chinese restaurant in Cambridge, Massachusetts, that was shaped like a ship and where whoever I was with usually ordered sweet-and-sour pork or General Tso's chicken but I always ordered the same dish: steamed pork wontons on a bed of bean sprouts covered with a watery red sauce of peppers and ginger.

Chow mein and *chop suey* were nevertheless familiar to me even before I ever ate them, epitomizing, somehow, a rich rightness that, as I matured, I would increasingly attribute to all things foreign. I suppose I imagined that Eddie, a portly happy boy who knew the answer to every question anyone ever asked him, was reared on such foods. Brain foods. Happiness foods. Foods that would keep my sister Joanie and me, as my father was always warning would happen to us if we didn't eat what was on our plates, from shriveling up to shadows of our former selves and blowing away. The very words *chow mein* and *chop suey* had a synaesthetic connotation in my childish ear—a quality akin to onomatopoeia, except that I didn't *hear* what the word signified; I *tasted* it. *Chow mein* was, in this gustapo-etic context, any filling and profoundly satisfying mixture of textures and tastes.

And *chop suey* . . . oh, can't you just taste those chopped vegetables, feel their sweet crunchiness contrasting with the chewy bits of meat in the salty sauce?

I read over and over again in those days a book called *Fifth Chinese Daughter*, the autobiography of a Chinese girl named Jade Snow Wong who grew up in San Francisco in a first generation immigrant family. I learned from her book so much about her culture and my own. How my culture tightened and restricted hers, consigning it to basement factories and narrow streets and a strangely separate world called Chinatown. But I learned too that there was no holding Jade Snow's culture in. It burst out of shop doors into sidewalk fruit and vegetable stands and flew out of windowless factories into the toys in every toddler's hands and fashions worn on every street in the United States.

Jade Snow's family made denim jeans and overalls. In Jade Snow's account, I tasted the differences between her large Chinese family and my large German-Irish-Scottish-English-Choctaw-Just-Plain-Poor family, and I savored the many similarities. I shuddered at her family's often cruel-seeming habits, such as referring to Jade Snow not by her name but by her low rank in the family—fifth in a string of useless daughters—and requiring the children to attend Chinese school after regular school in addition to working in the family clothing factory. The family was hard-working and frugal, saving denim scraps to make their own shoes. Twenty years later, having read Jade Snow's account throughout my youth, I constructed, with a confidence that startled me, my own cloth shoes, from memory.

And from Jade Snow I learned everything I would ever need to know about rice. How her family first tested free samples given to them at a store in Chinatown entirely devoted to the sale of rice, then bought a year's supply all at once. How they transported and stored the rice, talked about it, washed it, cooked it. I learned that rice changes over time—that new rice and old rice don't taste or cook up the same. And, more than anything else, I learned what rice meant to Jade Snow and her family and probably to many people all over the world: plain old ordinary rice steaming in a pot on the stove—the staple of their diet—had more value than flakes of gold glittering at the bottom of a pie pan full of creek water and sand.

Rice, now one of California's top agricultural products, was farmed in the Carolinas from Colonial times but took off out West in the early 1900s in response not only to the burgeoning Chinese population following the Gold Rush but to a new influx of rice-eaters from the U.S. Territory of Hawaii: hopeful indentured servants originally imported from Japan for backbreaking work on Hawaiian sugar plantations. They would find farm labor in California in many ways even less welcoming than working in Hawaii had been— the contracts they were forced to engage in even more Laban-esque, the rewards for hard work slimmer, and the laws governing their residence increasingly mean-spirited. Many would look back with regret on the lives they had left even further behind them in the southern Japanese farmlands of Kumamoto, Yamaguchi, and Hiroshima.

Although many of my classmates were Japanese-Americans, we never learned anything about their history as Americans. Or else I just don't remember. Instead, I somehow or another became aware of people in faraway Japan making yearly pilgrimages up snow-capped Mount Fuji and living in paper houses and folding up their beds when they got up in the morning. As I got older, I would come to have an appreciation for Japanese art, for fog-filled landscapes and the raw beauty of nature they often depicted. Once, when I worked in a bookstore as a teenager, I almost spent fifty dollars, which included my discount, on a coffee-table book called *How to Wrap Five Eggs*, a photographic exploration of Japanese packaging design. I wish I had bought it. It's out of print now and, when I can find it used, costs $300 or more. It is the most beautiful book I have ever seen.

What I actually remember from school, though, was the kimono-clad mother of a Japanese-American classmate coming to our room and teaching us how to use dainty, pointed chopsticks and how to mold in our hands balls of seasoned rice called *onigiri* and then decorate them with bits of brittle, smoky-tasting seaweed. I remember that when I made my *onigiri* into a white whale with teeth arranged in a big black grin, the woman clapped her hands in enthusiasm. I didn't want to destroy my artwork by eating it, but I did anyway. The rice tasted good, satisfyingly chewy and bland.

My classmate's mom also brought in other Japanese delicacies for us to try. One in particular—a dessert item, she said it was—has come to mean Japan for me in an elemental way that has nothing to do with any other experience I have had of the country or its people. It was a mossy jelly, also made of seaweed, that came in a can, like jellied cranberry sauce, only green. The woman cut it into cubes and then served them to us on fancy miniature napkins. My classmates made faces and expressed noisy reluctance to try theirs—even the woman's own son seemed unenthusiastic—but I was greedy to get my little napkin and disappointed that we only got to have one cube each.

Despite the woman's cajoling, most of my classmates wouldn't even taste the dessert as we went around the room, and those who did exclaimed "Yuck!" and dropped the cube, still intact, immediately back out of their mouths. Their disgust didn't daunt me, though. The transparent jelly looked like moss agate, my favorite gemstone: like a cube of pond water, dusky green, streaked with dark algae.

Beautiful. It would be delicious, I knew, and I waited with excitement for my turn.

I don't know what I was expecting when I put my cube in my mouth. Sweetness or some compelling flavor that didn't happen, I suppose. But it tasted terrible. Unlike Jell-O, it was strangely nonresistant to the tongue, crumbling under pressure. It tasted mildly salty, like snot, like congealed tears, and I, too, had to spit it out.

I did it stealthily, though. Guiltily. I could hear my father's voice in the back of my mind, admonishing the picky eater, pronouncing scornfully, with a groan, when one of us didn't like a food we were served, "Argghh! You just don't know what's good!"

I didn't know then that the desserts of other cultures are often their least likeable foods—too sweet, not sweet enough, too greasy, the texture too weird. And I hadn't yet learned that a display of one's culture's culinary artifacts among foreigners often meets with disgust. Or that the purpose of such public tastings may even be to elicit this disgust, this evidence of the precious difference between those who, in my father's words, "know what's good" and those who are on the outside and can never appreciate it. I was too embarrassed to look up and find out if the woman was angry or hurt by my rejection of her dessert. I only know how ashamed I felt that I couldn't like that green jelly. And somewhere, beneath my shame, I felt betrayed.

The unpalatable tastes of shame and treason in regard to all things Japanese have stayed with me, and I have to surreptitiously spit them out into my napkin whenever I learn anything new relevant to Japan and its people. I was an adult before I learned about the U.S. internment of Japanese-Americans during the Second World War—a historical event that had probably directly affected some of my elementary school classmates' families but was never discussed in class and even today remains virtually unknown to the majority of my college students—but when I did, I simultaneously tasted deep shame and had to bite my own self-righteous tongue and swallow all mention of Pearl Harbor and choke down the horror stories my students in Beijing had told me of Japanese brutalities in their country. It is, surely, not possible to excuse atrocities by comparison with others. What's cruel is cruel. And our evil is no less evil than anyone else's.

My father would say, "See, underneath all the talk, you're prejudiced, like everyone else." But it's not that simple, I think. Sure, we are all prejudiced, I wanted to tell him, even as a teenager. Sure, we all secretly think we are better than everyone who is not like us. We feel superior to them, and we want it to stay that way. Even individually, in our homes—our own private sanctuaries protected against all things foreign—we fight little identity fights, right down to how we pronounce certain words or lay out the silverware on the table or hang the rolls of toilet paper in our bathrooms. In my family nowadays, we argue about whether the hamburger is more properly dressed with ketchup, California-style, or with mustard, the default hamburger condiment in Oklahoma.

But it is education that cures us, I think. Tasting. Chewing. Swallowing. Changing our minds. Learning to love something new and different. And even, wadding up our failures in our napkins and hiding them away in the furthest corners of our schoolroom desks.

For much of my life, I have hated what I have known of my home state. The blinding white wealth of the cul-de-sac of my childhood. The sparkling supermarket where my clever teenage sisters and brothers earned twice minimum wage—twice what I earned at the bookstore in the mall—to bag groceries or enter into a cash register strings of numbers that meant tortillas, soy sauce, avocados, sugar. I hated California beach beauties, with their carefully nurtured tans and grapefruit diets. As a young person, I carried on a campaign of one against California and what I thought it represented by clothing myself in formless dresses my father called potato sacks and refusing to shave my legs. Throughout my college years, I owned no car and had to either bum rides where I wanted to go or else wait hours for one of Orange County's almost nonexistent public buses. I sought out the more authentic "ethnic foods" at greasy spoons in far-off neighborhoods I would never otherwise have visited. And I couldn't wait to leave home, leave California, leave the country of my birth to see other lands and other people and speak other languages than the one that had filled my mouth since childhood. But it is hard to reject your own culture. No, impossible.

Once, a friend of my parents asked me why I didn't shave my legs. I was home from college that weekend, and my parents were entertaining. I wore a summer dress for the occasion, and somehow I ended up alone with this man out on the patio, he with his martini and I with my sea breeze, both of us spearing rumaki with toothpicks from a shared plate.

"I'm revolting," I told him in all seriousness, staring down proudly at the thick black hair on my legs. I was not aware until he howled at the humor of it that I had punned my own cultural dilemma: To revolt against one's own culture is to be, at the core, revolting.

And California, which I ate of throughout my youth, is part of me. It is in my brain, my hands, my feet. I see and hear and taste through the filters of its myths. It is in the very muscle and bone and surging blood of who I am. Having learned California by mouth, I cannot undo in myself its history—neither its richness nor its cruelties—any more easily than I can remove the hardened yellow fat from a savory stew that I have already eaten.

PAN-FRIED MUSHROOMS

In my family we call these Irish mushrooms, for reasons I have forgotten.

Choose mature mushrooms that have opened up their gills—champignon-type is fine, but any sort will do, as long as they're the classic mushroom shape. Wipe the mushrooms clean with a cloth and remove their stems. Heat a skillet over a medium flame and lay the mushrooms in, gills up. Put a little pat of butter and some salt and pepper in each mushroom and continue to cook, undisturbed, until the butter melts and the brown mushroom juices run. Put a lid on the skillet until you're ready to serve them. Make sure you serve some good bread so you can sop up the buttery, mushroomy juices.

RAISIN PIE

Robinson Crusoe made me a lover of the homely raisin. One of my favorite ways to eat raisins is plain, by the handful, with a few unsalted almonds or walnuts. This is the perfect dessert, I think, after a rich meal—that and maybe the dark brown, crunchy oatmeal raisin cookie my husband and I share at Barnes & Noble after our weekly dinner out. I like raisins in fancier desserts, too. I rarely see raisin recipes in contemporary cookbooks, though. I especially love raisins in pie of any variety. Here are some of my favorites.

Double-Crust Raisin Pie

My mother-in-law first made me this pie early on in my marriage, unaware that raisins undid me. It was love after that.

Boil together:

> **2 cups raisins,** washed and drained
> **1/2 cup boiling water**
> **1/2 cup sugar**
> **1/2 teaspoon salt**

Mix together:

> **1/3 cup orange juice**
> **2 tablespoons cornstarch**

Add the cornstarch mixture to the raisin mixture and cook until thick. Then add:

1 tablespoon butter
1 tablespoon grated orange rind

Pour the filling into an uncooked pie shell (See page 29.), top with pastry, and bake at 450° for 15 minutes, then at 350° until golden brown.

Vinegar Pie

This pie is like a cross between a mincemeat pie and a pecan pie. It forms a wonderful brown meringue topping as it bakes.

Preheat oven to 450°. Chop briefly in food processor and set aside in a mixing bowl:

1 cup raisins

Cream together in a food processor:

1/4 cup butter
2 cups sugar

Add to food processor and process until creamy; then pour into the bowl with the raisins:

1/2 teaspoon cinnamon
1/2 teaspoon allspice
1/4 teaspoon cloves
4 egg yolks
3 tablespoons cider vinegar

In another bowl, beat until peaks form:

4 egg whites
1/4 teaspoon salt

Gently fold the egg whites into the sugar mixture, going around the bowl and stirring with a rubber spatula up from the bottom and over until you see no more clumps of frothy egg white. Pour the mixture into an uncooked pie crust (See page 29.) and bake at 450° for 15 minutes, then at 300° for 15 to 20 minutes. Cool the pie completely before cutting—at least 2 hours.

Raisin Cream Pie

Bring to a boil; then simmer, covered, for 5 minutes:

1 cup raisins

1/4 cup water

1/2 teaspoon finely grated lemon peel

Combine with a wire whisk; then cook over a very low flame or in a double boiler, stirring constantly with the whisk until thick:

1/2 cup sugar

4 tablespoons flour

3 egg yolks

1/4 teaspoon salt

1 teaspoon vanilla

2 cups milk

Add the custard to the raisins and allow filling to cool slightly while you make the meringue topping.

For the meringue, beat until soft peaks form:

3 egg whites

1/4 teaspoon cream of tartar

Combine and add 1 tablespoon at a time, beating all the while:

6 tablespoons sugar mixed with 1/2 teaspoon cornstarch

Pour the filling into a baked pie shell. (Follow the recipe for a single crust on page 29; then bake the empty crust at 350° for 15 or so minutes or until just beginning to turn golden on the edges.) Top with meringue, pulling the spoon up over and over again to make little waves and points. Brown at 400° for 10 minutes or until the meringue is golden. Cool well before cutting—at least 2 hours.

GAME

Traditional recipes for game typically involve marinating the meat first in everything from vinegar to buttermilk in order to "remove the wild taste." I think, though, that if you have the good fortune to get your hands on some wild meat, which has no hormones or antibiotics or salts or colors added to it, you should want to know what that tastes like. Gaminess is another name for the flavor of wild meat, a good clean flavor. Dark-fleshed game—such as venison, wild duck or goose, jack rabbit (North American hare), bear, moose, or elk—has a gamier flavor than the light-fleshed meat of rabbit, squirrel, opossum, and most birds (quail, pheasant, etc.). Game is typically very lean, even wild duck, so whenever one of my hunting friends or neighbors gives me game, I typically cook it wet. If the meat is in one big piece, I either pot roast it or slow cook it with celery and wine. If the meat is cut up in smaller chunks, I make stew. If the meat is a particularly tender cut, such as the entire back of a hare or a tenderloin of venison, I sear and pan roast it in its own juices and make a rich gravy. However you cook game, be sure to inspect it carefully and remove any shot and embedded bits of fur by carefully cutting into any purplish spot or tiny hole. If it looks as though it might be where a shot pellet entered the flesh, it is. Wash the meat in cold water and dry it with a clean towel. Specific recipes follow.

Game Pot Roast with Pan Juices

Sear the meat on both sides in a heavy pot or pan that's about the same size as the piece of meat. To sear is to panfry in a small amount of fat on a high flame until dark brown. I don't find that it makes much difference if you flour the meat beforehand or leave it as is. Add enough liquid—broth or water or black coffee or a mixture—to come halfway up the side of the meat and bring it to a boil. Season with a bay leaf and, if you can get them, a teaspoon of dried juniper berries, or else about 1/4 cup gin. Cover tightly and simmer over the lowest possible heat until the meat is easily broken apart with a fork—2 hours or more. Halfway through, if you want to have pot-roasted vegetables, add quartered onions, peeled carrots halved lengthwise, celery cut into long chunks, and—unless you're making mashed potatoes—quartered potatoes. Serve the meat and vegetables drizzled with the thin brown gravy from the pan. This recipe is also tasty with lean cuts of beef.

Slow-Cooked Game with Celery and Wine

Best for light-fleshed game, such as rabbit, squirrel, or fowl.

For three or four pounds of meat, chop at least a cup or more of celery. Put the celery in a lidded pan with a good 1/4 to 1/2 cup of olive oil and a mashed clove or two of garlic. Lay the washed meat on top of the celery, cover tightly, and simmer 2 hours without opening. After two hours, the meat and celery will have created a fair amount of liquid in the pan. Strip several sprigs of fresh rosemary onto the meat, add 1/2 to 1 cup of wine (red or white, dry or sweet), several coarse grindings of pepper, and about a teaspoon of salt. Cook over a high flame until about half of the wine and pan juices have boiled away; then add a beef bouillon cube and a dollop of tomato paste. Cover and simmer for 15 to 30 minutes. The best part of this dish is the sauce, so mop it up with good bread: the crustiest but plainest bread you can make or buy, preferably a saltless bread, like the bread of Tuscany. One of those scrawny free-range chickens, cut up and skinned, also works for this recipe.

Game Stew

Best for dark-fleshed game.

Cut the meat into largish chunks, flour them, and brown them in a stew pot in a little oil. Add coarsely sliced onions and continue to sauté until they are limp. Add meat broth from the boiled-down game bones or else chicken or beef broth that you have on hand or, if you have no broth, water and a couple of bouillon cubes. Regardless of how much meat you have, add enough water to make the amount of stew you need. Bring to a boil, cover, and simmer until the meat is tender—1 to 2 hours. Add salt to taste, cracked pepper, a few leaves of fresh sage if you have some, and peeled potatoes, cut into large chunks, one potato per person. Boil uncovered until the potatoes are tender. If the stew is too thin to suit you, stir in a thin paste of flour and cold water and cook until thickened.

Game Pan Roasted in Its Own Juices

I have this recipe from my friend Susanne, who lives in Berlin, where you can buy game in the supermarket. She uses the long, deep purple backs of hare, and it is my absolute favorite German food. This recipe can be used with large, tender cuts of any dark-fleshed game, such as venison or boar. As with most game dishes in Germany, it is served with wild cranberry sauce, which is chunky, not jellied, and comes in jars. Ordinary cranberry sauce will do: Boil fresh cranberries in enough water to see it through the top layer of berries and sugar to taste, and it will thicken quickly into a sauce the consistency of soft jam.

Heat 1/4 inch of lard or vegetable oil to smoking in a heavy-lidded pan just big enough for all of your meat to lie flat. Carefully lower the meat into the hot oil and brown on high until the meat looks just about burnt underneath. (If you have one of those screens that keeps you from spattering fat, now is the time to use it.) Flip the meat over and brown just as dark on the other side. When the meat is well browned on both sides, clap the lid on, turn the fire down as low as it goes, and cook without opening for about an hour and a half. Meanwhile, sauté a whole bunch of quartered mushrooms in butter until they are brown on the edges. Set aside. About half an hour before the meat is done, boil a big pot of peeled and halved potatoes in salted water. When meat is ready, remove it to a platter and put the pot lid on top of it to keep it warm and moist while you make the sauce.

For the sauce, whisk 2 to 3 tablespoons of flour into the drippings, and stir over medium heat until the flour is brown but not burnt. Add all at once about 2 cups of the water from the boiling potatoes, whisking and scraping the bottom of the pan well. You should have a thin gravy. Add more potato water if it seems too thick. Now whisk in one 8-ounce carton of sour cream. Stir smooth and let thicken over low heat. Add the mushrooms. Taste for salt. (Notice that you haven't used any salt at all except for what was in the potato water, so you may need lots, depending on how much natural salt your game had.) Serve the sauce over the meat with the boiled potatoes and cranberry sauce.

GUACAMOLE

You need the avocados to be perfectly ripe for this—firm but resistant to the pressure of your thumb. Because you do not want avocados that someone has already pressed a thumb into—they go bad, then—it's best to choose hard ones and let them ripen in your fruit bowl. When they're ready is the day to make guacamole.

Peel two avocados and mash them with a fork. Add:

**minced tomato and sweet onion, to taste—and/or 1 to 2 tablespoons
   salsa
salt
a squeeze of lemon or lime juice**

In my family, we always put an avocado pit back on top of the bowl of guacamole—supposedly to keep it from going dark. One kid always grabbed the pit at the table and sucked off the guacamole. I never do the pit thing now, though. Even if it does keep the guacamole from oxidizing, which I doubt, the guacamole always gets eaten so fast it doesn't have time to go dark.

ENCHILADAS

The best enchiladas are filled with chopped sweet onions and a grated white cheese, such as any firm white Mexican cheese or Monterey Jack.

Prepare the corn tortillas by softening them in hot oil in a skillet, then immediately removing them to a 9x13-inch baking pan. Roll each softened tortilla up with some of the cheese and onion mixture in it. Line the rolls up side by side as you go. Cover with a can of green enchilada sauce. Top with a little more cheese. Bake in a preheated 350° oven until the enchiladas are hot and the cheese is melted—20 to 30 minutes.

Note: When I am dieting (which is usually), I soften the tortillas by wetting them and then microwaving them for about 30 seconds rather than dipping them in hot oil. I also up the onions in the filling and put less cheese on top. It's not quite as good as the traditional way but satisfies my urge for enchiladas while lowering the fat considerably.

SCRAMBLED EGGS RICHARD NIXON STYLE

If I had to scramble an ostrich egg, I'd do it the way my mother once told me Richard Nixon liked his eggs—scrambled, with a tablespoon or so of cottage cheese per egg. For an ostrich egg, that would mean adding 24 tablespoons of cottage cheese—that's 1 1/2 cups. I don't know how my mom knew the way Nixon liked his eggs. It seems like an awfully intimate thing to know about someone. It must have been in some magazine she read. In any case, eggs are good this way, even if you don't usually like them scrambled.

MY FAMILY'S BEEF STROGANOFF

Remove the fat and any bones from a 1-inch thick chuck steak. Cut the remaining meat into bite-sized rectangular chunks. Mix the meat chunks in a bowl with enough flour to coat the pieces. Sauté a coarsely chopped onion in 1/4 cup oil or butter or a mixture of the two. Add 1 chopped clove of garlic just as the onions are getting limp. Add the floured meat and fry over high flame until browned. Add an 8-ounce container of sour cream. Season with salt and pepper. Serve with wide noodles.

German Potato Salad

This recipe is for the American dish. For real German potato salad, see page 167.

For 4 to 6 servings, boil in their jackets, then peel, thickly slice, and set aside in a bowl:

4 or 5 big potatoes

Fry in a skillet until crispy:

1/2 pound of bacon

Set the bacon aside, pour off all but 1/4 cup bacon grease, and fry in the remaining fat:

1 coarsely chopped onion

Add:

1/4 cup sugar—or less, depending on your taste
1/2 cup vinegar—or more; some potatoes just seem to suck it up, and the
    salad should be wet, so add more, if you need to
1 beef bouillon cube
1/2 cup water mixed with 1 tablespoon cornstarch—optional

If you want a thick sauce, use the cornstarch and water and cook till thickened. Otherwise, just heat the vinegar-sugar mixture, stirring well to incorporate the bacon drippings. Pour the sauce over the hot, sliced potatoes in the bowl. Taste for salt. Serve warm or at room temperature.

Chili con Carne

The perfect fast meal for a winter dinner. Serves 4-6.

Brown in stew pot:

1 pound ground beef
2 coarsely chopped onions
2 finely chopped cloves of garlic

Add to the pot and stir over medium heat until fragrant:

1/4 cup or more chili powder—it's impossible to use too much

Add:

2 cans of dark red kidney beans or red beans or a mixture of the two,
  with their juice
1 cup canned tomatoes
1 cup water

Bring to a boil and simmer, covered, for maybe 20 minutes—or longer if you like. Taste for salt and add some if necessary. Put a box of saltines, a bowl of chopped sweet onions, and a bowl of shredded sharp cheddar on the table and serve the chili in big bowls.

FRIED PIES

These are the turnovers my grandma used to make. My mother-in-law still makes them and calls them "fried pies." She rolls canned biscuit dough into thin circles and folds them over a filling of heavily sweetened, cooked-down, peeled and chopped apples. She crimps the curved edges of the dough tightly shut with a fork and panfries the pies two at a time in a little grease in her black skillet. When they're brown on both sides, she sprinkles them with sugar and piles them on a plate. Sometimes she spices the applesauce with cinnamon or nutmeg or both, but I like them best plain. Forty-Niner Mary Jane Caples would have had to make her own dough, of course—probably a simple mixture of that salt pork lard, flour, and enough water to make it stick together well enough that she could pat it out into circles.

I make these pies with my regular pie dough: 1/2 cup butter processed with 1 1/2 cup flour and enough ice water to make it just stick together. (See page 29 for more detailed instruction.) Then I bake rather than fry them. For a filling, I sweeten the pulp left over from making crabapple or plum jelly. Or I use applesauce made from surplus apples from an overproductive tree. Same folding of dough and crimping, only sometimes I brush them with milk or egg white and sprinkle them with big-grain sugar.

Steamed Wonton on Bean Sprouts with Chili-Ginger Fish Sauce

I made up this recipe from guessing so that I could still eat them after I left Boston. They are so good and relatively easy to make. I have a certain way of eating them: Holding the wonton in my chopsticks, I nibble the top open and spoon in, with my other hand, some of the gingery chili sauce. I eat the sauce-filled remainder of the wonton in one bite, then take a slurp of the crunchy bean sprouts in the hot broth. The sauce is pretty hot and gingery, though, and probably won't work for everyone. Serves 4 to 6 adults. (Not a good dish for most children.)

For the sauce, combine and set aside in a pretty bowl:

1/4 cup fish sauce
1/4 cup water
a grated two-inch piece of peeled ginger
2 or more tablespoons plain, red chili paste, such as Indonesian
sambal oelek—Asian markets have hundreds of chili pastes. Choose one that is bright red and doesn't mention garlic, beans, or much of anything but chili and salt in the list of ingredients.

For the filling, combine:

1 pound ground pork
several finely chopped green onions
1 finely minced garlic clove
1 teaspoon salt
1 teaspoon sugar

Fold 1 teaspoon of filling into a 2-inch square wonton skin. Fold the edges up past the ball of meat to make a sack or goldfish shape. Repeat until the filling is used up.

Heat to boiling:

6 cups chicken broth or a mixture of chicken broth and water

Drop in the wontons. Bring to a boil again and cook until the meat is no longer pink inside when you cut one open, about 10 minutes. Meanwhile, rinse and drain raw bean sprouts and distribute them between as many bowls as you are serving. As soon as the wontons are done, divide them up and put them and some of the hot broth on top of the bean sprouts in each bowl.

6

Three Bean Salad

Our dog Bingo was a mutt. Somehow this fact made me respect him more than I did other dogs. I considered myself a mutt, too, for one thing: the product of many breeds and ancestral homes. German. Irish. English. Scottish. Native American of some sort. Maybe even African, judging from an entry in a old census that listed as a "freedman" one female ancestor I was hoping might link me unequivocally to the Choctaw pedigree of my mother's stories. My parents came from New York and Arkansas, but I grew up in California and Connecticut. Bingo couldn't have been any more of a mongrel than I was.

Also, my parents said that mutts were healthier and better-tempered than purebred dogs. Certainly Bingo was healthier and better-tempered than our previous dog, Daisy, a beagle. According to family legend, Daisy cried all night for weeks after we got her, and I believe there were house-training difficulties. Daisy was my sister Sharon's dog, acquired when I was too small to remember her at all. As a child, I always associated the Daisy of our family stories with the Daisy in a song my dad sang: Everyone was half crazy over her, even though she never would give her answer true. Daisy was a prissy, coy creature, surely—in my imagination stout and flirty about the eyes. There are no family photos of her—or of Bingo, for that matter. And I don't know how Daisy left us—if she died or we got rid of her somehow. But Bingo, I knew, was a different sort of dog altogether. Certainly not coy or prissy. Not given to bingeing on the sly or withholding a straight answer. Bingo was rugged, male—insouciant, certainly, but single-minded in his interests. He kept his own counsel.

Bingo was lean and scruffy, with longish salt-and-pepper fur. Pepper for the most part, actually, but frizzled and whiter around the jowls and haunches and belly, like an aging man. He was part terrier, we had been told, but he didn't yap like one. His barks were throaty and mature-sounding. And rare. As I said, he didn't have much to say to the rest of us.

The cul-de-sac we lived on butted up against a hill on one side and a canyon on the other, and at the midpoint between hill and canyon was our backyard: a circle of prickly green lawn transcribed by a slope at the top of which was an asphalt drain ditch that rose in one direction to the blue lupines and rotten-sweet iceplant on the hill and descended in the other direction to the tall dry grass and weeds and rocks of the canyon.

According to my parents, the canyon was full of rattlesnakes and skunks. Also king snakes, which killed and ate rattlesnakes but were not poisonous. And coyotes. And scorpions. And spiky tumbleweeds. A dangerous place, in short. As a toddler, I once disappeared into it, and my father, who had been left in charge of us kids while my mother was shopping, searched frantically for me everywhere but there. I reappeared by the patio, wailing and covered with bits of canyon debris, just as my mother arrived home. Subsequent to that, the canyon was forbidden territory for us kids—and thus correspondingly romantic in our imaginations: an outback of huggermugger brush littered with half-eaten rattlesnakes, dead children, and a fabled glass house—actually an observation post of some sort—that the bigger kids of the neighborhood made up stories about and trekked out to in the summertime.

The furthest into the canyon I ever dared to go on my own was along the drain ditch just beyond our official backyard. There I stomped out multi-room forts and outfitted these retreats with cooking utensils and dishes and cutlery and other essentials I constructed from twigs, milkweed pods, broken toys, and treasures I had collected from the neighbors' trash. I prepared for myself half-pretend, half-serious meals of the local foodstuffs. Woody brown acacia beans. The sweet inner blades of grass from our lawn. Lupine pods, which really did look edible, but were actually scarily bitter. Triangular iceplant, the fleshy blades of which my mother once said would keep you from dying of thirst in the desert but which were strangely dry on the tongue. I seasoned it all with a sprinkling of the poppy-like seeds from scraggly bushes the neighbor kids and I called salt-and-pepper trees, and I enjoyed these meals alone, sitting on rock furniture, in the slithery quiet of the canyon's edge. The dry grass walls of my fort were taller than I was, impervious to all other company but Bingo, who emerged from between the stalks from time to time and then disappeared again moments later, like a ghostdog, visiting his former haunts.

Bingo was not subject to my parents' strictures and often went down into the canyon, disappearing for days at a time. He came back feral-looking and stinking of skunk, his hair matted with burrs and bits of tumbleweed. My mom scrubbed him down with tomato juice in our bathtub. Afterwards, his fur smelled metallic and tomatoey for a day or two and stuck out in stiff flames all over his body, like the fur of a cartoon animal that had suffered an electrical shock. No one knew why Bingo went down in the canyon. We guessed that he had a coyote lover. Or maybe he hunted and ate the wild beasts that lived there. Rattlesnakes. Skunks. Or perhaps he scavenged for the half-rotted bodies of any children who had wandered in and couldn't find their way back out again. Bingo was always hungry.

His favorite food was boiled liver, which my mother cooked for him regularly in our smallest Revere Ware saucepan. Sometimes, while she changed a diaper or resolved some dispute among my siblings, she made me stand at the stove and watch to make sure the liver didn't boil dry and burn. As it cooked, it went from purple-red to grey to greenish, and blood leaked out and coagulated into blobs and strings and made the cooking water yellow. I could barely stand to be in the kitchen for the smell, but, if he was around, Bingo would appear at my feet and moan for it. When it was totally grey-green and hard, my mother let it cool a bit. Then she cut it up into a bowl for him, poured the warm broth over it, and set the bowl on the floor. Bingo slurped it down in three or four shoulder-shaking gulps.

Bingo's passion for the nasty liver intrigued me. Although my sisters and I liked certain atypical kid dishes—like huge white lima beans cooked with ham hocks and the smoked baby oysters our parents ate with cocktails—for the most part our parents had to force us to eat what they served us. Of course, we engaged in the usual tricks for particularly objectionable foods: the wadded napkin, the potted plants, the rush to the bathroom with half of a deviled ham sandwich shoved down our underwear. Sometimes we got away with these subterfuges. And some monstrosities they served us were so noxious that our outrage outlasted even our parents' dogged insistence that we clean our plates. Tomato aspic, for example, a Thanksgiving requisite in our house: cream cheese and gelatin melted into tomato juice with bits of celery and black olive and onion and then poured into our fish-shaped Jell-O mold. Plopped out onto a plate, it looked exactly like congealed vomit. In an effort to preserve the conviviality of our Thanksgiving meal, my father gave up trying to make us kids taste it when we were still small and only commented, after exhaling a deep growl of disgust both of my daughters and I have inherited, that he'd know we were grown up when we finally agreed to try a bite.

For me, though, the absolute worst food in the world was something called Three Bean Salad, a mixture of canned beans marinated with onions and celery in a sour vinaigrette. I have seen this salad served elsewhere, and usually the beans involved are green beans, kidney beans, and so-called wax beans—long colorless beans that look like albino green beans. In my family, though, the bean mix was made even more atrocious by the substitution of garbanzo beans for the albino green beans.

No child likes garbanzos, in my experience. As an adult I would eventually come to savor their grainy, meat-like consistency with spicy sausage and tomatoes in a stew that a Spanish acquaintance served me one uncharacteristically cold winter evening in New Orleans. And they're good atop brown rice, with sour cream, Worcestershire sauce, and tons of chopped parsley in a variation of a comforting and addictive dish that my vegetarian friend Carla ate for dinner almost every night—using kidney beans, which are also good—when she came to New Orleans to nurse me after I was sexually assaulted. And in the hummus my friend Valerie taught me to make by putting the canned beans in a blender with lemon juice, garlic, and tahini.

As a child, though, I wouldn't touch garbanzos. I was put off by their creepy hue—called "flesh" color in my old Crayola crayon box—and their mealy texture and their bulging shape, so suggestive of mysterious anatomical parts. My daughters refuse to taste them to this day and have called them "butt beans" ever since they were small, but to me it was the little nub of embryonic root between the globes that offended. A blunt little hairless tail, perhaps, but secretly more like the unnamed part of my baby brothers' bodies I saw when my mother diapered them.

Garbanzo beans were enough of an oddity to be expensive in those days, so my mother typically bought them only when they were on sale. But when she did, she bought them en masse, three, four, five meals' worth at a time. Sometimes, rooting around in our pantry for the bag of lentils my mother had ordered me to find for our meal or little cans of tomato paste for spaghetti sauce, I would discover six or eight cans of garbanzos—stacked in ominous columns—waiting for the moment when my mother would assemble them into that evening's wretchedness.

Although not yet an actual participant in the cooking process, I was an interested observer even then and frequently called upon to watch a pot or locate whatever it was my mother was planning to cook. My presence in the kitchen gave me the opportunity to develop a more proactive, and effective, weapon of defense against punishment meals than whining and napkins: the preemptive strike. Daily, when I opened the pantry for the ingredients of that evening's meal, I searched the shelves for garbanzos. Whenever I found any, I hid as many cans as I could in my clothes and snuck out to the canyon. Edging down a little past the furthest I had last ventured, I hurled the cans, one at a time, into the tangle of tall grass and burrs and sage brush below. Bingo, if he was around, stood by and watched, scuttling briefly into the brush, as after some smelly animal, whenever he heard the muffled thud of a can tumbling invisibly against other cans, rocks, dry dirt, and the drain ditch. The next day, or sometimes later that evening, I returned to the pantry and disposed of a few more cans in the same manner, until they were all gone—at least until the next time my mother found them on special.

This subterfuge depended heavily on my mother's faulty memory—a good call, on my part. Over time, my siblings and I forgot to dread the dish, and my mother seemed to forget to desire it. She bought garbanzos less and less frequently and, when she did, forgot them immediately. She never seemed to notice their disappearance, even when I was cavalier enough to get rid of a few cans directly from the shopping bags upon her return from the supermarket. So, for a period of several years we had no Three Bean Salad, and gradually I, too, forgot about the cans in the pantry or the ones collecting beneath the weeds beyond our yard.

Until, one afternoon, we came home from somewhere in our station wagon to find a neat pile of dented cans in our driveway. The labels had mostly faded or rotted away, and the cans themselves were as unrecognizable as any other trash— deeply dented and rank-smelling, some of them split and rusting along the seams. My mom and my sisters and brothers and I all got out to look at them and speculate over where they came from, and even I didn't think of the cans in the canyon until Bingo appeared from the side of the house with another can in his mouth. He stepped delicately to where we stood and dropped the can on the pile with the other cans, then left us once more for the canyon.

I felt my throat grow hot and readied myself for the trouble I knew was coming, but none came. Even then, my mother did not appear to notice that all the labels still readable were for garbanzo beans or to remember the cans of garbanzos she had bought over the years that had disappeared. She just picked the cans up, one by one, and put them in the trash and then poured bleach water on the mess in the driveway to get rid of the smell. Later, when she told my dad, he seemed to have little impulse to analyze the situation either and no suspicion whatsoever of any misdeed besides Bingo's odd behavior in dragging up stinky garbage and piling it in our driveway.

Every once in a while, until we left that house and moved to Connecticut when I was nine, Bingo would deposit another can in our driveway. In the same spot. With the same dog nonchalance. And each time I underwent the same horrifying certainty, a feeling on the verge of shame, that I would be caught. And each time my family merely laughed at our dog's antics, and my mother cleaned up the mess.

"I wonder where he gets those cans," she mused. And we all joined her, me the loudest, in speculation. Bingo, we decided, was a strange dog.

Three Bean Salad

This really isn't a bad dish, unless you are a child.

Drain and combine in a large bowl:

a can of blunt-cut green beans
a can of dark red kidney beans
a can of garbanzo beans

Add, toss, and let marinate a while before serving:

chopped onion
chopped celery
salt
pepper
1 to 2 tablespoons oil
1/4 to 1/2 cup cider vinegar

Enjoy.

Garbanzo Bean and Sausage Stew

There are so many recipes for this dish, in so many cultures. Having only eaten it once, cooked by a person I met only once and never saw again, I can offer you only my guesses about what she put in it. Still, the dish was, for me, as a lifelong hater of garbanzos, transformational.

Soak overnight, then cook, partly covered, on medium low in *lots* of water—at least a quart and a half—till soft but not mushy:

1 pound of garbanzos

The cooking could take anywhere from 1 to 3 hours, depending on the age of your beans. Check them every now and then to make sure the water doesn't disappear entirely. Add boiling water if you need to—you want the beans to stay covered with water. By the time they are done, you should have enough of the liquid—a wonderfully fragrant bean broth that will jelly slightly when you put it in the refrigerator—to be visible, but not a lot more.

Sauté in olive oil, then add to pot:

> **andouille,** if you can get it, **or any good-tasting, firm, Cajun-type sausage** about 10 or so inches long, cut into disks about 3/4 inch thick
> **1 onion,** coarsely chopped
> **1 green pepper,** coarsely chopped
> **3 big cloves of garlic,** smashed with the flat of a knife

Add and stew, covered, for one hour:

> **1 large can of chopped tomatoes**
> **1 bay leaf**
> **a pinch of saffron strands**

Twenty minutes before serving, taste for salt and pepper and add:

> **3 large potatoes,** cut into large chunks

Continue cooking until potatoes are just done.

Hummus

Puree in a food processor or blender:

> **1 can of chickpeas,** drained—but save the liquid to add if you want the hummus thinner
> **1 tablespoon tahini**
> **1 clove of garlic** (My friend Valerie uses 2 cloves, but I find even one clove of raw garlic overwhelming. To lessen the effect, I smash the garlic lightly with the flat of a knife, mix it into the hummus, then remove it before serving.)
> **juice of 1 lemon**
> **a speck of cumin** (not in Valerie's recipe but I like it)

Taste for salt, lemon juice, and cumin and add more if you like. Parsley is also a good addition. Serve drizzled with olive oil alongside good, chewy bread and wedges of sweet onion.

7

Working Girls

I began working when I was eleven. It was at a resort a couple of miles from where we went to live when my mom grew unhappy with our life in California. Having grown up poor, she never really felt like she belonged in the ritzy suburban neighborhoods where we lived. According to family legend, she closed her eyes over a map of the United States and set her finger down on Connecticut. I always wished it had been a map of the whole world and she had put her finger down on Perth, Australia, or Paris, France, or some place I had never even heard of. Later I would conduct my own version of my mother's search for happiness over and over again in lands increasingly unknown to me. In any case, my father applied for jobs in Connecticut, and before too long we were living out in the country, in a tiny Polish-Italian town at the base of the Connecticut River.

We lived on a thinly populated dirt road that wasn't snowplowed in the winter, in a falling-apart house built in 1770 that my parents renovated and then sold five years later for twice what we had paid for it. It had a leaky basement, a broken heating system, and an attic full of treasures: long bearskin coats from the twenties, carnival glass candy dishes, rat and squirrel skeletons, a pair of rubber fly-fishing waders that must have been worn by a giant, and old records a quarter of an inch-thick with grooves on only one side featuring Jazz Age hits like "Mean to Me" and "Nothing Does-Does Like It Used to Do-Do-Do." The house sat on 5 1/2 acres: one acre of shaggy lawn, which in summer and fall we had to cut weekly with a riding mower, and the rest woods of mostly deciduous trees with a sparse underbrush of sassafras, poke, and wintergreen.

Those woods were my heaven. A fragrant place where dead leaves crunched underfoot and trees grew pink-and-brown shelves of woody mushrooms and you

65

never knew where you might trip on the lichen-covered remains of a stone wall. Along one edge of our property, the woods broke onto a tangle of black raspberry brambles, chokecherry trees, and elderberry bushes with their delicate umbrellas of tiny black berries. I collected all of these fruits to make jams and pies and cobblers.

My first couple of years in Connecticut—at nine or ten years old—I spent whole days exploring the possibilities of our woods and fantasizing about a life in which I never left them that involved collecting all the food I would need until my death: day lily roots and hickory nuts and berries dried like Robinson Crusoe's raisins. In a recurring dream that lulled me to sleep most nights, I gathered this sustenance and stored it in bins in an imaginary house that had no windows or doors. A stream ran through one corner. The inflow was my source of water, the outflow my toilet. In this hermitage, like some demented medieval anchoress, I would live forever.

I loved Connecticut from the second I set foot on its spongy soil, so full of mysteries, so full of life. Once, I found what looked like a massive rutabaga growing in the loam beneath the trees. I dug around it with a spoon for days before I finally figured out it was a swelling on the bright orange root of the maple tree above me. Southern California, in my child memory, seemed like a plastic toy by comparison: a made-up place out of Dr. Seuss or a sanitary outpost in outer space, its colors too bright to be of this world, its surfaces too shiny and perfect. The flora of our suburban landscaping there—birds of paradise, fuchsias, gerbera daisies—had been scentless. Even the purple acacia tree from which my mother had made my little sisters and me choose the switches with which she punished us seemed artificial and unreal in my recollection compared to the wet, odorous maples, oaks, and birches of our Connecticut woods.

The town was full of resorts built in the twenties and thirties. When we first moved there, in the midst of what we were told was an uncharacteristically severe snowstorm, a local arsonist was burning down abandoned resorts one by one. While my family and I huddled in sleeping bags around the fireplace in our otherwise heatless house, the big entertainment of local teenagers was to go sliding around the ice-covered roads in the night and watch the fires from their cars, in between necking and taking stealthy swigs from sloe gin fizzes.

Those exciting fires, which we heard about at school and our parents read about in the paper, were all my family knew of the famous resorts until, our first summer, the town swelled with vacationers staying at those resorts still in business. They roamed our country road in Bermuda shorts and Hawaiian shirts, gawking as we kids ran ahead of our dad on the mower to toss stones and twigs away from its blades. From beyond the low stone wall surrounding our yard, the tourists stared unabashedly at whatever we were doing and sometimes even pointed, as if we were picturesque cattle grazing or farmers going about our quaint chores.

The tourists were New Yorkers, according to my dad—the big city people of his past. My father modeled a studied ignorance of the resort crowd whenever they passed and referred to them afterwards as "Lard Butts," a venomous term we never heard him use for anyone else.

Nevertheless, with my parents' encouragement, from the time I was eleven or so, I walked to the resort nearest us in the early evening almost every day of summer to babysit those New Yorkers' children. I always brought along a book to read, in case I got the chance, and I read in the dimming light as I walked down our dirt road to the paved road and then to the turnoff that took me past the chicken farm where we got eggs and nasty manure for our garden and then on to the scraggly wooded grounds of the resort itself.

I was entering, in those years, the age of romance and lived in a fantasy of longing for a life I could hardly imagine, where mystery and danger lurked in the woods and the puzzling safety of love beckoned from the distance. I fed this fantasy with novels I borrowed ten at a time from the local library—pulp Gothics of Victoria Holt and Daphne du Maurier mixed in with sturdier selections from Thomas Hardy and the Brontës—usually about a young woman, orphaned or in some other way suddenly bereft and thrust into a harsh and scary work world for the first time. Often, like me, she took care of rich people's children. Invariably, she fell in love, typically with her forbidding employer. Or sometimes she was a young bride who had married too quickly, only to discover terrible crimes in her husband's past. Always the girl was smart and of course beautiful, but somehow helpless. Always the man was rich, abrupt in his habits, and given to inexplicable silences or absences or both. Always the book shimmered with a dark, sexy kind of independence that I craved at that age, in which girls first parted the curtain of adulthood onto the terror of aloneness and submission and thankless work, but then were rescued from it all through the alluring but equally terrifying panacea of marriage. Thus I sleepwalked to my place of employment, the book spread open in one hand and the other hand raised before me to brush away the gypsy moth caterpillars dangling from the maples.

At the front desk of the resort, I was given a cabin number, and I searched around among the moldy buildings until I found the one where I would spend most of that night. I arrived to find the family on the verge of parting. The parents, dressed up and smelling of makeup and cigarette smoke, were waiting at the door of the cramped space, impatient for me to get there, impatient to leave.

If the children were older, they were usually sitting in front of the TV watching *Laugh-In* or *All in the Family*. They barely noticed I was there. Toddlers and babies, though, clung to their mothers, and I had to be ruthless. When I pulled them away, they stretched like leeches and started up a wail that would continue until the parents returned, at two or three or four in the morning.

By eleven or so my older charges would slump over on the couch and I could carry them off to their bunks. But the little ones defied any effort to lull them. They screamed themselves purple and strained to the window, the door, stretching their hands open and closed toward the lit up buildings, just barely visible under the trees, where their parents drank Harvey Wallbangers and played bridge and shrieked happily into the dark night, ignorant—or perhaps not—of their babies' and my despair. It was not possible to read.

The parents paid me upon their return. Sometimes it was the woman, who fished around in a miniature handbag for the exact amount, filtering coins through long, painted fingernails into my sweaty palm. If I was lucky, though, it was the man who paid me, always rounding up to the nearest bill. Sometimes, in the generosity of drunkenness, he pressed into my hand way more than the resort's requisite $3.50 an hour, which was over minimum wage in those days and considerably more than one could make babysitting outside the resort. Unless the man insisted on walking me back, which was always awkward, I then zigzagged my way alone through the trees and dark paths to the front desk, invariably getting lost if I had been in one of the more remote cabins. The receptionist had long since gone home to wherever she lived, but usually one or two other sitters were there, waiting for the elderly security guard—a semi-retired policeman known as Pistol Pete—to drive them home.

I cringe nowadays to tell my own story. I imagine one of my daughters, now the age I was then, lost among those dark cabins full of strangers. Or, worse, one of those drunken husbands offering to walk her back through the dark. In my mind I see Charlotte's tiny face through the windshield of the sagging police car, the last girl to be taken home because she lived out in the country, sitting taut beside a sour-smelling old man she only vaguely recognized as the one who directed traffic on Sunday mornings and handed Wrigley's spearmint gum into the back of the station wagon. Or I see Lulu—a babyhater like I was in those days—in skimpy cut-off jeans, creeping in the back door not long before sunrise, so late that even my husband and I, despite our watchfulness, are asleep.

Although I have always been—even as a child—an early riser, during those summers of babysitting I slept until noon, sometimes later, emerging from my room numb-faced from sleep to breakfast all by myself on a stack of buttered white toast dipped in a cup of coffee leftover from my parents' morning that I warmed up in the percolator. After rinsing off my dishes, I put on my bathing suit, rubbed myself with baby oil, and fell back asleep again in the sun out on the concrete slab behind our house. I felt grownup, drinking coffee, eating alone, tanning. My dad would have been at work and Sharon who knows where with her teenage friends or perhaps at the supermarket three towns away where *she* worked, but my mother and younger sisters and baby brothers are all absent from my recollections. Where were they? At the town reservoir, swimming? Running errands? Trundling pails of water and manure up the hill to my mom's garden?

What if, back then, I had never returned home at all one morning? What if, while they all slept, I had been snatched up in the night—raped and stabbed and left to die in the woods? My parents and sisters and brothers might not have known until well into the next day that I was even missing. I imagine my parents at the resort, a place they had never really seen up close, weaving their way through the knots of vacationers to the now vacant cabin where I had babysat the night before, questioning strangers and sullen children who didn't even remember my name, searching between the cabins in the darkening light, in the woods, down at the creek.

Never, I think. *Never would I allow my children to roam the margins of safety as I did as a child. Never would I let them enter that world at that age.*

But all the girls in town babysat at one of the town's many resorts. Not surprisingly, like modern day governesses, we made up a tractable workforce, far more responsible than many of the adults we worked for. Sent out by our trusting parents into the night to labor for strangers. Counting our bills and change in our bedrooms. Bragging to our friends about the sums we had amassed during the summer. Just before the start of school, we bought new jeans, peasant shirts, and Indian sandals at Bob's Army Surplus, where our older siblings bought their roach clips and peace sign jewelry.

Four or five hours a night. $3.50 an hour. Just about every night of summer. Tot it up. Seven, eight, nine hundred dollars. In 1970, that was a lot of money.

At twelve, forgetting that I hated what I so far knew of resort life—hated shuffleboard and bingo, hated mildew and cigarette smoke and the distant shrieks of laughter in the dark, hated babysitting, hated children, hated my own younger brothers and sisters, much less children I didn't know and would never see again, hated spending my summers doing anything but wandering the shady woods alone and reading romances—I accepted a second job corralling children at the resort all day long as a day counselor, and from that point on I virtually lived at the resort every summer until we moved back to California.

Work started early in the morning. Together with several other counselors my age, I first oversaw the kids at breakfast, learning twenty years before I had children of my own how to eat my meal while at the same time grabbing hands out of plates and managing conflicts and seeing to it that everyone else at the table had what they wanted. After breakfast, we herded the kids out to the pool or the rec room or the creek. At a set hour that did not coincide with the parents' mealtime, we herded the children back to the dining room for lunch. Then it was more games or quieter crafts or naptime, depending on the ages of the children in our group.

I find it remarkable that I can remember so little of these summers. Not one girl that I worked with, no particular child I felt sorry for or older staff member that I liked. I didn't fall in love with anyone that I recall. I can summon the white suit and insinuating cologne of an older man who taught ballroom dancing, and, in some back layer of my mind, as scratched and foreign as a daguerreotype in my memory, I believe that fancily dressed adults bossa-novaed atop a raised outdoor dance-floor as I and a group of children watched from below. But these may be chimeras. In truth, I can recall no face or gesture or voice or even a name besides Pistol Pete, and that was just a made up name.

Once, having never rowed a boat in my life, I dumped a canoe full of children into the creek. I vaguely recall some of the other staff abandoning their own canoes to help me get the kids who couldn't swim out of the water, but I can't remember any more than that. I can't remember trudging through the water with the sopping, screaming children or my probable terror or any sense of guilt. I'm sure that we told none of the grownups about the accident and that, although the children likely chattered excitedly about it afterwards, none of them were really aware of the danger they had been in. I tremble now to think of it, though, or to imagine how my life would have changed had the shadowy memory coalesced into a drowned toddler, someone's child, dead. I remember the feel of the slick wooden oars, how I kept repositioning my hands in an effort to steer. What if one of my own daughters had been in that boat, pulled unsteadily forward by my own childhood attempt to row like the others?

What I do remember about the resort is the food. The breakfast menu featured items I had never heard of, and that meal became the highlight of my day. Chewy, donut-shaped hard rolls called bagels—they wouldn't become ubiquitous all over the country until years later—were served with an amazingly rich cream cheese flecked with green onions. Crusty potato pancakes with applesauce.

Matzos crumbled up in eggs and scrambled or soaked in a sweetened egg mixture as for French toast, fried, and eaten with syrup.

The children taught me to smear a crispy matzo with butter and sprinkle it with salt, and even now, out in the country in Oklahoma, I crave that combination of elemental flavors, nothing at all like saltines or ordinary bread, and I have to drive over an hour to a store that sells matzos.

My favorite breakfast at the resort, though, was eggs scrambled with bits of a salty pink fish and onions. When I told my dad about it, he laughed and said it sounded like lox and eggs. Jewish food. Lox, he said, was smoked salmon. He liked it, too, had eaten it as a child. I wanted to get some and make the dish for us at home, but he told me lox were too expensive. And he didn't know where we could buy them anyway.

Lunch at the resort was just sandwiches, although occasionally there was a soup I liked made of beef broth with barley, carrots, and briny canned mushrooms. And dinner was what anyone might imagine at a resort or at a country club or on a cruise ship or any place where opulence is the main gastronomical goal. Grilled meat, the fat blackened and crispy from the fire. Wedges of iceberg lettuce with thick slices of Bermuda onion and blue cheese dressing. Tray upon tray of fruits viewed as exotic in my family's frugal household: strawberries, grapes, melons in all colors, pineapple wedges with the rind still attached and a decorative sliver of green spiky leaves.

So as not to look greedy, I took less than I wanted and snuck off with my plate to a remote empty table, away from the families, where I ate, once again, alone. To me, the extravagant food meant not just luxury but license, carnality, escape—a culinary equation that, despite my objections then and now to the life the resort represented, I must have carried with me into adulthood: When my husband and I go out for the evening, leaving our children at home, these are the foods I crave.

The foods eaten by real governesses were another thing altogether, my romances told me. Oatmeal. A bit of cheese. A slice or two of bread and a pot of tea taken alone in a draughty room. I craved these foods, too, and still do. The barest scrapings of enough, but satisfying somehow, like the sustenance diet of my house dream. The foods of true independence.

Poor, orphaned and despised Jane Eyre, in her moment of flight, passes out from hunger and would have died had she not been discovered by other orphaned girls in more fortunate circumstances: with a brother to provide them with a home. The sisters nurse Jane, first with a piece of bread dipped in milk, then gruel and tea, and then "a little cake, baked on top of the oven," which I decided was some sort of pancake.

And there's the even poorer Lucy Snowe of Charlotte Brontë's barely fictional autobiography *Villette*. Lucy, like Charlotte, has not even beauty to carry her forward when she is cast out into the want ads and her uncertain dreams of something better than babysitting. What does she eat in her heaven of independence—the school of one's own that her fellow teacher and almost lover, Monsieur Paul, surprises her with at the end of the novel? They share one meal there, we're told—hot chocolate, soft rolls, and a "plate of fresh summer fruit, cherries and strawberries bedded in green leaves"—before the frequently absent Monsieur Paul leaves on another trip and dies in a shipwreck. But what about afterwards, after the novel ends and Lucy finds herself, once again, alone in the little schoolhouse? I'll wager, in a pantry somewhere, she stores up flour and beans and raisins in bins. Enough to feed her students till the end of the school year. Enough to get by on herself after that—maybe, if she lives very frugally. Enough, if she is careful, for a lifetime of spare, solitary meals, consumed with gratitude.

My mother did not find happiness in Connecticut. And later, I did not find it in my journeys abroad. There, I met many like us, women in flight from every sort of dependence, searching for love, working hard, earning just enough to keep on working and to savor, on occasion, the scraps of someone else's prosperity. In their stories, in my own, I hear the voice of Charlotte Brontë herself, about to leave her teaching post at the Pensionnat in Brussels. No sooner did she arrive than she fell in love—with her employer, of course. Like the taciturn hero of a romance, he first nurtured her affections, then, apparently remembering his wife and reputation, spurned them. Thus, work became for Charlotte, not escape, not opportunity, not freedom, certainly not romance, but merely work, and she was miserable, the more so because she had nowhere else to go besides back. Back to her childhood, to the parsonage where she grew up. To her aging father, who would soon die, and to her younger sisters, Emily and Anne, both sometime governesses. To the very life she once fled, now her only refuge, one she looked on with all the longing and uncertainty of the prodigal, returned home.

Not long before she returns to England, Charlotte writes Emily:

> I should like uncommonly to be in the dining-room at home, or in the kitchen, or
> in the back kitchen—I should like, even, to be cutting up the hash, with the clerk
> and some registry people at the other table, and you standing by, watching that I
> put enough flour and not too much pepper . . . How divine are these recollections
> to me at this moment! Yet I have no thought of coming home just now; I lack a real
> pretext for doing so; it is true this place is dismal to me, but I cannot go home

without a fixed prospect when I get there. . . Tell me whether papa really wants me very much to come home, and whether you do likewise. I have the idea I shall be of no use there—a sort of aged person upon the parish.

And indeed she does sound aged, far older than her twenty-seven years. And in five years Emily will die. And the next year Anne. And a few years after that, at thirty-eight, Charlotte herself—having months earlier finally married her father's curate, a man in whom she found, as she wrote from her deathbed, "the best earthly comfort that ever woman had."

Lox and Eggs

I make this dish without dirtying a chopping block.

Pare half a small white onion in curved chunks into some butter in a frying pan and sauté until barely translucent. Turn the flame to low. Add 2 to 4 eggs beaten with a little milk; then immediately cut in as many slices of lox as you can afford—1 slice per egg, if you need a number. Stir slowly to scramble. To make the eggs prettier, use green onions instead of white. To make it richer, cut in some cream cheese just as the eggs are beginning to set and toss lightly. Serve with toast or a bagel.

Mushroom Barley Soup with Carrots

Add to a pot of boiling beef broth:

a handful of pearl barley
1 or 2 finely chopped carrots
1 chopped rib of celery
1 chopped onion
1 or 2 cans of sliced button mushrooms

Serve when barley and carrots are soft.

PANCAKES

The ultimate food of aloneness. Makes three or four pancakes—enough for one hungry governess.

Melt in a bowl or glass measuring cup:

1 tablespoon butter

Add and mix well with a fork:

1 egg
2/3 cup milk
1 tablespoon sugar

Add and mix with a fork:

2/3 cup flour
1 teaspoon baking powder
a few shakes of salt

The batter should be thick, but not too thick to pour. If it is, add a bit more milk. Lightly grease a griddle or frying pan, heat it to medium-high, pour three or four cakes, and cook them until brown beneath—check with the edge of a spatula—and just beginning to bubble on top. Turn and brown on the other side. Eat, in the hand, plain, or with a little butter—or, if you must, on a plate, covered in maple syrup or honey or jam.

HASH

Hash is a leftovers dish made from the finely chopped remains of a traditional Sunday dinner of roast, potatoes, vegetables, and gravy. Nothing is measured. Use all the leftovers that you have.

Sauté in butter:

a small onion, minced

Finely mince, add, and continue sautéing until the raw potatoes are glassy looking:

leftover roast meat of any kind
leftover potatoes cooked any way
1 or 2 raw potatoes, pared

leftover, cooked vegetables (Roots, like carrots or turnips, are especially good
for hash, but you may also use green beans, broccoli, zucchini, etc.—anything
that can be chopped up. Avoid unchoppable vegetables, like peas and corn.)

Add and cook until the raw potatoes are just cooked—not mushy:

leftover gravy (Or, lacking that, sprinkle the sauté with flour, stir it well, and
then add enough liquid—broth or milk—to make a somewhat gloppy
mixture.)

salt and pepper to taste

The hash may be served now, with a fried egg and toast. Alternatively, you may
brown the hash in butter or bacon grease in a skillet, first on one side, then the
other, and serve it with a poached egg on top.

8

Food Fantasies

Food has raw romantic power, especially for children. It is not merely the tame romance of the familiar, of mom-love and home and cherished memories, but the wilder allure of what is not known at all. Exotic foods. The foods of other lands, of other people a child must strain to imagine. Illicit foods even, foods from not only outside one's culture but outside all sense of what is right. Taboo delicacies never before seen on one's plate or in the grocery store. Offal. Insects. A sorcery of flavors known only in dreams.

It is for this reason, perhaps—the sheer romance with which foods can evoke our inevitable longing, even in the most congenial of upbringings, for what is *not* what we already know—that the foods we read about in books as children so excite us. Fairy tales—although among the darkest stories children will ever read and articulating some of their deepest fears—offer the most obvious examples. In tale upon tale, sweetmeats and feasts manage to supplant cruelty, condemnation, and abandonment with the lure of potential salvation from these realities, however ephemeral. In mouthfuls often nibbled on the sly or stolen from others more fortunate than they, half-starved characters—and, by extension, half-starved readers—sample not merely hope of something better but heaven itself.

Consider the gingerbread cottage that Hansel and Gretal find in the woods. In the original story, it's made of bread, with clear sugar windows and a roof paved with cookies.

"How is that possible?" Every-Child breathlessly wonders . . . and promptly forgets the loveless mother—so horrifying a character that the Grimm brothers changed her to a stepmother in later editions—who sends her hungry children into the woods to die. And the possibly worse father, who—as so often happens in cases of child abuse—witnesses his spouse's cruelty but takes no action on his children's behalf.

And then comes the meal that the witch serves the starving children once she gets them in the door of her enchanted house. So homely and strange and perfect a feast: milk and pancakes, with sugar, apples, and nuts. Who would ever eat such things together? Who could dream up anything better? In this simplest of repasts, the past is erased so completely that we read on into the reality of the hungry children's situation with new horror. They are trapped by someone whose intentions are as evil as their parents', if not more so. Hansel is caged and fattened, destined to be eaten himself, and his sister becomes the witch's unwilling henchgirl, tending the oven in which her own brother will be roasted. Thus the storyteller by the fire teaches the innocents at her feet two spiritual truths in one blow: the promise of good things to come and the likelihood that evil people will try to hijack and pervert our desire for good things along the way.

I fantasized as a child about the food mentioned in every book I read. I longed to try green eggs and ham, which I decided must be wonderfully flavored from the addition of a luscious herb that grew wild and fragrant in one of those weird Suessian landscapes, which always reminded me of Africa as depicted in *National Geographic* magazines and in the Catholic Missions pamphlets my parents got when I was little. In Maurice Sendak's *Where the Wild Things Are*, I either didn't notice as a child or else forgot the child-rage that precipitates Max's journey into the unknown. Instead, what linger in my memory are the far-off "good things to eat" that Max smells—or remembers or imagines—in the wild outpost to which he has fled. A bowl of soup, a glass of milk, a wedge of cake. Simple comforts of a home Max has forgotten—or perhaps never really valued before he left them—that appear at his bedside, as if conjured by his longing, when he finally returns.

From another of Sendak's books, I unconsciously memorized a culinary anthem to the ultimate comfort food, which in those days I knew only out of a can:

> In January
> it's so nice
> while slipping
> on the sliding ice
> to sip hot chicken soup
> with rice.

I dreamt of the cheese the Grandfather roasted for *Heidi* and the raisin cake that the five little Pepper children struggled to make for Ma's birthday and then ended up

burning in their broken down oven. And, from a story I read in school but don't otherwise remember, I retain the aching memory of an apple and a hunk of bread tied
into a checkered kerchief—unfamiliar and appealing not only as a meal I never
enjoyed in childhood but in its form: the apple the happiest green, the bread not
sliced or hygienically packaged but grabbed up in happy-looking cloth, the Old
World word *kerchief* suggestive not only of another time but another world entirely,
where happy-go-lucky young people embarked into the unknown and routinely
encountered the supernatural. Reading became the road ahead of me in edible form,
and the food passages in the books I read as a child made me nervous with desire.

One of the *Childcraft* books that came with our *World Book Encyclopedia* featured an episode, rewritten for the child reader, from Mahatma Gandhi's autobiography. In the story, the boy Mohandas, a strict vegetarian, is wheedled by a
friend into eating meat. He immediately becomes wretchedly ill. It's hard to
explain how this story affected me, how it made me crave meat, which I have
always loved above all other foods, and simultaneously hunger for a life of meat-
lessness. In my mind, I snuck off with Mohandas into the jungle and there, in the
half dark, beneath a canopy of trees, chomped down on my morsel of the forbidden substance—the flesh of a living creature cut apart and burnt in a fire—and
then vomited it up again and was immediately, perversely, ravenous for the food
that awaited Gandhi when he got home, whatever that might be. Some sort of
grain, I guessed. Salad. Vegetables in a sauce. Lentil soup, one of few meatless
meals in my own house and a dish that I usually despised.

Until my children entered the world of chapter books, I thought my childhood
obsession with food in books was just a quirk of my own, that I was the only one who
strained outward past known experiences and into the world in this way. Then
Charlotte started reading historical biographies and fictional diaries from *American
Girl* and asking me to fix foods I had never made before: *Marillenknödel* (apricot
dumplings rolled in cinnamon-sugar from Austria) and some Japanese rice snacks
that we eventually found a recipe for online. And the other day I overheard Lulu and
her friends discussing the Aztec hot chocolate mentioned in their sixth grade
English book. One of them had even copied off the recipe into her notebook—just
as I would have as a child—and tried to make it at home. It turned out darker than
regular cocoa, she said, and cinnamony, with crunchy little bits of nuts in it. The girls
all murmured in awe. These are twelve-year-olds, mind you. Rural kids whose
plebian tastes, when I run through possible dinner menus, rarely stray far beyond
the culinary kid-boundaries of spaghetti or chili. They usually profess to hate
school, Lulu especially, and here they were remembering something from an earlier
year's English book, in yearning voices that made me want to cry. Although Lulu

loves to read, it was the first time I ever heard her mention that she even *had* books at her school.

Many years ago, to make some extra money when I was a graduate student, I took off a semester and substitute-taught seventh-grade English at a tiny rural school in southern Arkansas. My students were boys mostly, or so it seems to me in my memory, but I may just remember the boys more clearly because they were so fully present: loud and smelly and ceaselessly active—forever jabbing, jiving, jumping. Knuckleheads, the principal called them. That was a good name for them. Always cutting capers and making offensive gestures and fighting and getting into trouble. One day, I had to go to the office for a few minutes, and when I got back all the boys in the class were gone. The girls sat there, their faces painted with a nonchalance as unnatural looking as their makeup. I was just about to run back to the principal's office to report the boys missing when there was a noise in the ceiling and one of the tiles moved. One by one, shrieking like birds, they dropped back into the classroom. I could never figure out how they had managed to organize the stunt so quickly. Probably they had done it before. Many times. Probably every time there was a substitute teacher. They were wild boys. They smelled like gym shoes and sharp pubescent boy-sweat and hair that hasn't been washed in a few days. In winter, they came to my desk for assistance and brought with them the distinct whiff of burnt wood or wet dog or swamp.

I liked one boy in particular, a short, delicately made boy named Tyrone whom the other kids called T. It was T's great dream, he wrote in essay after essay, to play NBA basketball. He was indisputably the best player on the junior high team and so devoted to the sport that it seemed possible that he might actually achieve his goal, except that he was so small.

"He may grow," the other teachers told me, but I guessed from his delicate bone structure, his petite hands and feet, that he probably wouldn't. At games, he skimmed in between the other boys' lumbering forms like a lizard among cabbages, arching up around a massive-seeming elbow or belly to sink the ball, impossibly, from right beneath the enemy. It broke my heart to watch him.

I taught mostly writing that semester, partly because it was the only thing I knew how to teach and partly because the teacher I was replacing—she was having a baby—had left me a note saying she always skipped the writing exercises in the textbook. She advised me to do the same. Writing wasn't tested over, she wrote, so it wasn't important. As a grad student in creative writing, I was outraged. And I saw right off that none of the kids could write. So we wrote.

T was simultaneously the worst and the best writer in class. His sentences were appallingly miswritten, lacking all punctuation but what was entirely unnecessary, and his compositions were as short as aphorisms. But everything he said was so concrete you were right there with him. In one essay he went with his family on the big trip of his life thus far, to California, where they went to Disneyland and Universal Studios and, most wonderful of all, stayed at a fancy hotel where he and his brothers—there were two younger boys just like him—ate club sandwiches stacked five layers high. There were several ingredients in each layer—different kinds of meat, sliced avocado, sprouts, cheese—and the whole thing was skewered together so that it didn't fall apart with long toothpicks decorated with a frill of colored cellophane on one end.

On the second day there, as the brothers were touring the hotel, they spat over a high balcony into the reception area below, and one of them managed to hit a doorman or a bellhop or a maitre-d'—someone in a short coat with gold buttons, T wrote—square on the top of his shiny bald head. What ensued in T's essay was like a scene from *Curious George*: men in uniforms running and pointing and closing in from all directions, shouting in foreign languages, the brothers scattering, and, in the end, a burly security guard seizing T up by one arm as if he didn't weigh anything. And, in the midst of all this, T wrote—contemplatively, lovingly, deliriously—that this wonderful hotel smelled like coconuts.

There was another student I didn't like so much, a hulking boy named Lewis with straight yellow hair cut like a bowl around his head. Lewis routinely brought in essay drafts written in old-fashioned curlicue handwriting and tried to substitute them for the nearly indecipherable clumps of words he just barely managed to produce in class. He looked genuinely perplexed as to why I wouldn't let him type up these neater drafts, even when I explained that the writer hadn't followed the assignment's instructions.

Lewis was finicky about many things. He didn't bray in class like the other boys when someone did something crass, and he never ate in the lunchroom because of his weak stomach. Seeing other kids' chewing with their mouths open, he said, made him feel like throwing up. So, he brought a sack lunch every day and got special permission from the principal to eat in the hallway outside my room. Lewis was also what I called an eraser, one of those students who, upon discovering an error, erases everything on the entire page and starts over. His in-class assignments were grey and pilly from erasures, and, when he handed them in, his handwriting looked carved, like cuneiform.

Lewis was rumored to be a bully, but I found this hard to believe at first. To adults, especially adult women, he was smarmily polite, calling us "Ma'am" or

"Miss" and racing to open doors for us when we approached. But then I started noticing him looming menacingly around the younger kids before school, out in the parking lot, where no adults were on duty. And once, on a class visit to the school library, I caught him.

"Him and me was just fooling around, Miss," he told me as I pulled him off a boy half his size that he had managed to corner. It unnerved me how the younger boy nodded in agreement, but it was Lewis's politeness that made the brutality all the more loathsome. Not just ordinary boy-meanness but genuine cruelty cloaked in a courtly-seeming pretense of candor and deference. From that day on, I couldn't stand the boy.

My whole attitude toward Lewis changed one day, though, when, in a brainstorming session for a writing assignment, he told the story of how he had visited his grandparents, who lived outside of Little Rock, over the weekend. He begged them to take him to a fancy Chinese restaurant in the city, a restaurant he had seen advertised on TV. Although suspicious of anything that wasn't the country food they cooked every day, his grandparents had finally given in. It was buffet-style. Lewis spent probably ten full minutes in class that day describing each dish he sampled. He detailed them so minutely I could name them back to him. Kung Pao Shrimp. General Tso's Chicken. Moo Goo Gai Pan. Egg Drop Soup.

The end of the meal was the best, though, he told us. Not only the steamed-looking cakes that Lulu would later become enamored of in Chinese restaurant buffets—dense of crumb and layered or rolled up with pastel icings and creams— but *two flavors* of soft-serve ice cream and an amazing palette of bright-colored sauces and glittery sprinkles to put on top.

"And you got to serve yourself from the machine," Lewis told the class, with reverence.

Imagine, if you will, this brawny boy, a little beige Melamine bowl in his big hand, at the soft-serve machine, craning back at Grandma and Grandpa across the restaurant and pointing as he pulled the crank delicately to extrude a loopy swirl of vanilla ice cream. Lewis was in his stomach's heaven, surrounded by wonderful foods from the foreign land of TV.

And then, the crank stuck.

The ice cream came and came and came and came. Lewis didn't know what to do, he said, and he nearly cried in the telling. He balanced the bowl with its growing swirl in one hand while he hammered discreetly on the crank with the other. Then he gave up on the crank to concentrate on containing the ice cream that kept coming out to keep it from ending up on the floor. Just as the swirl was beginning to droop over and fall, he caught it with his other hand—his bare hand, he told us—where it piled up in slow circles beneath the spout.

"I didn't want nobody to notice," he told us piteously. But it was no use. Other people were arriving with their bowls and their advice, and Lewis could hear people in the restaurant behind him laughing and saying, "That boy needs some help." His hand was full and dripping down his arm, so he set the bowl of melting ice cream down on the little ledge in order to switch hands and catch the ice cream in the other bare hand. All the while he looked for somewhere to dump the first handful of ice cream, which was melting and getting on his shirt and pants.

"All these waiters come over then," he told us, "jabbering and swatting at me with their towels, and they turned off the machine somehow." Afterwards, he said, he had ice cream all over him, and he no longer wanted any, even with sprinkles. His granddaddy got mad at him, he told us. Said, "Now you got it, you don't want to eat it." But Lewis just wanted out of there, and he didn't ever want to go eat Chinese food again.

The process analysis lesson in the seventh-grade English book featured a recipe for deviled eggs with the steps all mixed up for the students to reorganize chronologically. They were miserable at logical thinking, and their resulting recipes left out steps and were as mixed up afterwards as when they started out. Nevertheless, I boiled up a gigantic pot of eggs and brought in mayonnaise and mustard and relish and paprika and let the students follow the recipe we all decided was correct.

Judging from the groans of disgust at the sulphury smell and the fussy way the students tapped their eggs on their desks to shell them and held the bowls of yolks and condiments so far from their bodies that they could barely mix the ingredients, you would think we were making something truly foreign and revolting. Blood puddings, perhaps. Or head cheese. When it came time to eat the eggs, I had to let Lewis go down the hall to do some photocopying. He was overcome. Everyone else, though, ate at least half an egg—the girls like cats in small wet bites and the boys without chewing in one excited gulp. T and his basketball buddies devoured the halves left over, and we all went home smelling like eggs.

Food, I have found as a teacher of writing, is a magical topic. Most students like to write about it, even if they hate to write about anything else, and everything they write is interesting. When they read their food essays aloud—and they all want to—everyone in class pays attention.

Many of the stories my daughters have demanded of me from childhood are food stories. How I used to taste all the wild plants wherever I lived to find out if they were edible. And how I once, having heard about sailors who had died from eating hotdogs roasted on oleander twigs, ate an oleander leaf to find out if the plants really were poisonous. And about the time, not long after we arrived in Connecticut, when a girl I met on the bus came home with me and we made, at her suggestion, penuche—the foreign-sounding word as wonderful to me as the chocolate-less fudge. We used a whole box of brown sugar plus two little cartons of cream, and afterwards we ate the entire pan all by ourselves.

My daughters' favorite food story from my childhood is about how, at a camp-out in junior high school, I made frog legs for my friends. One girl's family had a cabin beside a frog-filled pond in the woods. As a newcomer to the region, I was fascinated with frogs. Every spring, I trespassed in the swampy field across the road from my house to witness and consider the horror of sexual reproduction. For a few weeks, the shallow ponds there writhed with thousands of frogs, glued together in sickening pairs. Not long after, the muddy green water was jellied with their eggs and then, weeks later, jiggled with pollywogs. Throughout the whole saga, terrible dreams plagued me. Of the frogs' slick blotchy skin. The intentness with which the frogs held on to one another. The monstrous smell of pondwater and mud and sex.

In science that year, my friends and I had skewered frogs between the eyes and then dissected them and watched their hearts continue to beat. We were proud of not being squirmy and disgusted like the other girls in class. In our French class, we learned that frog legs—along with snails and mysterious internal organs called sweetbreads—were considered delicacies in France. I longed to try them.

So, when we began planning our camping trip, I looked up frog legs in our *Joy of Cooking* cookbook, and, sure enough, there were instructions on how to cook them. "They are usually bought skinned and ready to use," Irma Rombauer begins. "If the frogs are not prepared, cut off the hind legs—the only part of the frog used—close to the body. Separate and wash them in cold water. Begin at the top and strip off the skin like a glove." From that point, her description of frog butchery veers into the macabre. "Through an experiment with a twitching frog leg, Galvani discovered the electric current that bears his name," she writes. Evidently, the legs might continue to move after we severed them—just as the dissected frog's heart continued to beat. As there was no refrigerator in the cabin, we wouldn't be able to follow Rombauer's advice to prevent this eventuality: "Should you prefer keeping your kitchen and your scientific activities separate and distinct, chill the frog legs before skinning." I read the passage aloud to my friends, and we shuddered with anticipation.

Once the frog legs were prepared, though, the recipes—there were four— sounded doable. As we would be camping in the forest, I selected the recipe Rombauer called "Frog Legs Forestière," which I streamlined and simplified for ease of preparation over a campfire to become an elegant sauté of the prepared legs in butter, with lemon juice squeezed over them in the pan. I pilfered a stick of butter and a lemon I had talked my mom into buying and brought along, as an accompaniment to be reheated in the same pan, an already cooked vegetable dish I had invented that summer, made by sautéing a mixture of coarsely chopped vegetables from our garden—eggplant, squash, peppers, onions, tomatoes—and cubed bread. The two dishes, I told my friends, would be our supper.

The other girls must not have believed I would go through with it, or else they were secretly reluctant to actually eat frog legs, because they also brought wieners and marshmallows, which we roasted as soon as we arrived over a fire we built in a ring of stones left by campers before us. Nevertheless, when it started to get dark out and the bullfrogs began bellowing, we paddled an old rowboat around the edge of the pond and collected two big bullfrogs per girl. We hadn't brought a gig, but the heavy paddle worked just fine as an instrument of death. We steered the boat toward the frogs' deep voices, and whenever we saw a set of eye-bumps break the surface, we whacked at them as hard as we could with the flat of the paddle. The frog turned white belly up as soon as we hit it, and we were able to lift it out of the water by one limp leg and drop it into our bucket.

At our campsite, I took charge. Using my family's big butcher knife that I had brought along, I sawed the first frog's legs off at the point just above where they joined together and the frog's abdomen swelled outward. It felt different from dissection, somehow—more like murder than science—and I had to consciously fight down a gag. The frog's skin ruched down a little around where I had severed the legs from the body. I janked it inside out and off. It was more like removing panty hose than stripping off a glove: The frog's legs looked disturbingly human, pale and shapely as a dancer's. There was no twitching. Still, I was leery of separating the legs from each other, so I left them attached.

After the first frog, the process got easier, and after a few more, the other girls, as a point of honor, each cut apart one frog. We left the legless bodies and skins in a pile near the fire and went down to the pond to wash off the parts we would be cooking.

We returned to a horror that would so haunt all of us for the remaining years of our friendship that we never once talked about it. While we were rinsing the legs in the pond, the frogs in the pile had woken up. Apparently, we hadn't killed them with the paddle but only stunned them, and now they strained, minus their powerful hind legs, to leap away from the heat, or us, or both—a sight so pitiful that we wailed into the night. We were too cowardly to end them with the butcher knife, so we dug a hole and buried them alive—or, surely dying, we hoped, as we heaped dirt and dead leaves over their writhing forms.

After the burial—because, I told my friends, it would be worse than meanness not to consume what we had killed to get—I sautéed the frog legs and made us eat them. Point of honor. They tasted like catfish but felt more like chicken in the mouth. Hardly worth the effort, we decided. Or the additional horror of watching the legs spread open as if alive again, kicking apart and twitching lustily, when I laid them in the hot butter. Later, far from the frogs' bodies, we buried their bones and what we couldn't eat. We let the fire die down and told no ghost stories that night but just got into our sleeping bags and listened to the noises from the woods around us and slept until first light.

It would not always be like this. The romance of the world beyond the fire, beyond what we could imagine, would not always horrify and disappoint us. Some realities, I know, turned out much better than I could ever have dreamt them. But for a time, when I was growing up, there was an elusive deliciousness of *not* knowing— of not even being able to imagine—that surpassed what could be tasted and chewed and swallowed. A gastronomy of curiosity and anticipation for what the world might offer that conjured dishes known to no tongue, yet known, somehow, to all.

These are the fantastic foods young men and women of fairy tales wandered from home to find. For one it was out-of-season wild strawberries beyond the path in the woods; for another the stolen liver and heart of a rich uncle's chicken. For Gandhi, it was meat. For T it was coconuts and club sandwiches, and for Lewis, Chinese food from TV. For me, it was roasted cheese. A magically comforting soup of chicken and rice. A cake studded with raisins baked in a broken oven by children who knew a poverty richer than the wealth I enjoyed. The frightful delicacies of lands I longed to see with my own eyes. Somehow I seek it still, I think, this cuisine of hope. Perhaps we all do. And in this life we will, perhaps, taste nothing more delicious.

Chicken Soup with Rice

I make this soup from broth (see page 22) that I keep frozen to use when one of my children stays home sick from school, the family needs comfort, or it's cold out and feels like soup weather. It is a very bland, warming, reassuring meal, quick to make and low in calories.

About half an hour before you want to eat the soup, heat chicken broth in the amount of soup you want to make. Add chopped onion, celery, parsley, carrot, a small amount of raw rice, and chicken breast meat (or meat picked from the trimmings and frozen with the broth). Chop the meat up into 1/2- to 1-inch cubes, and the vegetables in neat 1/4-inch cubes. For 6 cups of broth, use:

1 onion

3 to 4 ribs of celery—cut each rib first lengthwise in thirds and then
    crosswise at 1/2-inch intervals

1 carrot

1 good-size branch of parsley

1/4 cup rice

1 boneless, skinless chicken breast

Bring to a boil and then simmer until the rice is just done. Season with salt and,
if you like, pepper.

Heidi's Grandfather's Roasted Cheese *(Raclette)*

For this dish you need a special cheese from Switzerland called Raclette. *It's
expensive and hard to find where I live, and it smells terrible—or, to turophiles like
me, divine. Many Swiss people have a special appliance for making* Raclette: *a
kind of tabletop grill with flat plates on which to melt several slices of cheese
individually. But a frying pan will do. Nonstick is best, enabling the melted cheese
slices to slide out easily, but I don't have one and have found that my seasoned cast-
iron skillet works fine. Alternatively, you could make* Raclette *as Heidi's
grandfather does, by roasting the cheese in one big hunk on a long fork over an
open fire. As it browns on the outside, scrape the roasted part off onto someone's
potatoes; then roast the remainder.*

Drain and set out on the table in little bowls:

a jar of cocktail onions

a jar of sweet gherkins

any other pickled items you happen to like

Boil a pot of smallish potatoes in their jackets—two or three per person. When
the potatoes are done, drain them and put them, wrapped tightly in a clean cloth,
in a basket or bowl and set on the table.

While the potatoes are boiling, slice the cheese 1/4- to 1/3-inch thick. You will
use about 1/4 to 1/3 pound—or about 3 or 4 slices—per person. Lay a few slices
of cheese in a heated skillet, leaving lots of room between them so they don't melt
into one another. Melt over medium heat until bubbly all over and browned on
the edges. Some people put spices such as paprika or marjoram on the cheese as
it melts.

Meanwhile, each diner takes a potato, peels it if desired—the Swiss do, but I don't—and mashes it slightly with a fork, then scatters a few pickled onions or gherkins over it. Using a solid—not slotted—spatula, lift or slide a melted slice of cheese out of the pan onto each person's potatoes.

This is so good. Serve it with dry white wine and a big salad dressed with vinegar and the slightest skim of oil. So good.

Lentil Soup

These two recipes couldn't taste more different. Both are good.

The Lentil Soup I Made Growing Up

Put a pound of ordinary gray-green lentils in a pot with twice as much water. Chop and add:

> **carrots**
> **celery**
> **onions**
> **potatoes**

Cook until done—about an hour. Season to taste with salt. Serve with Worcestershire sauce.

The Lentil Soup I Make Now

If you want to make this soup and have never cooked red lentils before, I need to prepare you for one of the two great disappointments of Indian cooking: The gorgeous, bright orange of the lentils will fade as they begin to cook. When they are done, their color will be a wheaty yellow, which the turmeric in this recipe—a yellow dye—will brighten considerably. (The other disappointment of Indian cuisine, by the way, is that when Indians make the clarified butter they call ghee, *they throw away the tasty milk solids that collect at the bottom of the pan. Every recipe I have ever read says to discard them, and I have verified this directive with all the Indian-Americans I know. There is hope, however. I have not yet consulted the masses of native Indians—and it will take masses to convince me—all averring the same thing. I simply cannot believe a culture could be so wrongheaded as to discard the best part of the butter. I can't do it. I skim the solids from the top of the* ghee *and scrape them up from the bottom of the pan and savor them as I cook, just like that.)*

Boil in 5 to 6 cups of water until done—about 1/2 hour:

1 cup red lentils
1/2 teaspoon turmeric
1 teaspoon salt

While they cook, prepare what in Indian cuisine is called a *tadka*—a mixture of whole spices and/or onion or garlic fried in a few tablespoons of oil or *ghee* until browned, crisp, and fragrant. Common spices include cumin, mustard, and coriander. For some *tadkas*, cilantro is added at the last second. For red lentils, I like a *tadka* of either garlic or onions, but a combination of just a few cumin seeds with minced ginger and garlic is also interesting. Whatever you use, slice or mince the garlic, onion, or ginger as finely and evenly as you can and fry them over a low flame until very brown but not burnt—a minute or two for garlic, longer for onions. Let the *tadka* cool and serve it at the table in a pretty bowl with a spoon for those dining to drizzle, at will, onto their soup.

DEVILED EGGS

Boil a large egg or two per person for twelve minutes. Drain the cooked eggs and soak them in cold water until cool. Carefully peel the shells from the eggs; then cut them in half lengthwise, popping the yolks into a bowl as you go. Arrange the whites on a pretty plate. (Unless you have inherited one of those wonderful deviled egg plates with the little depressions in it, you may want to cut a little slice off the bottoms of some of the eggs to keep them from sliding around on your plate.) Mash the yolks, and mix in mayonnaise, good relish or finely minced pickles, and Dijon mustard in quantities that taste good to you: add a little, taste, add a little more, etc. Add salt, if you think you need to. Mound the yolk mixture into the egg-white halves and sprinkle with paprika.

PENUCHE *(Brown Sugar Fudge)*

This is easy if you use a candy thermometer.

Boil in a large saucepan over medium-low to soft-boil stage (236° on a candy thermometer):

2 pounds brown sugar (approximately 4 1/2 cups, packed)
2 8-ounce cartons of heavy cream

a good pinch of cream of tartar
a good pinch of salt

Add 2 tablespoons butter and stir slightly until just starting to melt.

Put the pan in the sink in a couple of inches of cold water and let the contents cool to 150°. Meanwhile, butter an 8 x 8 or 9 x 9-inch square pan (or two loaf pans) and coarsely chop about a cup of walnuts and have them ready. As soon as the brown sugar mixture has cooled to 150°, start stirring it. Pay attention to how shiny the mixture is as you stir. As long as it's shiny, keep stirring. Very suddenly, it will look slightly less shiny and/or ever so slightly lighter in color. When this happens, stir in the walnuts just to mix, and scrape the mixture into your pan(s). Don't think about it too much. If it seems to you that the dulling and/or lightening may have begun, it has. Get the walnuts into the fudge and the mixture into the pan(s). It goes that fast. That's the only trick you need to know for making this fudge or any other cooked-sugar (as opposed to marshmallow) fudge. That and don't refrigerate it, which makes it gritty.

Garden Vegetable Dish

Sort of a cross between ratatouille and the Tuscan bread and tomato salad called panzanella. *Make this when your summer garden is overflowing and you're tired tired tired of each vegetable on its own. Don't worry about amounts. Use what you have.*

Cut into large cubes and sauté in olive oil until slightly softened but not mushy:

eggplant
summer squash of any kind—zucchini, yellow crookneck, pattypan—
   at best a mixture
onion
peppers of any kind—bell, ancho, banana, jalapeño, etc.—at best a
   mixture with some hot

Add and continue to sauté briefly until just hot:

tomatoes, cut into wedges

Stir in salt and pepper to taste and then add fresh bread cubes in a quantity of about 1/4 the volume of vegetables. Stir just to mix. Good immediately or the next day, warmed or room temperature. This dish is especially nice gaarnished with a spoonful of fresh rosemary sprigs sautéed in olive oil.

9

In Which I Consider Zeal, Restraint, Sandwiches, and What It Means to Be Holy

Growing up, I hated the concept of bread with meat or cheese or peanut butter or anything else. The only sandwich I consented to take in my bag to school was a staid "baloney sandwich" that I made myself, featuring a round of bologna with the merest skim of mustard on one slice of white bread and butter on the other. On weekends, my siblings longed for our mother to go shopping so that our dad would make us the sandwich he always made in her absence: peanut butter and banana, with the bananas cut lengthwise so they wouldn't fall out as easily and make a mess. But I barely tolerated this treat. And I disassembled every other sandwich I was forced to eat. On the rare occasion when my family ate at a fast food restaurant, I peeled the hamburger patty from its spongy bun and eschewed all condiments. I especially hated one of my mother's favorite meals: bacon, lettuce, and tomato sandwich on toast, oozing with mayonnaise. Most times, if sandwiches were on the menu, I just didn't eat.

I'm not sure why this was. Perhaps it was a texture thing. Children are very texture-conscious. The oozing. The disturbing combinations of crunchy and soft, slimy and dry. The adhesive nature of the bread we bought, which left a wet white film on the surface of any moist item, such as lettuce or lunchmeat, when you pulled the sandwich apart. Or it may have been that, even as a child, I unconsciously considered the sandwich a private, solipsistic way to eat a meal and therefore not really what food was about. It's not inconceivable that I might have intuited from an early age what I later came believe about food: it was meant to be shared. Children know more than we give them credit for, I think.

At some point in my childhood, in any case, I saw a picture of a particularly noxious sandwich that summed up my feelings about sandwiches in general. It was in a Catholic missionary tract my family had received in the mail. In the black-and-white photo, a missionary was offering a starving African girl what the caption said was a tomato sandwich. She drew back in horror. The magazine caption seemed to think her response a tragic indication that, having starved so long, she was no longer capable of recovery. As a child myself, though, I read the picture totally differently. What child anywhere in the world would eat such a monstrosity? Bread all gloppy and gooey with mayonnaise and tomatoes. I completely understood her horror.

The girl was almost naked, and, even though her belly was round and tight-looking, her arms and legs were like sticks with skin on them, the joints outsized in comparison, like a Tinkertoy person. It was hard to tell her age. Perhaps much older than I was, perhaps only five or six. Although her hands and stance and gestures were those of a young child, her face looked more mature, like an adult's face, like an old old woman's face. But it was her expression that stayed with me: at once ravenous and recusant. Hungry and in sore need, but obstinately rejecting the offer of sustenance or comfort.

Somehow that girl's face summed up something crucial in my mind, something I was considering in those years, and I identified with it deeply. And reluctantly. *I would not want to be like her,* I thought. Or prayed. It may have been a prayer, even then. Somehow, I recognized something familiar in her wide eyes. A hunger I, too, had felt, although I had never really been hungry. An outrage that, despite my much shallower experience of suffering, I shared. Some part of me— the "little Indian" deep within me that I had inherited from my mother, perhaps—knew what she knew, and I thought, *I am like her. We are the same.* This revelation filled me with dread.

I underwent a spate of piety in my early adolescent years. It crept upon me like a headache. Or a pimple. Or like the breasts of my friends, which had surely been swelling steadily for some time but to me seemed to sprout up overnight, on every theretofore flat expanse of ribs and skin except my own. So it was with my faith— or rather, with my *awareness* of such a thing as faith, which in those days I considered to be nothing less than the sacrifice of whatever one valued most—love, money, dignity, purposeful work—in the service of God. To selflessly reject whatever one especially craved in the pursuit of holiness.

The Catholic missions pamphlets were full of stories about people who did this. People who gave up jobs and families and all sense of home in order to tell others about God. Who lived in filth and poverty, voluntarily. Who, like Father Damien of Molokai, died even, in the service of those less fortunate. I scoured their stories for instruction on how to be like them. I dreamt of living among the incurably sick, bathing the heads of the dying in some stinking and miserable foreign place. Or succumbing to death myself, on a foul pallet, in a dark hut made of palm branches, alone.

In the absence of ready opportunities to sacrifice myself in some more dramatic fashion, I took to reading holy books. I pored through our illustrated children's Bible and looked for models of godliness in books popular among teenagers at the time: *The Cross and the Switchblade*, *The Greatest Story Ever Told*, *The Exorcist*. In the missal at church, I paged past the Mass we celebrated every Sunday, which I knew by heart, past the liturgies for baptism and confirmation and marriage, to study the mysterious services we never celebrated: ordination and extreme unction. I wondered about these rites of passage into holy worlds beyond the ones I knew.

One day, on my way out of church, I put a dollar of my allowance in a box in the entryway to buy a copy of *The Life of St. Teresa of Avila*. To my mother's wonder and admiration, I read it cover to cover, and then—without really getting much from it beyond a general sense of the tedium of her life as a nun—I read it again and again. I skimmed past the ecstasies of God-love she described—which sounded almost sexual and alarmed me considerably—and lingered instead on the few passages that confirmed my expectations of the holy life: fasting, kneeling for hours at a time, scrubbing the rough stone floor of the convent until one's fingers bled.

From childhood on, I had tasted the odd pleasure of hagiography in our household copy of *Little Pictorial Lives of Saints*. It featured uplifting stories of the martyrs' lives and the gruesome details of their torture and murder, all clothed in the pretty language of nineteenth-century moral tales, with quaint engravings depicting their ghastly deaths. I loved this book—the true crime of an older, more reverent era. And in the library of my Catholic high school, I discovered even gorier hagiographies of the early church. In these, ancient eyewitnesses offered such disconcerting details as that, when St. Polycarp, the bishop of Smyrna—whose feast day was my birthday—was lit on fire at the stake, his body smelled not like burning hair and flesh, as one would expect, but like a loaf of bread baking in the oven. I sought out biographies of more contemporary martyrs, among them savoring especially the account of one early American woman—possibly fictional, as I haven't managed to rediscover her in subsequent research—who witnessed the scalping and murder of her entire family and then went on to become a nun and live among their murderers, serving them, loving them.

Not long after that, when I was fifteen, we moved back to California, and I got a job at a bookstore. One of my first purchases with my discount was the New American translation of the Bible, which I read sporadically for a few years, starting with the Old Testament and never actually making it to the New. Unlike the illustrated Bible of my childhood, this was an entirely adult Bible, filled with stories of heroes of the faith that made me queasy. Onan spilling his seed on the ground. Ehud sinking his sword so deeply into the king of Moab's belly that the fat closed over his hand on the hilt. Jael welcoming the fleeing Sisera into her house, giving him milk to drink and covering him with a rug, and then, while he slept, driving a tent peg through his temples.

About that time, I became friends with a group of young seminarians who hung out at my church. They were on leave from their school to conduct a research project on how best to pastor and work with older, often difficult parishioners and church staff, who were devoted to the Roman Catholicism of an earlier era. The seminarians—all of them handsome and smart and funny—split up to live at churches in our area. One of them, the unofficial leader of the group, chose my church as his home, and I got to know him better than the rest. He served in various assistant capacities during the Mass and sang in our church folk group, where I also sang and played the banjo. Church members referred to him as "our seminarian," and he lived at the church rectory, an ordinary house just down the road from my house.

I was in the rectory a lot. Our church, in those days, didn't have its own church building—we shared the Methodist church in town—so most of the regular activities of a church took place at the rectory. We had our folk group practices there on Wednesday nights, and the other seminarians often joined us.

The seminarians, it seemed to me, were always happy. They often spoke of their daily exploits in the churches where they worked, and every story they told had a ribald moment. Every misery of their trade—and there were many, everything from mean remarks and unrealistic expectations to what I imagined must be the sheer boredom of the day-to-day practice of goodness—every routine irritation that would have made another rage and complain seemed to provide, for them, an opportunity for tomfoolery and wit. Even the most holy appointments of the church—the as yet unconsecrated bits of bread called "hosts" that the priest would hold up during Communion and place on our outstretched tongues and that would eventually incarnate our Lord and Savior in our own bodies—even these provided opportunities for humor. The hosts arrived in a big box at the rectory, separated by size and type into plastic bags. During folk group practice, if the pastor wasn't around, the seminarians let us tear open bags of hosts to snack on. We could choose between white and whole wheat, and we sometimes smeared them with peanut butter or dipped them in French onion dip. It was just the sort of iconoclasm that defined these young men for me.

The seminarians discussed and argued and talked all the time—with one another, with us kids, with whoever was around—and it was talk like I had never heard before. No topic was forbidden. No subject too improper—or "nasty," as my mother would say—for open discussion. I was aghast when they started talking about a then popular R-rated movie called *The Sailor Who Fell from Grace with the Sea*, the story of a widowed young mother and her sailor lover, who is murdered in the end by the widow's adolescent son and his friends.

My friends and I had snuck into a theater to see the movie, and I had found it profoundly unsettling, not only for its peculiar brand of violence—the boy murderers also torture and kill cats and birds—but for its relentless sex scenes. The lovers go at it again and again, at length and noisily, while the boys watch through a keyhole. Worse, in an endless scene I found too embarrassing for words, the mother masturbates alone in her room.

The seminarians argued, in detail, as though it were the most natural thing in the world, about whether or not the sex and violence in the movie were justified. They asked our teenage opinions and carefully considered them. They offered their own. And through it all I wondered, but never asked, *Why had they gone to see such a disturbing movie to begin with? And why had I?*

When I questioned them about the Bible stories I found disturbing—Jael, Onan, Abraham sacrificing Isaac—they told me that they found them disturbing, too. They joked about whatever we—whatever anyone—hallowed. And yet, in another sense, they took it all seriously. I could see that. Holiness, the way they lived it, was another thing than the holiness I had been considering all those years. It had nothing at all to do with avoiding or rejecting what one desired but instead with embracing it wholeheartedly.

I'm telling you all this because I want to show you another image—in addition to the photograph of that starving little girl rejecting the sandwich—that accompanied me through those years of aspiring holiness, and it is this: the picture, captured in no other medium than my own probably unreliable memory, of our seminarian eating a hamburger. I don't think you can see this picture as I saw it, though, unless you know something of my confusion in those days, my yearnings. And I need to tell you some more about this young man, too, for you to get there.

Our seminarian's name was Dave. (Now he's probably Father Dave and pastor of some large congregation.) He came from a huge family, with eight or ten or twelve kids—an Old World sort of Catholic family I guessed to be more like the Polish and Italian families I had known back in Connecticut than the modern Catholics of Southern California, who shared church buildings with Methodists and were always talking about ecumenical this and that and clearly practiced birth control. I think I recall mention of other priests and nuns among Dave's relatives. In my mind, I saw his massive family as a mini-parish, served by homegrown priests and brothers and a whole convent of sisters. He was raised, in my drastic imagination, literally *in* a church, was already a priest as a boy. This was how I understood his wanting to give up all possibility of marriage— of children and sex and the kind of love I was beginning to be interested in—in order to serve God. It was a decision that made me sad and kind of angry, if I let myself think about it too much. I was a little in love with the seminarians, and with Dave most of all.

I corresponded with the seminarians after they returned to the seminary to complete their degrees, and I attended Dave's ordination, a big church event involving bishops in all their finery. Dave's whole family was there, no doubt, but I don't remember anything but the overlong ceremony and a big procession out of the church when it was all over. Before long, Dave was a priest and had started work at an established parish that, from the cagey details of his new life I gleaned from our waning conversations, I guessed might challenge all the strategies he and his classmates had experimented with for getting along.

We met for lunch a few times after I started college, at a coffee shop near my university called Bob's Big Boy that served breakfast foods, burgers and fries, a forward-looking fusion monstrosity of the seventies called chili spaghetti— topped with a square of American cheese—and a dessert Dave loved that involved brownies, vanilla ice cream, and a thick, hot chocolate sauce covering everything. This was not my kind of food. My favorite lunch items, in those days, were more exotic: sushi, Vietnamese summer rolls, a California sandwich of avocados and sprouts. But Bob's Big Boy was nearby and cheap, and Dave always liked to go there, so we went. I ordered a chef salad: iceberg lettuce, halved eggs, and strips of ham and cheese, drenched in bright orange French dressing. Dave usually had the hamburger and then that brownie dessert.

Dave looked older and more haggard than before, but was otherwise the same: that is, the opposite of what one would expect in a priest. The opposite of well-behaved. Full of the same gassy jokes and stories as always. He was happy, he said. He liked his parish. Liked his boss, the head priest. His new work. We talked about my school and my family's struggles following my mom's brain tumor surgery and the people he remembered from my church, which I had stopped attending. I didn't quite realize it yet—or we probably would have discussed it—but I was losing my faith in God in those days. Or perhaps I did realize it, even then, and we did discuss it. Perhaps Dave sought, in his big brotherly, priestly, godly way, to win me back. Arguing. Cajoling. Teasing. But I don't remember any of that.

What I do remember is Dave eating. While we talked, Dave used both hands to ferry his overloaded burger to his mouth and, almost simultaneously, pinch up three or four fries dripping in ketchup. He ate fast, and he dribbled and dripped and dropped his food, getting it all over himself before he finally mopped it all up, laughing, with five or six of the diner's skimpy paper napkins.

I am not a slow or delicate eater, but I found it amazing to watch Dave eat. He ate like five people at once. Like ten. I imagined him at his mother's table as a boy, his two grasping, shoveling, wiping hands multiplied by ten, eleven, twelve. Having grown up in a biggish family myself, I understood the subdued frenzy that develops right before the blessing and as the dishes are set down on the table, the inevitable competition for the breasts and wings of the barbecued chicken. But this was something else. Never before or since have I witnessed such a candid appetite or such determined pursuit—unrestrained by politeness, entirely unadulterated by guilt or embarrassment—of whatever would satisfy it.

The image of Dave's eating stayed with me, gaining as firm a place of consideration in my sense of what is right as what was, for me, its opposite: the photo of the little girl from Africa, refusing the tomato sandwich. In my memories of those years, the pictures merge, somehow, and I cannot sort them from each other. The insatiability of the one who was not, technically, hungry. The restraint of the one who was. In each image, in each equally honest response to the frightful provision of manna, I see, as in a vision from God himself, the dilemma of our existence: the competing sanctities of enjoyment and abstinence. This mystery of holiness was, finally, the answer that I carried with me from my teenage years into adulthood, and it has flavored, in some sense, every bite I have taken since.

Vietnamese Summer Rolls

Get the Vietnamese ingredients in just about any Asian store. Makes about a dozen.

Filling

Prepare and arrange in separate piles on a large chopping block or platter:

2 carrots, peeled and then, with the peeler, shaved into long strips

1 cucumber, thinly sliced, lengthwise, then cut into long, thin strips

6 green onions, trimmed, then quartered lengthwise into long strips

12 cooked shrimp, deveined and halved lengthwise (double the shrimp if you leave out the pork)

12 pieces of red cooked pork or leftover pork roast (optional)

1 section of a package of the Vietnamese noodles called rice sticks, softened in hot water

1 bag of very fresh bean sprouts, well rinsed and drained

1 handful each of mint and cilantro leaves, pulled from their stems

Assembly

Soften the larger size of Vietnamese summer roll wrappers—called "rice paper"—one sheet at a time by placing it on a wet towel and spraying it with water or tamping it all over with wet hands. The wrappers are not really paper but a brittle membrane of rice noodle—very fragile when dry—so be careful. As the rice paper softens, within a matter of seconds, it becomes sort of sticky and stretchy. That's how you want it. On the edge nearest you, make a long, tidy pile of some of each ingredient of the filling; then fold the sides of the rice paper inward, over the filling. Then, beginning with the edge nearest you, roll the heaped ingredients gently up. If you've let the wrapper soften enough, it will stick to itself and hold. Your first one or two summer rolls will probably be too loose and fall apart or else too tight and tear open, but you'll soon get the hang of it. Keep softening rice paper sheets and filling them one by one until all the filling is used. Pile on a pretty plate and serve with the sauce, which you will stir at the table. Everyone will love these. They don't keep well—the softened rice paper, in the refrigerator, gets opaque and tough—so eat them all.

Sauce

Combine in a small bowl:

1 cup hoisin sauce

1/4 cup water

1 to 2 tablespoons fish sauce

2 tablespoons peanut butter

Arrange, each in its own spot, on top of the hoisin sauce mixture:

> 1 *finely* grated carrot
> 1/4 cup roasted, unsalted peanuts
> 1 jalapeño pepper, seeds removed, finely chopped

Stir the sauce at the table and allow diners to serve themselves.

THE CALIFORNIA SANDWICH

This is a perfect meal for two. I'm not dogmatic about very many recipes, but about this one I am. DO NOT use any of the following:

- *any other kind of bread than what I describe*
- *one of those weird, shiny, green Florida avocados that taste sweetish, have a white sap, and get gritty little tumors in their flesh*
- *any other kind of cheese than provolone—well, except maybe Jack—but definitely not the pretend kind of cheese that comes individually wrapped in cellophane*
- *anything but very fresh sprouts—they get weird tasting if they're even slightly old*
- *a typical supermarket tomato*
- *any other brand of mayonnaise besides Best Foods (called Hellman's on the East Coast)—Don't even think about it!*

Assemble your ingredients:

> 4 slices of sprouted wheat or whole-grain bread (with visible nubs of grain throughout)
> 1 perfectly ripe, black-skinned avocado, peeled and sliced
> 1 big handful of the freshest alfalfa sprouts or several well-washed and dried Romaine lettuce leaves (or both, if you like crunchy sandwiches)
> 2 slices of provolone cheese
> 1 vine-ripened tomato, thinly sliced
> Best Foods mayonnaise (Called Hellman's east of the Rockies. There's only one kind of mayonnaise in my book. Other brands are sweet: Yuck!)

Spread each slice of bread with the mayonnaise. Arrange avocado slices on two of the slices of bread. Top with cheese, a few slices of tomato, sprouts and/or lettuce, salt and pepper, and finally the other two slices of bread. Halve to make 4 triangles.

My Family's Oven-Barbecued Chicken

This recipe results in one cut-up chicken, enough—including the back pieces and a diner like my mother or mother-in-law humble enough to choose a back—for my family of eight growing up. Although I give the barbecue sauce recipe that I used growing up, actually any homemade sauce will work. All are pretty much a mixture of ketchup and mustard, vinegar, and something sweet. Nowadays I still make my own barbecue sauce, but instead of following a recipe, I approximate whenever I clean out the refrigerator and find that I have redundant open jars of jelly. I melt the jelly with a bunch of ketchup, a little mustard, and some finely chopped onion and garlic and cook it until the onions are soft and the sauce is thick. Then I thin it down considerably with whatever vinegars are hanging around that I have accidentally bought before using up an old bottle. I then cook the sauce some more until I like how it tastes, doctoring it with additions of brown sugar or maple syrup, leftover canned tomatoes, flavored salts, Worcestershire sauce, and hot sauce. You'll notice that I leave out the butter or oil in this version entirely. Chickens these days are fatty enough, in my opinion, and all that the added fat in the sauce does is sully the good pan juices with icky red grease.

Sauté in 1/2 stick of butter:

> **1 onion,** finely chopped
>
> **2 cloves of garlic,** minced

Add and simmer until it's about the consistency of barbecue sauce from the jar (tasting from time to time and adjusting to make sure it's as sweet or sour or hot as you like it):

> **1 cup ketchup**
>
> **1/2 cup brown sugar**
>
> **1/3 cup vinegar**
>
> **2 tablespoons mustard**
>
> **1 tablespoon hot sauce**
>
> **1 tablespoon Worcestershire sauce**
>
> **1 teaspoon cracked black pepper**
>
> **salt to taste**

Cut up a chicken into two breast halves, two thighs, two drumsticks, two wings, and—unless you have only four or so people eating or guests you are embarrassed to serve backs to—the two back pieces. Arrange the chicken pieces in a baking dish big enough to leave a little space between them and pour some of the sauce over them. Bake in an oven preheated to 375° for about one hour (or higher for less time) or until beginning to burn* on the edges. At intervals during the baking, turn the pieces over and spread a little more of the sauce over the top. Serve with salad and rice and scrape some of the caramelized pan juices on top.

---

* A note on burning the edges: I love my beef and lamb deep pink and juicy and savor both meats raw every chance I get: on the sly and also officially in foods like Italian carpaccio and Ethiopian kitfo. I also love sashimi and even the raw ground pork that, in Germany, was often served as a breakfast item: salted and peppered, spread on a chewy roll, and topped with diced onion. Nevertheless, I grew up believing that a bird the slightest bit wet at the bone was an abomination under heaven, and I still think so. If I roast a chicken in the oven, I do it on high and serve it brown and crusty. If my husband grills chicken pieces outside, I like it burnt on the outside and dry within.

10

The Abalone Story

One of my daughters' favorite stories is about the time I collected abalones with my high school boyfriend. I'm not sure what about the story attracts them, whether it's the sensual undercurrent of the adventure, which we have never really discussed, or the story's implicit lawlessness: I roamed beaches and freeways and dangers with a boyfriend, which Charlotte and Lulu are not yet allowed to do, and we broke laws, which they are never allowed to do. Possibly, though, the abalone story is just a good story.

The girls know little about the characters in the story: the solitary, quiet girl I was at fifteen—a literal outsider, which it's not good to be in the tenth grade, just recently returned to suburban California after a five-year hiatus in rural Connecticut—and James, my first real boyfriend, a skinny mongrel of a man-boy, smart but badly behaved at school, six foot four at sixteen but too gangly and awkward to do well on the basketball team. I never told Charlotte and Lulu about the heishi beads and macramé bracelets he wore or that he took his guitar everywhere and sang "Lay, Lady, Lay" incessantly.

James' parents were divorced and both pursued other relationships, but the resulting families were all on friendly terms with one another. His stepfather—a happy, portly man named Frank—believed in the power of olive oil. He drank it and preached about it, cooked wonderful cioppino with it, and bathed soy-soaked chicken thighs in it before laying them on the grill. He oiled himself with it daily, then sat almost naked in their leafy backyard, after work every afternoon and all day long on the weekends, happy-faced and shiny and big-bellied out under the palm fronds and bougainvillea, like a statue of the Buddha.

I have never told my daughters that almost everything about James and his world scared me back then. The suddenness with which he entered my life. The pot he liked to smoke and the psychedelic drugs he was keen to try. His younger sister, who had an eerily beautiful soprano voice and was always singing, skipped school almost daily to be with her boyfriend, ten years her senior. The house had the lakey smell of sex whenever the two were around. They were both what we called back then "Jesus freaks": They spoke of Jesus as if he were a personal acquaintance, an actual person who might walk in the door at any moment. Their terrifyingly frank sexuality notwithstanding, they seemed oddly beatific to me. They had the sweetest, most innocent and congenial faces of any young people I had ever seen, not a hint of sullenness or uncertainty. Maybe it was the perpetually post-coital state in which I always encountered them.

My first date with James was to the Strawberry Festival, held annually at a university near where we lived. The university and our ritzy new housing development were still surrounded, in those days, by cattle grazing and cultivated fields of strawberries and tomatoes. The festival celebrated the traditional harvest-time in May. School was almost out. It was almost summer.

My parents fell mysteriously in love with James from the moment they met him. It was three or so on a Saturday afternoon. They had invited over some people from my dad's work and were in the cocktails phase of the evening meal. I was cooking dinner: pork roast powdered with ginger and spiked all over with garlic and served with potatoes roasted in the drippings and red cabbage. My whole family—sisters, baby brothers, parents—straggled to the front door when the doorbell rang. We were still so new in the neighborhood that we knew no one, and our doorbell ringing was a curiosity.

There stood this incredibly tall boy with a six-inch Afro that I just barely remembered the name of from one of my classes. I was so embarrassed I felt sick. My mom and dad immediately gave their permission when James asked them, not me, if I could go. I remember this searing tableau as an emblem of my entire teenage experience: my parents standing at the wide open door, Manhattans in hand; my siblings snickering into their shoulders; and this odd-looking stranger, the joker at school, his guitar slung over his back and his mom's little green car running at the curb, asking my parents if he could take me somewhere. Before I knew what was happening, we were in the car, barely talking, then wandering side by side among the booths.

The Strawberry Festival was actually a Renaissance fair of sorts—not one of those elaborate fictions they call a Renaissance Faire these days but an open air market with madrigal singers from the university and shabby hippies in the same torn dresses they always wore meandering among tawdry stalls offering not only fruits and vegetables but homemade toys, pottery, embroidered scarves, and intricate silver roach clips laid out on black velvet boards. There were little knots of college students here and there and, from out by the port-o-potties, the faint whiff of marijuana.

I couldn't figure out why my parents just let me go off with a guy I hardly knew and didn't even know if I liked, much less wanted to hold hands with in a public place, but by the end of the afternoon, when he brought me back to my parents, we were a couple and would continue so throughout the remainder of our high school years. We met at out neighborhood pool every day of summer, took most of the same classes, and attended the prom together as seniors. Frequently I ate at James' house, and once his dad took us to a little hut of a restaurant in Newport Beach that served what he said was the most authentic Mexican food outside Mexico: tacos in un-fried tortillas—otherwise unheard of in those days—filled with stringy shredded beef, white cheese, lettuce, and fresh green and red salsas full of cilantro.

James and I had one key interest in common, and this is where the story starts for my girls. We were scavengers. Just as I had foraged for food in our Connecticut woods—finding fruits for jams and pies and once poisoning my family on Jack-in-the-Pulpit roots that I had read Native Americans boiled and ate like potatoes—I scoured my new neighborhood for ignored foodstuffs. I eyed the olives dropping everywhere but didn't know how to cure them. The sidewalks near my house were lined with ornamental trees heavy with loquats, and many of my neighbors' citrus trees dropped fruit outside the walls surrounding their yards. I collected these treasures with enthusiasm. Somehow, the availability of such comestibles, abandoned to birds and rats and whatever other foragers happened by, made them taste better to me than any food you could buy in the supermarket.

James favored nearby beaches as his source of wild food. He worshipped his dad, who taught scuba diving for a living and owned a sailboat with which he roamed the Pacific coastline for months at a time, like one of the early explorers. He taught his son everything he knew. Sea creatures. Mexico. Strange foods. Scuba.

I never liked the idea of depending on a tank of air for survival, but James and I often went skin-diving off the beaches near where we lived. James could name every animal we saw: limpets, chitons, anemones, periwinkles, sponges, Garibaldi, the various jellyfish and octopuses that pulsed up from below us, little brown rays, and once a striped fish about four feet long that he insisted was a tiger shark. He had seen, he said, the telling dorsal fin and the curved air slits behind the head as the creature slid past. All I saw was that it was big. I was too busy trying to get away to notice the details.

"Are sharks mammals?" I wanted to know afterward. We had taken biology by then, and I told James about how once, back in Connecticut, my dad had gone deep sea fishing for bluefish and returned with a small shark. The other fishermen had laughed at him for not throwing it back in, but I guess my dad was a scavenger, like me. In any case, he gave it to me to clean for our supper that night, and when I cut it open, I found a baby inside it, still squirming.

"They're fish," James told me. "Cold-blooded trumps live birth."

James took me to beaches in Laguna that none of the kids at school went to, where the sand was covered in stinky seaweed and the only other humans we saw were occasional surfers in wetsuits, paddling alone on their boards. We also went to all the local marine life refuges, where posted messages threatened fines if you took any wildlife away from the beach. At these, like Caliban introducing Prospero and Miranda to his island, James showed me where to find the fattest mussels and taught me to sauté them first in olive oil, garlic, and parsley and then cover the pan to steam them in their own juices. We caught crabs and little octopuses to put in Frank's cioppino and cracked open spiny-shelled sea urchins to scoop out their gonads—as James called the bright orange substance inside—which we then mashed with garlic and butter and smeared on sourdough toast.

"You ate them raw?" my daughters asked when they were little. "What did they taste like?" The idea of eating raw things has always excited them. They liked to hear about the raw clams I ate at shad bakes in Connecticut: They throbbed and wiggled as they went down my throat. And about the sushi and sashimi—still unthinkable in Oklahoma—that I learned to love in college. The cockles and winkles I used a pin to pick raw from their shells on a chilly beach in England. The Steak Tatar I ate in Germany: raw lean ground beef nestling a raw egg yolk, onions, and an anchovy.

"Sea urchin gonads are just salty and fishy-tasting," I explained, "but mixed up with garlic and butter they taste, well, garlicky and buttery." I always expected them to ask me what gonads were, but they never did. I had had to ask James myself, who told me they were the male urchin's testicles. I thought it odd that this organ took up so much of the sea urchin's insides. When the urchin turned out to be female, we ate the roe, which tasted about the same.

James longed to try grunion, small silvery fish that flop up yearly, en masse, onto certain Southern California beaches to mate. James' dad, who had witnessed this event many times and eaten the little smelt-like fish and pronounced them good, reported that conditions had to be just right for the grunion to "run," as he called it. A moonlit night. A certain tide. The right kind of soft sand. No lights or obvious predators or noise or other disturbances. And absolutely perfect conditions for the resulting eggs to hatch out two weeks later and for the babies to swim out to sea on another certain tide.

Somehow the grunion knew all this, and, if you were lucky, you would witness tens of thousands of them flopping up the beach with the tide. The female grunion arched and twisted themselves tails first into the still semi-liquid sand at the furthest reaches of the water to lay their eggs, and the males wiggled around the half-burrowed females, drizzling their milt—fish-speak for sperm—all over the wet sand to fertilize the eggs. James' dad told him there was so much milt that the sand would glisten with it. In a minute or two, the fish would flop back down to the ocean and disappear into the surf.

James sought out insider information on when the fish might run on each of the likely beaches. It was always after midnight. Ideally, you were the only one on the beach. You built a fire and had a frying pan ready. When the fish came squirming up the sand, you grabbed as many as you could with your bare hands; dusted them in flour, salt, and pepper; then pan-fried them live—head, guts, and all—and feasted on them then and there. Every time James and I went, though, there were already dozens of drunken idiots shining their flashlights around when we arrived. Even though nights are cold in California, people were wading in the surf, scaring away any grunion even thinking about sex on the beach. Typically, beach police would arrive on their bicycles. We were afraid we'd get arrested if we made a campfire, so we just sat on the hard sand, huddled under a damp blanket that smelled like dirty car, and I never got to see the frenzied males curling themselves around the female grunion erect in their holes or the sperm-glazed beach. Grunion-hunting was always a disappointment.

The best story of our scavenging days on the beaches of California, though—and the girls' favorite story—was the time we were skin-diving at the Marine Life Refuge, in full view of the lifeguard on her chair, and came upon an amazing treasure bed of green abalones. Dozens and dozens of them. So many they were climbing up one another's backs in their eagerness to find a rock to clamp down on.

Abalones were the highpoint of seafood cuisine, according to James, but the poor creatures were already relatively rare in those days, even before over-fishing and a disease called Withering Foot Syndrome ravaged the abalone population along the coasts of California and Mexico in the 1980s. During my teenage years, you were lucky to come upon even one in the wild, and then only in water too deep for skin-diving. In the warmer shallows, they were nonexistent.

James gave me a breathless short course on the abalone. The gastropod—or, single shell mollusk—moves along the ocean floor on its muscular foot. Once it latches onto a rock, no amount of prying will loosen it and the only way to extract the meat would be to smash the thick shell with a rock, which, even if you have a rock, is hard to do underwater. The best way to catch an abalone is to swim up on it as motionlessly as possible and then, while its frilly mantle is still blithely extended, thrust a knife under its foot, flipping it over onto its back.

The problem was that, although we did have a knife—James never went anywhere, even swimming, without his pocketknife—we had nothing to collect abalones in. They were big, too, many of them seven or eight inches across. James could fit maybe a couple of the smaller ones in the pockets of his swim trunks, but we wanted more. We stood a long time in the chest high water debating whether one of us ought to go back to the beach and get a towel to use as a sack, but we finally concluded that it would be too unwieldy and the lifeguard would likely figure out we had something anyway and make us throw it back in.

Finally, we decided to use my swimsuit, which was luckily one piece. James would sneak up on the abalone colony, flip over as many abalones as he could, and I would swim after him, gather them up, and hide them in my swimsuit. Afterwards I would be able to come up on shore without anyone noticing anything besides that I looked a little bumpy.

It worked. As soon as I put one in my bathing suit, it fastened itself onto me, and I was able to add another without losing it. It felt a little strange, and at times I could sense the abalones shifting around on my body, but soon we had over a dozen big ones and hurried up onto the beach. James draped my towel around me, then returned to the water to soak his towel so we could keep the abalones wet in the car. Then we trudged up the long path to the road to unload our catch.

Once in the car, I unwrapped my towel and worked at removing the abalones while James spread the wet towel out on the sandy floorboard of the back seat. The abalones were stuck on tight by this time, and it took effort and a little pain to get them loose, but I managed to do it without taking off my suit. When we had them all rolled up in the towel, we wriggled into our shorts and T-shirts and raced to James' house, where we immediately set to carving them out of their shells, cleaning them, trimming off the mantle, and then slicing them against the grain into tough, pinkish-yellow medallions. James was ecstatic. We would cook them the next day. He would invite his dad—who would be impressed—and his dad's latest girlfriend. We put the abalone meat in the refrigerator and made our plans.

Neither of our families had a meat mallet, but I told James how my Arkansas grandmother had used the edge of a plate to tenderize beef for chicken-fried steak, and we decided that would work. We would coat the tenderized medallions in flour seasoned with salt and pepper, then brown them in lots of butter, and finally squeeze a wedge of lemon over each one as we served it.

"Parsley would be good," I suggested, but James was against it. He was a purist about some things. To accompany the abalone, I would make buttered rice and a salad. We would eat in his family's fancy dining room, instead of at the bar in the kitchen as we usually did. We would light candles.

The best part of this story—the part that the girls begged me to tell again and again when they were little and that made them shriek with horror and delight—was not the big abalone dinner, of which I remember little except that his dad *was* impressed and the tough foot of the mollusk, hammered tender and then flash-fried in butter, was velvety and sweet and tasted like nuts. Rather, it happened the night before, when I got home from James' house and was getting ready for bed. When it was my turn to use my siblings' and my shared bathroom and I finally peeled off my bathing suit to get into the shower, I discovered that my entire torso, every part of me that had been covered by the bathing suit, was one big, purple-red bruise. Over the weeks that followed it faded to gray-violet, then blue, and finally, after about a month, to those faint blotches of green and yellow discoloration you see on little kids' shins.

"It was a hickey," I told my girls when I knew they were old enough to have heard that word whispered among their friends. It was a word from my own adolescence, a word I only ever encountered in adolescence, a word that seemed, in those days—and even now—to hold in its etymology all the obscurity and substance of carnal experience. And where the shrieks once came was now silence. "The only hickey I ever got," I added. "Maybe the biggest one anyone *ever* got."

They contemplated this mystery in the depths of their minds. And they said nothing. The older they get, the more wonderful it is, the more horrific. It is a thought too astonishing and too horrific for words.

Frank's Cioppino, as I Remember It

I made these instructions vague to emphasize the "as I remember it" quality of the recipe and because it was originally a fish stew from the wharfs of San Francisco, made from whatever the fishermen were hauling in. Frank probably had some secret ingredient that I have left out here or a proportion of something to something else that I have gotten wrong. Your goal is a thick, dark, tomatoey stew packed with fresh seafood.

Select at least three different types of fresh fish/shellfish—ideally fresh, but use frozen seafood if fresh is not available. Prepare the fish/shellfish ahead of time so that you can use the trimmings for broth:

Clams, scallops, and/or mussels in their shells: Scrub them well first. You might want to steam them first in a little water to make sure they all open, although lately I've read that unopened ones being bad is just superstition. If you do precook them, strain the resulting broth through a fine sieve to remove any sand and add it to the tomato mixture as it cooks. Frozen shellfish will work, too, in which case just throw them in the pot frozen.

Shrimp: Remove heads and most of the shell except for the tail and put them in the broth pot. Then devein the shrimp with a knife tip along the back and rinse.

Fresh or frozen meat of scallops: These need no preparation, but put any juice that collects from them in the broth pot.

Whole crab or crab legs: Scrub well and steam in a little water as for clams, reserving the strained steaming water for the broth pot. When cool, remove the meat from the crab's body in chunks as big as you can manage. Crack the legs here and there to make removing the meat easier, but leave them whole. If you are using frozen crabmeat and legs, you don't need to prepare them.

Squid or octopus: Over a bowl (to catch the ink), cut off the tentacles as one piece. Squeeze out the hard center (the squid's mouth) between your fingers and throw it in the broth pot. Skin the squid's sack-like body by scraping at the purplish outside where you cut off the tentacles until you can get hold of it and then pulling it off as you would a sock. Throw the skin in the broth pot. Strain the ink into the stew mixture and cut the sack into rings. Use the rings and the tentacles in the stew. Frozen squid and octopus also come already cleaned and cut up, in which case, simply add frozen to the stew.

White sea fish of any sort: Remove head, bones, and skin and throw them in the broth pot. Cut the fish into biggish chunks, just big enough to be manageable in a bowl. Fish will go in the stew last of all, shortly before serving.

For the vegetables, use quantities that seem right to you, saving the trimmings for the broth pot and putting the chopped vegetables together in a bowl:

onion, chopped
garlic, minced
celery, chopped
carrot, chopped
a good-sized bouquet of parsley, stemmed and chopped

Some recipes call for green peppers, fennel, and/or leeks, but I don't remember these tastes in Frank's cioppino. They might be good, though.

Broth

Boil in plenty of water for at least an hour:

> **all the fish/shellfish trimmings**
> **2 bay leaves**
> **all the vegetable trimmings except the hard, papery onion skins**

Strain the broth into a large container. Freeze any you don't use for later use.

Assembly

Sauté all the vegetables in something like 1/2 cup olive oil—or whatever seems to you like a lot—in a big pot. Add:

> **2 big cans crushed or coarsely chopped tomatoes**
> **1/2 bottle red wine**
> **2 cups fish broth**
> **1 bay leaf**
> **a few chopped basil leaves** (or 1 teaspoon dried basil leaves, crushed)
> **the leaves from 2 or 3 sprigs of thyme** (or 1/2 teaspoon dried thyme)
> **cracked pepper**

Simmer, partly covered, all afternoon, adding broth as needed, until it is very dark and thick, about the consistency of spaghetti sauce. Half an hour before serving, add the shellfish you are using; then, ten minutes or so before serving, add the fish. Serve in shallow bowls, with good, crusty sourdough bread and any dark red wine that you like.

FRANK'S GRILLED CHICKEN THIGHS

These are amazingly good and so easy. Frank would marinate a 9 x 13-inch pan full of thighs only. Serve with rice and salad.

Marinate chicken thighs (chicken was always skin-on in those days, but I don't see why you couldn't do these skinless, if you wanted to) in the refrigerator for a day, in a mixture of equal parts olive oil and soy sauce. Grill the thighs until black—burned!—on the outside. Mmmm.

Roast Pork with Ginger, Garlic, and Potatoes

This is probably my dad's original recipe. We ate it as a special festive meal. Select a big, bone-in pork roast with fat on the outside. The best cut is a loin roast, the one that chops are cut from, but just about any cut of pork will work as long as it has some fat on the outside. You can use the same recipe for a leg of lamb. Either way, roast quartered potatoes along with the meat, around and under it, so that they are bathed and browned in the juices.

Preheat the oven to 375°. Slit the surface of the roast all over with the narrow point of a knife and insert slivers of fresh garlic into the holes. Make lots of holes—in the fat and the meat—and use lots of garlic. Salt and pepper the meat all over; then powder it thickly with ground ginger. Wash as many medium-sized potatoes as there are people eating and cut them—peeled or unpeeled—into quarters. Set the roast on some of the potatoes in a big roasting pan and arrange the rest of the potatoes around the meat. Roast until the meat is crusty all over and firm when you press on it, approximately 20–25 minutes per pound. Stir the potatoes around in the juices a couple of times as the meat roasts. The potatoes will be browned on the edges and quite soft. Make sure each person gets part of the crispy, spicy fat on the outside of the roast, the best part.

Red Cabbage

Fry chopped onion and a sour apple in a little bacon grease or oil or butter. Add a bay leaf, a few whole cloves, 1/4 cup each of sugar and vinegar, and a big jar of pickled red cabbage. Simmer for about half an hour. You can also make this recipe with fresh red cabbage, in which case shred and sauté it with the onions and apple; add a few juniper berries or some gin; and double the spices, sugar, vinegar, and cooking time.

Soft Tacos

As soon as you read this recipe, before you undertake to make soft tacos, you need to locate the nearest tortillería, which is a store that makes its own tortillas fresh daily. There is one near you—likely in the Hispanic part of your town. Go there and buy a dozen or two freshly made corn tortillas. They will be soft and pliable and soooo good. You will want to eat a few then and there, hot from the griddle, and then a few more in the car as you drive home. Leave them on the counter for your family to sniff out and eat; then have any that remain with dinner that night—warmed slightly in the microwave, with butter—accompanied by a pot of beans, maybe, or some eggs scrambled with chorizo. If you went crazy and bought way too many, store the leftover tortillas in a plastic bag in the refrigerator. They will harden to the consistency and taste of ordinary supermarket tortillas by the next morning—still edible, but nothing special. Plan to buy fresh corn tortillas at that tortillería on the day you make soft tacos, as they will be far better than any you could buy in the supermarket or even make by hand.

Condiments

Prepare and set out on the table in pretty bowls:

fresh salsa (see page 4)

guacamole (see page 52)

crunchy lettuce, such as Romaine or green leaf or iceberg, finely shredded

mild white cheese—one of the firm white Mexican cheeses, Monterey jack, or cheddar will all work, finely grated

Meat

Simmer in salted water to cover for 1 1/2 to 3 hours or until it pulls apart easily:

1 pound cheap beef, cut into 2-inch chunks

Cool the meat in its broth; then shred it with your fingers and/or a fork, removing any fat or gristle as you go. (You can refrigerate the shredded meat in a little broth up to 3 days. Freeze the rest of the broth for later use.) Sauté in a little oil:

1 onion, chopped

2 cloves of garlic, minced or pressed

Add and continue sautéing for a few minutes:

the shredded meat

1 chopped tomato (fresh or canned)

some finely chopped green chili pepper, such as ancho (mild) **or serrano** (hot)**, or jalapeño** (fresh or canned)

chili powder and/or a bit of cumin

salt

Put the meat in a bowl and set it on the table.

At the very last minute, warm the fresh corn tortillas by wrapping them, stacked, in a damp towel and microwaving them for about 30 seconds. Set them out on the table, on a plate, still wrapped in the towel.

Eaters assemble their own tacos by piling first meat, then cheese, then lettuce, and finally salsa onto a tortilla and squeezing it together in one hand. Keep the remaining tortillas wrapped up to keep them from getting cold and stiff.

11

Salmagundi

The drinking age is twenty-one, but none of the Salmagundi staff seem to notice anything amiss when I put in my order: a bowl of mushroom soup, a sourdough roll, a glass of chablis. They see my high-heeled boots and plucked eyebrows, the book in my hand, and above all my solitariness—read: a working girl from one of the stores—and they never guess that I am only sixteen. Or perhaps they do guess and don't care. No one's checking. The security guards at this mall are there to ensure the orderly sort of pleasure I enjoy, not forbid it.

The soup is nothing like mushroom soup from a can, nothing like any soup I have ever tasted. It is dark, thick with sliced mushrooms, and topped with sherried whipped cream and shaved almonds. And the butter that comes with the sour roll is, unlike any other butter I have eaten in my life, unsalted. I savor these, almost forgetting the wine, the substance that marks me as grown up and was my initial reason for trying Salmagundi for the first time months ago.

I have been working at a bookstore at the mall for about a year—long enough to acquire the $250 boots and the solitary affect. I lunch in the mall restaurants often, using up a good portion of my minimum wage salary, but it is worth it. For the spinach salad at the Magic Pan, dressed with bacon, crumbled egg, and sweet vinegar. Or their Crêpes St. Jacques. For a Kaiser roll with a thick slice of liverwurst from the Jewish deli. For the bitter hot chocolate, made with steamed milk and almost no sugar, from the Italian espresso bar next door to the bookstore. I once dumped a tray of hot chocolates for myself and my coworkers down the front of Alan Alda on my way back to the store—a brush with fame I cherish, although it won me only a grimace.

But by far my favorite restaurant at South Coast Plaza Mall is Salmagundi, where the selection of soups, each with its own elegant garnish, changes daily. Later in life I will try—mostly in vain—to recreate them, but for now, I just enjoy them. Gazpacho. Avgolemono. Mulligatawny. Borscht. Cheddar soup with perfect rectangles of carrot. A tart cold soup of grapefruit and mandarin oranges, topped with curried sour cream. A clear brown broth filled with zucchini slices and clumps of ground beef and decorated with broad shavings of Parmesan. And with each meal the slim glass of sour wine, beaded with cold. The chewy roll. The rich, unsalted butter.

Once I brought a coworker along—a woman older than I was, as almost all my coworkers were. Sandi was studying law at Pepperdine University and also had a lucrative summer job at Disneyland. She worked at the store to keep herself in books, I think. I would be grown, working at a Christian university myself, before I realized that the university she attended was Christian and that Sandi herself may have belonged to a brand of Christianity that regarded drinking alcohol as a sin. But, if she did, she said nothing about my wine. Not even about the fact that I was not old enough to legally drink it. She just ordered a Coke.

When we sat down to eat a few minutes later—I recall the moment, for some reason, with great clarity—she took a bite of her buttered roll, chewed, looked at it wonderingly, then lifted the salt shaker from the table and salted the butter before taking another bite. This action shocked and disappointed and impressed me all at once, bypassing, as it did so neatly, a fraught dialogue that was beginning to draw me into itself about the conflicting appeals of the familiar and the exotic, about beauty and truth and yearning. About home. About leaving home. About newness.

"Behold, I make all things new," I remembered hearing quoted at church once, one of those God promises you didn't really know if you wanted fulfilled or not. Is what is new always better than what is known? Sandi, evidently, didn't think so. She sat across from me with her Coke and her salted roll and chattered on about our shared friends at the store, our boss, our coworkers, our regular customers. I liked listening to her talk. She had only cheerful reports to offer. Amusing incidents that implicated no one. Kind words where others might complain. Her face, when she talked, glowed.

GRAPEFRUIT AND MANDARIN SOUP WITH CURRIED SOUR CREAM

Combine in a small bowl and refrigerate:

1/2 cup sour cream (or plain, whole milk yogurt)
1 tablespoon curry powder

Prepare as follows:

3 juicy grapefruits
2 cans mandarin oranges

Peel the grapefruits, separate them into sections, and—working over a big bowl to catch the juice—use a knife to cut away the chewy membranes from the sections. Drain the liquid from mandarin oranges into a small bowl and put the mandarin sections in with the grapefruit sections. To the small bowl of mandarin orange liquid, add and stir until smooth:

1/2 cup orange juice
1/3 cup sugar
2 tablespoons cornstarch

Heat the cornstarch mixture over a low flame in a nonreactive pot, whisking all the while. When it is thick, whisk in, little by little, the grapefruit juice from the bowl. Stir until thick. Grapefruits vary widely in size and juiciness, so you may need to add a bit more liquid (such as orange or grapefruit juice) if the soup seems too thick, or more cornstarch—mixed with a little juice or water first—if the soup doesn't thicken up nicely. When all the juice has been added and the mixture is at least the thickness of buttermilk, let it cool. Then add the fruit sections, adjust the sugar to your taste (but keep it tart), and refrigerate until cold. Serve the soup cold, with a dollop of the curried sour cream.

12

The Summer Before the Jubilee

When I was seventeen, I made my first trip abroad. As a graduation present to myself, I decided to spend the three months before college exploring England with my friend Lynnet. Lynnet wanted to see the sights. Prior to our departure, she bought a number of guidebooks and developed a plan, complete with a penciled map and even timetable information, for seeing everything England and Scotland had to offer—museums, every literary and historical site, and especially anything related to old musical instruments, for which, as an amateur bassoonist, she had insatiable interest.

My goal was simpler. In a book somewhere, I had seen a picture of Hadrian's Wall, and I wanted to go there. It was one of those vivid, inky-looking color photographs you see only in old books nowadays: a rocky pile traversing a grassy expanse so green it looked wet. I didn't know anything about Northumbria—although just the name of the county bordering present day Scotland where the Wall was located did sound quintessentially English—and I knew little about Hadrian and his doings in England besides what I had memorized for a test in a high school English literature class: that the Romans had conquered the Angles and Saxons and occupied the area around A.D. 100 and that they were always fighting with the Picts in the north. Nevertheless, I wasn't interested in researching the region. I never read in our *World Book Encyclopedia* that Hadrian was one of Rome's "five good emperors"—i.e., wise, civically productive, and tolerant toward Christians—nor would I have cared if I had. I just wanted to see that lush green grass and those broken stones with my own eyes.

It was the summer of 1976: the summer of our Bicentennial back in the States and a summer England spent madly preparing for Queen Elizabeth II's upcoming

119

Silver Jubilee. To get our feet as first-timers in another country, we went directly from the airport to the home of an Irish engineer who used to work with my dad and had subsequently taken a teaching position at the University of Southampton. The man and his family lived on a tiny island called Hythe, off England's south-western coast. We didn't know it then, but our visit there was perhaps the purest introduction we could have had to plain old ordinary life in England. Although connected to the mainland via ferry, Hythe had no hotels or roaming tourists or anything like the big-city frenzy we had left behind us at Heathrow Airport. Just weed-bordered streets and grouchy mums with prams and endearingly shabby cottages with gardens out back. A small collection of business establishments—a bakery, a grocer, a butcher, a post office, a pub—served the locals, and there were a couple of churches. Hythe that summer was like walking into one of the Jane Austen novels Lynnet and I had read in English Lit.: a world utterly foreign to us characterized by the leisure and quiet pleasures of an older time.

Our stay there, as it would turn out, was a sweet interlude in what would become a hectic and an increasingly distressing summer. Traveling by train and finding cheap B & B's to stay in each night became dreaded daily burdens far more exhausting than any of Lynnet's travel guides had warned. Lynnet was a picky eater as well as a vegetarian and a teetotaler, so every restaurant or pub or even booth selling street food was for me an exercise in tolerance and restraint. My own foibles were equally distressing to us both. Unlike Lynnet, who didn't care much about how she looked and was able to carry in her brown backpack everything I had ever seen her wear back home, I had packed so many clothes I had to wear several layers whenever we changed towns because it wouldn't all go into the three gigantic suitcases I schlepped along with us everywhere we went.

We also travelled further afield than was originally the plan. Lynnet, it turned out, would not feel that she had truly been to Europe unless she saw the mainland—Frankfurt and Paris at least—but I was against it, so we fought about it for a while and ultimately ended up crossing the Channel early in our trip to get that obligation out of the way. The unanticipated expenditures of our whirlwind visits to Germany and France depleted our resources and made the daily search for accommodations back in England even more onerous. Lynnet and I eventually came to despise each other beyond endurance and parted ways until the day of our flight back home. So, in the last month of the trip, I was entirely on my own in a strange land, which had been my secret terror all along.

But Hythe was a happy, sleepy dream that stayed with me after the chaos of our travels subsided and Lynnet and I made up and settled into our four busy years of college and then parted for good after that. Eventually, Hythe came to mean not only "England" in my consciousness—a country I wanted to return to someday—but summer and calm and a merry woman I hardly knew and would never see again but would never forget and one particular teatime meal she served us during our stay.

It was unusually hot in England that summer. I had anticipated the cool weather, rain, and chilling fogs of Dickens and had brought with me a heavy coat and sweaters and turtlenecks and an enormous umbrella, but no real summer clothes. I could probably have borrowed some from my Irish hosts, but, at seventeen, I was too shy to do other than pretend I liked warm clothes in hot weather—that this was how I dressed back in sunny California and that I was perfectly comfortable.

The father of the family was one of those rare people you meet in life who knows more than you do about any topic you might bring up. He conversed with authority about not only Lynnet's bassoon but the ancient ones she longed to try: *bombardes* and the great bass shawm. He had opinions about all my favorite books and could tell me the name of every wildflower and any plant or tree I saw in any garden on the island.

One afternoon, he took Lynnet and me with him to what he said was the best fish and chips shop in Southampton to fetch a huge, newspaper-wrapped package for the family. On the ferry ride there he described in detail every fish on the menu—cod, haddock, plaice, skate, hake, dogfish, sole, whiting, huss—noting which ones were local and which had to be shipped in. Aiming an imaginary paring knife against an imaginary potato and into the roiling water of the channel, he demonstrated how the British cut their chips, which are not long and skinny like our French fries but irregular, like wood chips, so that they get crispy on their thin edges but stay soft and moist in the thick parts. In the fish and chips shop, he explained what was in the batter the fish was fried in, and he had a quicker command of which of the identical-looking fillets in the refrigerated case were from which fish than the man who ran the shop. Plaice, he told us, was unequivocally the best, so we ordered that, and even Lynnet ended up eating some and liking it.

She did not like a delicacy advertised on the menu as "mushy peas." She had insisted on buying some, in opposition to our host's dubious recommendation, which amounted to a comical expression and the explanation in some sort of dialect that wasn't his usual one—something like Pogo in Irish—that "you gets what you arsk for here." And he was right, of course. Mushy peas taste exactly like they sound. The man knew, in short, everything there was to know about every topic under discussion. Musical instruments. Engineering. Fish and chips. The history and politics of England, Ireland, and the United States.

Mostly, though, he was funny. He told raunchy jokes in his thick brogue and made his children howl at the faces he pulled. He nuzzled into his blowzy jolly wife, who was at least six feet tall, chucking her under the chin as one would a small child and making her seem tiny and amazingly cherished.

When he came home from work in the early evening, we always sat down all together—he and his wife, the children, Lynnet, and I—and had tea, the main meal of the day. If it was fine out—as they always decided it was whether it was sunny or drizzly and threatening to come down in a hard hot rain—we ate outside in the garden.

"Drink another cup," his wife was always telling Lynnet and me, pouring the steamy tea from a huge flowered teapot stained an indelible brown along a network of fine cracks around the spout. "It will refresh you."

But there was no refreshing me. I was hot that summer, in my woolens.

"Tea," the way this family seemed to be using the term, was what we might call dinner or lunch or brunch, depending on whether the father was at home in the evening or in the middle of the day, as he was on the weekend. It wasn't when or even what we ate that defined the meal as "tea," although we did always drink enormous quantities of tea and had to keep getting up and refilling the pot with more boiling water and tea from the kitchen. But there were no scones or cucumber sandwiches, as I was expecting. The meal featured boiled potatoes with parsley and butter. Or we might have a soft-boiled egg each. Or fish and chips, that one time.

As an American, I thought tea was a quaint British between-meals refreshment—"taken," not eaten, between lunch and dinner, or in late morning, when we might have brunch in the States. But this family didn't use the term that way at all. Most times we ate no lunch, unless, as I said, lunch *was* tea. And we also didn't usually eat again after this meal, except maybe a piece of bread with a half pint of cider or beer. The word was my first conundrum of a foreign tongue, my first experience of being culturally at sea, and I tried hard to sort it out in my head. I finally decided that "taking tea"—in this displaced family, at least—meant sitting down all together as a family and eating—really relishing—whatever there was in the house that day to eat.

Tea on one particular day during my stay there was special. We drank the usual tea, of course, and sawed slabs from the loaf of bread the mom and Lynnet and I had bought at the bakery that morning, towing the children along behind us for their exercise. The youngest was potty-training and insisted on wearing his little plastic potty on his head like a helmet wherever we went—even to Mass on Sunday—and no one seemed at all bothered by it.

In addition to the bread there was also, of course, butter—a deep yellow topping for everything that tasted like no other butter I had ever eaten. It was yellow not from dyes, as it often is in the U.S., our hostess told me, or because it was from some strange breed of cattle, but because it was summer, when cows eat fresh grass, which has more carotene than hay and feed. In winter, she said, when the cows eat straw, the butter is white and tastes different. Not bad. Just different. I remember being impressed with this information no less than by the fact that this woman and I were having a substantial conversation just about butter.

In any case, on this particular day, we were having a feast. That morning, the children and I had selected a cauliflower from the garden and their mother had broken it into flowerets and boiled them till just tender in salty water. So, we were eating—in addition to our tea and bread and butter and some wedges of tomato— that cauliflower, plucked from the dirt a few feet away in the garden where we sat. Plain, cooked cauliflower at garden temperature, dressed in homemade yogurt and curry powder. Even the children dug in with jubilation.

We sat in the searing sun, tore off chunks of our bread and dragged it through the curried yogurt and tomato juices on our plates, and laughed at the funny stories the dad told. The smallest boy got up midway through the meal with a reflective look on his face and went off between the lettuces with his potty on his head, and we all laughed about that. After a while, the sun started going down, but the air remained hot and still and heavy with the moisture that would come pouring down later that night. And I was sweating in my long-sleeved shirt and wool skirt.

"You need another cup of tea," the mother of the family told me, leaning in to pour from the steaming pot into my cup. So I sugared my tea and added some cream—which, like the butter, was also yellow—and I drank. And I was refreshed.

CAULIFLOWER IN CURRIED YOGURT

I just guess this dish, as I expect my hostess did. Ideally, you would have grown your own cauliflower and, as she did, made your own yogurt from the milk of local cows. I regret to say that I have never made my own yogurt or bought local milk. Even my curry powder is surely different from what she used in Indian cuisine-savvy England. Still, this is so good that it's worth trying a close approximation using store-bought, American ingredients.

Break a good-looking cauliflower into flowerets and steam or boil them in a little water until just tender. Let cool completely, but do not refrigerate. Combine:

1 1/2 cups good, sour yogurt (Get some at a health food store if your supermarket only has the bland, creamy kind.)

2 rounded teaspoons of not overly fiery curry powder

a good pinch of salt

a good pinch of sugar

Stir the yogurt into cauliflower. Sprinkle with a little finely chopped parsley. Serve.

13

Hand Cheese

I spent the better part of my twenties living abroad in a futile attempt to flee various life problems: my mother's struggle with a brain tumor, my family's resulting misery and confusion, a sexual assault of which I was the victim, and the resulting existential morass in which I found myself. I moved a lot, as fleers do—from California to Switzerland then New Orleans; New Orleans to Berlin then Boston, then back to Berlin and later to Beijing and Hong Kong—never finding enough pleasure or comfort or answers in any one place to allay the furtive appeal of home, for all its problems. I attended universities, worked at various jobs, read novels, and skimmed life the way a tourist does in art museums, parks, and zoos. My years abroad were lonely ones, peopled mainly by students in the language courses I took and taught, inconstant boyfriends, and roommates or friends with classes or jobs or lives that took them away for large periods of time from the echoing, usually cold apartment we shared or where I lived alone.

Loneliness in a foreign land is a strange business of letter writing and waiting and pleasurable sloth. It breeds ritual, changes the tenor of the most minor act, and imbues every sense with the piquancy of self-consciousness. *It is time to take my walk down the avenue of lindens at the park,* I would think. *I can stop along the way at the Markhalle for some of that wet, crusty bread full of sunflower and flax seeds from the natural foods booth.* Or, *now I will lie in my hammock by the open window and read* Effi Briest. I lived my life as though I were reading about it in a novel.

Germany being a place where it is possible to buy only half of a fresh loaf of bread or a single brown egg stamped with the date it was laid, I shopped daily for food when I lived there and bought cheap bunches of flowers every weekend. I

125

lived frugally, supporting my solitary life by teaching English at language schools and community colleges in far-off districts that took over an hour to get to using public transportation. After class, my busy students would hurry off to their busy lives, while I took my time going home, observing the other people on the train, noticing smells and funny advertisements, planning in my head my next activity, my next meal, my next thing to think about.

Never in my life has food tasted so good as in those simple, solitude-basted days—perhaps because my relative poverty made each meal seem like a miracle. Or perhaps it was because I ate less regularly and had more time after one meal to think about the next one. In any case, I reined my zeal and ate with uncharacteristic decorum. I used tablecloths and preferred a certain overlarge silver fork I'd bought at a flea market, a certain pink-and-green majolica plate left behind by a friend who'd moved away, a certain super-thin Turkish tea glass for whatever I was drinking. I ate slowly, reflectively, often listening to music or reading from a book propped against the butter dish. A particularly good meal might inspire an entire letter to some distant friend detailing what I had just eaten.

I ate simple foods. Bread, sometimes with just butter and dark grainy honey, other times with German sandwich meats. A soft-boiled egg. Simple salads and soups. Frequently I looked forward all day to a meal of nothing but a delicacy to which I was addicted that is known only in the Germanic countries of Europe: skim-milk cheese. As far as I can tell—which may not be very far at all, as I now live on a farm in Oklahoma and have to drive an hour just to buy a little container of goat milk yogurt—skim-milk cheese is not available in the United States. It is an unusual cheese. Because it has no fat content whatsoever, it has a translucency and a texture unlike that of any other cheese—like nearly congealed pork fat, ranging in hue from whitish to yellowish to grey. Depending on its age, it has the bite of one of those rubber art erasers that crumble as you use them or else the sticky chewiness of Gummi bears.

Although the version of the cheese I found most frequently in my local market was called *Korbkäse*—or basket cheese, referring to the fact that it is molded in small baskets, which leave their woven wrinkles in its yellowish skin—it's generic name is *Harzerkäse*, after the Harz region of Germany, where it probably originated. Actually, skim-milk cheese is called something different wherever you go in German-speaking countries, often some ridiculous-sounding nickname known only to locals: *Spitzkäse, Harzbube, Düsselbude, Olmützer Quargel, Labkäse*. The cheese is typically a private food for those who eat it—like, for some of us, Moon Pies or RC Cola or khaki-colored English peas eaten cold from the can: a delicacy typically loved by only one member of a household and loathed by all others and referred to by that person's name as if it were a brand name, as in Dad's stink cheese or Dorothy's peas. It is, in short, a homely domestic sort of pleasure, not expensive or fancily named, generally savored in privacy and, I think, with slight shame.

In Austria, where I first ate skim-milk cheese, it is called *Handkäse*, or hand cheese, because it is not molded at all but just globbed by hand into a greyish pile about the size of half a cabbage. I was in Austria for only a couple of weeks, staying in a medieval town at the home of a baker and his family, who lived in the shadowy, low-ceilinged upper story of the bakery, a *Fachwerk* building four hundred years old on a narrow street darkened by the inward tilt of the ancient buildings on either side. The business of baking seemed not to have changed in all those years. The tiled ovens were fueled, as of old, with wood, and the shop was outfitted with tools that looked like torture instruments from the Dark Ages: coarsely hewn troughs, wooden peels in various sizes, and iron hooks and spikes and long-handled shovels used for handling and displaying the loaves and retrieving them from the fire.

How I came to be in that storybook bakery at all is something of a mystery to me. I was accompanying—and sharing a bed with—a Swiss woman I barely knew named Elke, the cheerless mother of an ex-boyfriend of mine. The baker was Elke's brother, whom she hadn't seen in many years. Before the boyfriend and I had parted ways, I had stayed on and off at his family's house, which was a couple of hours away, by train, from the town in Switzerland where I worked. While the boyfriend worked at his father's joinery, I slept in late, wrote letters home, took walks all over their tiny town, and generally hung out.

I was thrown upon his mother's company a lot, and I was sure that she disliked me. Her fragmentary, heavily-accented Swiss German was as incomprehensible to me as my elementary High German must have been to her, so we gave up early in our acquaintance on everything but essential words and rudimentary sign language. Elke let me watch her bake the rich, braided Swiss bread called *Zöpfli* or assemble the fruit-and-custard tart they usually ate for their main meal on Sundays or prepare the soup her husband required as the first course of every meal but breakfast. Sometimes I accompanied her to the market or helped her collect little black plums from their tree. But I felt tolerated more than genuinely liked during these activities, useless and in the way, like a tourist who shows undue interest in all the wrong details and hasn't a clue what's really going on.

And I *didn't* know what was going on in that house. A door off the kitchen led to the joinery, a cavernous workroom full of planers and routers and saws of all sorts. The workroom floor was matted with wood shavings, which the men tracked in when they came in to eat their meals and which another woman who lived in the house—a maid, I decided, although that seemed unlikely for economic reasons—spent most of her time sweeping up. I figured out on my first visit to the workroom that women were not welcome in that place. The men, who wore loose work coveralls with large gaps at the sides and nothing but underwear on underneath, got nervous whenever I neared a machine. So I kept to the living portions of the house.

Even those spaces bewildered me. On one of my early visits, Elke noticed me staring when her husband went off to bed with the woman I thought was the maid, and I could tell that my confusion upset her. It turned out the woman had been the man's live-in mistress for as long as his son could remember, a situation Elke apparently endured without opposition. Nevertheless, there was a thick, brooding tension in that house.

Somehow, in any case, after I had broken up with the boyfriend, the trip evolved—perhaps out of my interest in baking or my pretended interest in a collection of picture postcards Elke had brought out to show me on several occasions. She evidently liked to travel and had been to numerous countries all by herself—the great achievement of her life, I got the impression. She sent home a postcard of each place she visited: no message, just the address on the back. When she got home, she rounded up the postcards that had arrived in her absence and put them in a shoebox with the others. Postcards from Elke to Elke. She lingered over each one, almost smiling, pointing to this lake or that monument to indicate that she had been there, had seen it with her own eyes.

Some months after my last visit to her house, in any case, Elke and I were on a train together through the Alps. I saw the Matterhorn in the distance—just like the one in Disneyland, I thought, although possibly more fictional-looking against the bright blue sky. Soon we were in Austria, dragging our luggage from the train station down the cobbled streets of Elke's hometown, then standing beneath the bakery awning, and finally passing through a door behind the counter to the stairwell leading to the rooms above.

The baker's wife and three grown daughters—along with most other women in the town where they lived—wore *Tracht*: the local costume of a dirndl of contrasting calicos with decorative chains and charms dangling from the waist, somehow prim-looking even though the tight bodice generally displayed a good deal of bosom. The daughters were expressionless, strong-looking women about my age with their brown hair in heavy braids. Attractive, all of them, although there was something strangely asexual in their demeanor. They could perform any task a household required—cooking, cleaning, sewing, knitting, washing clothes, hanging them to dry, beating heavy rugs in the dark alley behind the shop, kneading bread, making sausage. Probably slaughtering swine and chopping wood, I guessed. Although the girls were as yet unmarried, their ample, broad-hipped bodies seemed to me to have been expressly formed to supply the needs and desires of a family. In my mind, I saw them lugging babies around, busily providing their husbands and grown children with food and warmth and other comforts, sitting hunchbacked beside the fire telling stories of a world full of dangers beyond the bakery door. They knew nothing of such a transient life as mine. They were not even curious about it. Everything was home, belonging, stasis.

In the few days I was there, the daughters gave me garbled cooking lessons in their sing-songy Austrian German. We made an herb-covered pork pot roast, potato dumplings, and a variety of dense cakes that used finely ground nuts and/or bread crumbs instead of flour. Elke sat at the table in silence and watched or dozed as I rinsed off slabs of meat in the deep sink and ground almonds in a little hand-turned nut grinder. When everything was in the oven, we took off our aprons and joined Elke at the table, and the women chattered incomprehensibly over pastries and tiny bracing cups of coffee until the meal was ready. There was bread from the bakery with every meal, of course, as well as homemade beer and usually an assortment of sausages and other home-cured meats that felt raw on the tongue.

On my last day there, along with the bread on a wooden trencher came an alarming and smelly pile of variegated grey-and-yellow called, they told me in their Austrian lilt, *Hond-Kaysi*—hand cheese. They cut half-moon shaped slabs almost an inch thick, one for each plate, and sprinkled each slab with salt and crushed caraway seeds, then poured enough oil and vinegar over the cheese to leave plenty to mop up with one's bread.

I cut off a tiny bit—pressing it with my knife, as my hosts did, onto my backwards fork—tasted and was immediately an enthusiast. It was room temperature and pleasantly fetid, like the pungent smell of a lengthy car trip with a nursing mother and her newborn. The tart warmth of the caraway and vinegar offset the cheese's odor somewhat and heightened its creamy, bland resistance to the teeth. Some of the family ate the sour assemblage on bread, as an open-face sandwich. The others ate it on its own, like meat. In the windowless, low-ceilinged kitchen of that ancient house, eating slabs of a smelly greyish mass of indistinct origin served on a wooden platter by large-limbed men-women in aproned costumes and heavy braids, I felt as if I had traversed every boundary of who I am—place, time, gender, status—to a dark, enchanted world where life in all its arduous fecundity was both treasured and abased, where princesses and trolls exacted their outlandish fealties, and everything beyond the hearth was feared.

Elke and I took some of the cheese back to Switzerland with us and lunched on it on the train between slices of the black bread the baker's daughters had sent along with it. We ate in silence, as usual, by unspoken agreement looking away from the other passengers' glances when they got a whiff. Afterward, we took long swigs from a shared bottle of the baker's homemade cider, which was dry and just barely effervescent. Then, we were back. I stayed in Elke's unhappy house just long enough to say hello to the boyfriend and watch Elke gather up the postcards she had sent and put them in the box with the others. Then I returned to my job and not long afterward left Switzerland for good.

Years later, when I lived in Berlin, I rediscovered the cheese in less unsavory gestalt in the refrigerated section of my grocery store. After buying it that first time, I got sudden cravings for it—what the Germans call a *Heißhunger*, hot hunger—and always kept some in a little cold storage cupboard, intended for potatoes and other root vegetables, that was built into the wall of my kitchen and had a vent to the courtyard. The two types of skim-milk cheese widely available in Berlin were bratwurst-sized logs referred to as *Stangenkäse* (rod cheese) and harder, pillow-shaped patties that came pressed together in a roll and were labeled, generically, *Harzerkäse*, the cheese of Harz.

Harz is an untamed mountainous expanse known during the Middle Ages as a meeting place for witches and associated to this day with dark stories and strange doings. One of my German friends referred to my smelly little stash as my *Hexenkäse*, witch cheese.

Harz also means *resin*, though, and throughout my years in Berlin I persisted in mistranslating *Harzerkäse* in my mind as "resin cheese." It looks like resin. It looks, in fact, just about exactly like the waxy cake of resin I used on the bow of my viola when, as a child, I tried to learn that instrument. In the tidy rolls or patties from the supermarket, the variegated color of the Austrian version I first encountered was regularized to a creamy yellow, and its odor was sealed up in cellophane packages sporting a date when best consumed and a list of its simple ingredients: skim milk, rennet, salt. I discovered that, opened as is, cold from the grocery store shelf, it was rubbery and tasteless and had very little smell, a faintly yeasty dampness was all, like an adolescent boy, like something not quite mature. And it *wasn't* mature, I learned from its surreptitious admirers. *Harzerkäse* has to be aged.

"Leave the package unopened in a cupboard," a German fellow turophile told me, "and as soon as you can smell it, it's ready to eat." The smell, when it came, reminded me of diaper pails, a feature of my childhood that, with the advent of disposable diapers, is destined to be entirely forgotten by current and future generations. It is a visceral, human, embarrassing smell that thickens past bearing in the space of a few days. By that time the cheese has changed in consistency and opacity, too. It is chewy and transparent. I sliced then marinated it briefly in oil and cider vinegar and salt, but instead of caraway I used lots of crumbled marjoram and a little black pepper.

I ate it—on *Doppelkrustbrot* ("double crust" rye bread) from a nearby bakery—in my cold narrow kitchen, which looked out on the enclosed courtyard of my apartment building in the proletarian district of Wedding. Living alone as I did, I never had to apologize for the cheese's stink to anyone else or explain how a sudden hunger for it had awakened me from some magical slumber on my futon on the floor. In the grey Berlin night, I would stand at the kitchen window, tented for warmth in a boiled wool blanket, and take small reflective bites, making up stories about the people hidden behind the dark windows across from me, below me, above me. Chewing thick slabs of bread thickly smeared with the odorous cheese, I imagined their lives, their worries, their torpid dreams. I imagined my own life twenty years hence. Where would I be living? Who would I be? Would I still be alone?

My most outlandish ruminations could not have projected the peculiar course of God's grace. A husband. A farm. Dogs. A set of All-Clad pots and pans that match. Daughters of my own, half-grown already and utterly unskilled in the household arts, incapable of cooking, sewing, creating order and peace. This life would have been too strange then for me to imagine. Dangerous even. Outside my circle of enchantment. Back then, in my twenties, I imagined every motion but stopping, every time but now, every impulse but constancy, every known delight but home.

Swiss Braided Bread (Zöpfli)

This makes one massive and shiny, dark brown "braid"—or, as it's called in Swiss German, Zöpfli (pronounced Tzoopfully).

1 kilo flour—about 8 cups if you don't have a scale

2 yeast cakes (or 2 packages of dry yeast—41/2 teaspoons, if you buy it in
   bulk—dissolved in 1/4 cup water; decrease milk by 1/4 cup)

3/4 cup unsalted butter (11/2 sticks)

1 cup milk

2 teaspoons salt

2 eggs plus one egg white

2 to 3 tablespoons sugar

1 egg yolk mixed with 2 tablespoons water

Heat the milk with the butter until the butter melts; then let the mixture cool to no more than 110° (warm). Mound the flour in a big bowl. Crumble (or pour) the yeast into a well in the center of the mound and stir into it a little of the warm milk mixture and flour. Cover the resulting dough with a little of the flour from the mound. Let this sponge rise for 15 minutes. While the yeast is working, set the eggs and egg white, the salt, and the sugar around the outer edge of the mound of flour, along the sides of the bowl. When the yeast mixture has risen—which will be evident from little cracks in the flour on top, like pictures of Death Valley, and from the popping noise the risen place makes when you press down on it—stir in enough of the milk mixture to make a heavy dough. Ideally, it should take every bit of the milk to make a kneadable dough. If the dough starts to seem too gloppy to knead, use less. If the dough is too tough to knead, add a little more warmed milk. Knead for 10 minutes. I mean it. Your arms should ache when you're done. Put the dough in a great big buttered bowl, turning to coat all sides, and rubber-band plastic wrap over the top of the bowl to ensure that the atmosphere in the bowl remains moist. Let the dough rise until it is double or more. As the bread rises, so will the plastic wrap, making a bubble. Children will enjoy this.

Divide the dough in half. Carefully stretch and squeeze each half into a snake as long as you can make it, slightly fatter in the middle. My kitchen table is 4-foot square, and I try for two pieces that are almost as long as the diagonals of the table. Your goal is not merely length but that the dough, through the stretching and squeezing, develops unbroken fibers throughout. Crisscross the two strands in the middle of your kitchen table; then fold each over the other to form two upside-down *V*s, intersecting at the top, with their open ends facing you. Braid the four resulting strands. The braid will be much bigger on one end than it is at the end where you finish. Carefully pick the bread up and put it on a parchment-covered cookie sheet (or on a parchment-covered peel, if you have a big baking stone in your oven). Tuck the loose ends under and let the dough rise again until doubled—about an hour. Half an hour into the rising, preheat the oven to 400°. Just before putting the braid in the oven, brush it with the egg yolk mixture, covering the braid completely. (I sometimes sprinkle it with poppy seeds.) Bake the braid until very dark brown and hollow sounding when you knock on it, about 45 minutes to an hour.

Swiss Fruit-and-Custard Tart

Such a pretty dish. Very filling. This really does function as a meal—perhaps brunch?—on its own.

Preheat the oven to 350°. Arrange fruit—such as halved plums or apricots or quartered peaches (cut side up), sliced peeled apples or pears, pitted cherries, etc.—prettily in a pastry-lined pan, preferably a shallow, ripple-edged, European tart pan. Follow some sort of organizational scheme, such as concentric circles of overlapping sliced fruit, to entirely cover the bottom of the pastry. The Swiss use a sweet pastry, but I just add a tablespoon or so of sugar to one full recipe of my regular pie dough. (See page 29.) Put the fruit-filled pastry in the oven and bake for 15 minutes. Meanwhile, mix together until smooth:

> **1 cup heavy cream**
> **1 teaspoon cornstarch**
> **3 eggs**
> **1/4 cup sugar**

Pour the cream mixture carefully around the fruit, return the pan to the oven, and bake until the custard just sets, about another half hour. Cool completely and serve.

Austrian Pork Pot Roast

A thick, flat cut of pork, such as a blade roast, is best. Trim off extra fat beforehand, as the roast does not get brown and crispy on the outside.

Salt and pepper a pork roast on all sides, then coat—and I mean coat—the pork with any dried herbs you like. I use marjoram, thyme, and a little rosemary. A few broken-up or ground bay leaves is also nice. Heat a little oil in a covered casserole or Dutch oven as close to the size of the roast as possible and brown the herb-coated roast well on all sides. Add hot water to a depth of about two inches. Cover. Bake at 375° for 2 or more hours. (Alternatively, you can cook this on top of the stove for 2 or so hours.) The meat should be just about falling apart when it's done. Remove it gently to a warm platter and put the platter in the oven while you make the gravy. Serve with potato dumplings (recipe follows) or boiled, peeled potatoes.

Gravy

This gravy is different from a typical gravy because the drippings you start with are liquid, not pure fat.

Pour the liquid from the roast into a small pan and skim as much visible fat as you can by pressing a spoon to the surface over and over again. Mix a little cornstarch—maybe 1 heaping tablespoon—with a little cold water to make a smooth paste about the thickness of cream. Whisk it into the liquid in the pan, bring it to a boil over a medium flame, and cook until thickened, whisking all the while. Make more cornstarch paste if the gravy is not thick enough. Taste for salt.

POTATO DUMPLINGS

When making potato dumplings, your goal is to get as much moisture as possible out of the potatoes before making the dough; therefore, the process of pressing or grating the potatoes and then spreading them out to cool is important. Steaming— rather than boiling—the potatoes also results in less moisture. Any vegetable steamer or pasta pot with a holey insert or even a small colander in a big pot will do. Lacking these, go ahead and boil the potatoes, but don't overcook them or constantly poke them with a knife. You do not want their skins to burst open.

Wash well, then steam or boil:

> **1 1/2 pounds unpeeled, starchy potatoes, such as Idahos** (about 4 or 5 good-sized ones, if you don't have a scale. Don't worry too much about amounts. The process and the resulting consistency of the potato dough are what matters, and you can adjust accordingly.)

While the potatoes cook, cube a few slices of bread and fry them in a little butter until golden. Set aside.

As soon as the potatoes are done, while they're still hot, press them through a potato ricer or sieve. Alternatively, let them cool enough that you can just barely hold one; then peel and grate them on the fine holes of a grater. Spread the pressed or grated potatoes out on a chopping board and let them steam and cool completely. Add and mix well:

1 large egg
a good pinch of salt
the tiniest grating of nutmeg
enough flour to make a dough that you can form easily with your
hands—3/4 cup or so

Set a large pot of salted water to boil. Meanwhile, flour your hands and form the dough into golf balls, pressing into the middle of each two or three of the fried bread cubes and then closing up the hole. When all the dumplings are formed, turn the boiling water down to a simmer and carefully lay the dumplings in. Let them cook for about 10 to 15 minutes—just until dumplings rise to the top. Serve with any sauced roast.

SUNKEN APPLE CAKE (*Gesunkene Apfelkuchen*)

This makes an exceptionally pretty, rustic-looking little cake that will impress everyone—an especially apt cake for afternoon parties. Europeans can buy nuts already grated in the store, where they are called, in English, nut-meal. Buy that, if you can get it. If not, grate your own. The grated nuts must be light and fluffy. To achieve such a consistency, use a nut grater, available in fancy kitchen stores. I've also heard a parmesan grater will work. (A food processor will not work: It mashes the nuts, making them oily.)

Butter a 10-inch cake pan with a removable bottom and sprinkle the inside with fine dry bread crumbs. If you don't have a pan with a removable bottom, butter a regular 9 or 10-inch cake pan, fit a circle of parchment into the bottom, and then sprinkle the sides with dry bread crumbs.

Peel, quarter, and core 4 sour apples, such as Granny Smiths and sprinkle them immediately with lemon juice to prevent browning. Slice each quarter several times from the outside most of the way down toward the core to make little layers that look like a partially opened book.

Cream:

1/2 cup butter
1 cup sugar

Add and beat until smooth and no longer gritty sounding against the bowl:

4 eggs
a few drops of almond extract
the juice of half a lemon

Combine and add to the butter mixture, mixing well:

2 cups flour
2 teaspoons baking powder
2 cups grated almonds or hazelnuts

Spread the batter in the prepared pan. Press the apples down into the batter, core side down, such that the slits in each one are visible. Bake at 350° until brown around the edges, about 50 to 65 minutes. Remove the cake from the pan after 10 minutes and let it cool on a rack. When completely cool, remove the cake from the pan to a plate and sprinkle it lightly with powdered sugar.

14

Bitter Sweet

Working in another country is the quickest way to enter a culture. I learned this not only from a summer department store job—arranged through a work experience abroad program—that I held in Switzerland after my first year of college but again a few years later in 1981, when I got an under-the-table job as a cook in a restaurant in Berlin. West Berlin, in those days, was an incomprehensible outpost of Germany full of reminders of its martial past: elderly war widows and allied soldiers—American, French, and British—who roared their tanks through the streets on occasion and young men from distant towns in West Germany who were studying in Berlin to escape their required military service, from which Berlin residents were exempt. I was twenty-two, with a mostly completed graduate degree in English behind me in New Orleans. I had decided to continue my studies at Berlin's arts and sciences university, the *Freie Universität*, which, like all universities in Germany, was paid for—even for foreigners—by generous German taxpayers. Before I could take any classes in my field, however, I first had to pass an intensive, five-hour-a-day course called *Deutsch für Ausländer*, German for foreigners.

I learned pretty quickly that attendance was not required in the course: You could come in the last half hour to take the daily quiz, and the only grade that mattered anyway was the big written and oral test at the end of the semester. If you passed that, you could matriculate in your course of study. If you didn't, you'd have to spend another semester with other foreigners, learning their mistakes.

I had taken a lot of language courses in the States and learned nothing of much use to me when, in some emergency, I had to speak the language to native speakers. I never needed to find Sylvie or anyone else at the swimming pool and certainly never wanted to talk to other people in depth—in any language—about their hobbies. To really learn a language, I decided, all I needed was to grope my way through it with native speakers in the ordinary business of life. I figured if I was able to have a meaningful conversation by the end of the semester with a German stranger—one who would not lapse into English or cut me any slack— I'd be able to pass any test, with a little cramming.

Through friends of friends of friends, I managed to get a job at what I have always erroneously referred to as a cabaret restaurant, whatever that might mean to my listeners. Actually, *Zartbitter*, which means Bittersweet, was most of the time just a café that happened to be attached to a cabaret theater. At night it metamorphosed into the cabaret's requisite bar—a loud, smelly clot of people smoking and holding beers and bright-colored cocktails, all talking incredibly fast and laughing about stories that, if some kind English speaker took the trouble to explain them to me, didn't seem funny at all. By day, though—which was when I worked—Zabi, as everyone called the restaurant, served a traditional plate lunch and what Germans call their *zweite Frühstück*, or second breakfast. For ten marks an hour, I cooked the stodgy foods of the patrons' childhoods: either the heavy, filling meals their mothers had made them at midday, when they came home from school for lunch, or else the omelets and salads and soft-boiled eggs of holiday breakfasts— in either case, comforting family foods familiar to the patrons but strange to me.

I didn't remember in those days my own childhood pickiness—how baloney sandwiches, the only kind I would ever eat, had to have the thinnest possible smear of butter on one slice of white bread and an even thinner smear of bright yellow mustard on the other. Nor had I yet learned what I know now, from having children of my own: that the exacting nature of a child's breakfast establishes the emotional foundation of the entire family's day. The ten commandments of my daughters' breakfasts carry about the same degree of punishment when they are violated as the ones on Moses' tablets. Thou shalt not run out of roast beef-flavored (not plain old beef—it's not as good) ramen noodle. Thou shalt not inadequately sugar my tea. Thou shalt serve the milk separately from the Cheerios so that I can change my mind about whether I want any. Thou shalt remind me if there's any leftover shepherd's pie *before* I order toast with crabapple jelly—that's thy job, not mine. And so on. To my newly arisen children, at least, my provision of their daily bread *is* our relationship. If I don't supply not only what they need but what they want, what they long for as solace for having survived the night, if I get it even slightly wrong or forget that their desire has changed and that now they like *shrimp* ramen noodle and not roast beef at all, then I am an unjust and unloving parent and they don't love me anymore.

In truth, cooking the comfort food of other people just the way they imagine or remember it is never really possible. My mother-in-law often laments that she can't even recreate her *own* comfort foods from childhood—probably because, as comfort food researchers have discovered, the foods we crave exist primarily in our memories. Comfort foods are constructed from irretrievable events and people from our pasts, like being cared for by a loving parent when we were sick or eating special Sunday dinners at Grandma's house or sharing smelly cheese and homemade cider on a train through the Alps. Our resulting craving—our *Heißhunger*—is deeply lodged in our memories and larger existential longings. The patrons of Zartbitter—mostly men in their twenties, cut off from their families, living alone or in groups with other students—came to eat their pasts. Pasts foreign to me that they had left behind them in faraway parts of Germany I had never visited. Pasts they had themselves rejected through lifestyles their parents and grandparents wouldn't have approved. Pasts viscid with complicated smells and textures and relationships that a stranger could never understand and that, in any case, I had to recreate using only limp vegetables, cold slabs of meat, a few dented pots and pans, and a stove whose oven didn't work properly.

And, of course, the patrons' comfort foods were nothing like the foods of my American childhood. Soft-boiled eggs, for example. Although I had eaten them for breakfast growing up (scooped into a small dish and spoon-chopped with butter, salt, and pepper) and at teatime in England (barely cooked, eaten directly from the shell) I was unsure how Germans liked theirs, and my German cookbooks made no mention of anything so obvious. Cooking the pasts of Zabi's patrons could not be learned from a book, in other words, and Eugen, the Bavarian owner of the restaurant and cabaret, had to teach me how to make most of the dishes I cooked.

Eugen, whose passion for German cabaret had given birth to Zartbitter in the first place, evidently believed in the simple power of desire to accomplish miracles. On this principle alone, he managed to maintain and nurture an amazingly long-term relationship with a man half his age who had many other lovers. If they both simply *desired* a stable live-in relationship but also wanted to leave room for the flirtation and passion and excitement of new relationships on the side, then they could accomplish it, and, for the most part, they did. Similarly, if, as an American with little German and no formal cooking experience, I *desired* a job as the only cook in a tiny kitchen where Eugen and his waitstaff and even patrons were constantly sticking their heads in the door to shout their orders and complaints in gritty street Deutsch, then I would be able to do it. The same went for the Icelandic girl who cleaned the place and fantasized about finding the perfect German mate and leaving Reykjavik forever. And for Eva, the feisty lesbian manager of Zartbitter, who longed to have a cabaret of her own. Somehow—I'm really not sure if it was a fluke or if Eugen's belief was actually true or if it was his own belief in our desires that empowered us—we all accomplished our little dreams. By the end of the semester I worked at Zartbitter, Cecilia had found her man, Eva had opened her own bigger and more successful theater, and I had passed *Deutsch für Ausländer* and moved on to my *große Matrikel* while learning how to cook Germany's past.

Eugen was a loving, sweet-tempered, and widely beloved man. He was forever dragging visitors from his own past into my kitchen to introduce them to me. Lovers from long long ago. Women he had worked with in various capacities, who now had businesses of their own. Escapees from East Berlin who talked endlessly about their mental and physical illnesses. Street people he had met on the subway and developed friendships with that involved me cooking them up whatever they desired every once in a while. After I cooked whatever it was and Eva served it up, Eugen always made me come out into the restaurant to have a beer or a mimosa or some bright-colored cocktail with them.

Eugen had an incredible stomach for alcohol. He could drink it at any time of the day or night and in incredible quantities for his small size without throwing up or even seeming drunk. When we opened up in the morning—at nine o'clock, if he was on time—he never seemed to notice the nauseating belch of foul beery air from the cabaret bar that overcame me and made it hard for me even to think about consuming *anything* for a while, much less something alcoholic.

Eugen was typically cheery in the morning, unless he and Jürgen had had a fight. He was always looking for a reason to celebrate immediately with whoever was there. It was opening night or someone's birthday or Cecilia had come in sleepy-eyed and smiling shyly and smelling of sex. Eugen's favorite way to celebrate was to layer vodka or sekt in pointy glasses with a sugary liqueur—Campari and bright blue curaçao were his favorites—and then to pass the tray of drinks around for us to enjoy on the house. We crowded together at the corner table of the as yet empty, ill-lit restaurant and clinked our glasses together. Cecilia and Eva always dutifully drank their flutes of the concoction, but I snuck back into the tiny triangular kitchen as soon as we had toasted and poured mine down the sink. By then I had my metal work surface wiped down and the kitchen's one window open as wide as it would go to let in the dank coaly air of the courtyard behind the restaurant. I was, I explained to my coworkers, "*ein Morgenmensch*," a morning person, and I felt bad if I didn't get the day started right away.

Eugen's cooking was as strongly influenced by the rustic kitchen habits of his Bavarian childhood as by the exacting culinary procedures of my old-fashioned German cookbooks. *Das fränkishes Essen*, the Frankish meal, as he called the food of the region of Bavaria he came from, was a reckless some-of-this and some-of-that chaos of tossing things into bowls and massaging squishy mixtures with your bare hands. In the midst of some such task, though, he would suddenly employ a standard gastronomic term that it irritated him to have to explain and order me to throw together a *helle Einbrenne*—literally, a "light browning"—or to "sweat" the onions or to "refine" the dish before serving it. An "*Einbrenne*," I quickly learned, was a roux—light, medium, or dark—to which was added a liquid such as broth or milk or the water in which potatoes had been boiled. In other words, a white sauce or gravy. And to "sweat" onions was to sauté them until just transparent. And "refining" a dish meant adding a little cream or butter or wine or schnapps, depending on what you were cooking. Of course, having cooked my families' meals from the time I was nine, I knew well how to make a gravy and sauté onions. What I didn't know was what, exactly, Germany's traditional dishes were supposed to end up looking and tasting like.

"A 'light browning' out of what?" I would ask. "And how thick?" My questions would sink Eugen into a wordless Bavarian despair, and he would have to go pull himself another beer from the tap before he could even attempt to explain it.

Also, although Eugen, like most Germans, could speak some English, he had never used it for cooking or for anything but small talk, so we had to converse in the loopy circles of language-learners lacking vocabulary at crucial points.

"*Du mußt die Fleischkugel erstmal braten*," he would say, first in something I could never understand that was his Fränkish dialect and then, super slowly, in high German with a Bavarian lilt.

"*Weißt du? Bra-ten*." (Get it? *Bra-ten*.) He said it even more slowly—"*Braaaah-ten*"—and made a downward shoveling movement with his hands to clarify.

But it was the word *Fleischkugel* I was stuck on, not *braten*, which meant bake or roast or fry or grill or broil, a conflation of culinary terms I had long since gotten used to. In this case it was clearly bake or roast, since the first thing Eugen had ordered me to do was preheat the oven. I was making a German meatloaf, or *Hackbraten*, the literal translation of which is "chop roast," in reference to the ground—chopped in the old days—meat used to make the roast. I had already kneaded a massive pile of ground pork—wherever we Americans use beef in a recipe, Germans use pork—together with eggs and onions and herbs and water-softened rolls to make what Eugen kept calling the "dough." I just couldn't figure out what I was supposed to do next. Americans, I knew, baked meatloaf either in a loaf pan or else formed a log shape on a roasting pan and baked it that way. I paged with meat-sticky fingers through the phrasebook I kept in my apron pocket and found that *Kugel* meant *ball*. *Fleischkugel*. Fleshball, meatball, I pondered. Was I supposed to make it into meat balls first? Or form the meat into a ball and bake it? Was a German meatloaf spherical? Eugen, meanwhile, was almost out of the door in vexation.

"You *know* eet," he tried again from the doorway, in English this time. He shoveled the air together with his open palms. "You must"—here he shoveled downward again—"like a fish, you know, in ze pan, and zen you will put it"—here he shoved angrily in the direction of the stove—"in ze oooh-ven." His English had the exaggerated cowboy accent many Germans used in discourse with Americans, but it hiccuped along with a decidedly Bavarian-sounding rhythm.

"*Aber die Kugel*," I said. "*Was ist Kugel?*"

"Ze meat! You *know* it! Ze meat!" Here he slapped the meat mixture in my bowl with his unwashed hand.

Half an hour later I was actually doing this impossible task: frying the unwieldy, kilo-sized glob of ground pork—a long, flattened "ball" of meat, if you used your imagination, about the same shape and size as two or three of our meatloaves end to end—in the biggest skillet I had and then shoveling it over with two spatulas to fry it on the other side. It broke apart, of course, but I reassembled it in the roasting pan before I put it in the oven, and I covered the whole thing up afterwards in an *Einbrenne* made from the drippings, and nobody ever found out, not even Eugen. To this day I think the American method of letting the oven do the browning is superior.

After the first few weeks, Eugen left me alone in the kitchen most of the time. The orders were predictable. I developed a rhythm for the day that pleased me. In the first hour or so, people would order drinks from the bar: coffee drinks, teas, or hot milk with honey—a morning drink slurped two-handed from a bowl and popular, for some reason, among hippie-types. Whoever was available—usually Eva in the early hours because the young men Eugen hired to wait tables were always late—filled the drink orders at the bar. That left me free to prepare the lunch special for that day before the breakfast crowd arrived at ten or ten thirty. The special was almost always a big meat dish like pork pot roast or Sauerbraten or Kassler Rippen, a corned and smoked pork rib roast served on a bed of pineapple-sweetened sauerkraut. Whatever else I was cooking for lunch, I generally had to peel ten or so pounds of potatoes to go with it, so I peeled throughout the morning and between breakfast orders and threw the peeled, halved potatoes into a massive pot of water.

"Second breakfast" was not just a term but, for the patrons of Zartbitter, a concept I had to get used to, just as foreigners working in American restaurants probably have to accustom themselves to the special meaning of a Mother's Day brunch. I've never worked in a restaurant in the U.S. that catered to a large Mother's Day crowd, but I recently made the mistake of taking my mother-in-law to one and recognized, in the fractious families and their picky elderly parents, my old Zabi customers. You need to understand that Zartbitter's patrons had already all eaten their *erste Frühstück*, the regular or first breakfast of the day: a thick slab of the best bread in the world—heavy and moist with visible whole grains and a thick chewy crust—smeared with butter and maybe honey or jam or *Rübenkraut*, a pungent molasses the consistency of caramel made from cooked-down sugarbeets. (The name of this Germanic delicacy literally means "turnip herb," for reasons not entirely clear to me, but, like skim-milk cheese, it is called something different wherever you go, including *Rübensaft*—turnip juice—*Sirup, Bimbes, Krock, Peckeleck, Stroop,* and *Hoink*.) The word *Frühstück* breaks down into *früh* (early) and *Stück* (piece), and it means just that, an early piece of bread. Bread, in Germany, is eating in its most elemental form, so much so that Germans often refer to their meals as simply "bread"—*Morgenbrot* (morning bread), *Mittagsbrot* (midday bread), *Abendbrot* (evening bread)—just as the Chinese refer to their meals as "rice."

Breakfast, in any case, is at best a private business of ritual and nourishment, even when others are present. In my household now, when my husband serves up my coffee and frothy milk and then, for himself, his usual one-egg omelet and buttered toast, there are strict rules of engagement. Planning for the day is forbidden, at least out loud, and discourse is limited to commentary on what we are reading—his newspaper, my book or magazine, the Bible. Even then there is no talk at all before we are both seated and I have partly drunk my coffee.

The German second breakfast, in some sense, is the opposite. An occasional meal in the ordinary household, it is an elaborate assemblage of all the good things Germans might put in their miniature refrigerators in anticipation of a holiday and special visitors: all manner of coldcuts and cheeses; eggs no more than three days old for soft-boiling; *Kräuterquark*, a sour cheese spread with fresh herbs in it; freshly squeezed juices; butter; jam. At the last moment, the host runs down to the bakery on the corner for a fresh loaf of bread and an assortment of little rolls. My roommates only ever ate a second breakfast with new lovers or when friends from faraway came to visit or when they went home to their families in West Germany for holidays. Second breakfast is a celebration, a pandemonium of riches designed not to satisfy hunger—the eaters, having already broken their fast with their first breakfast, are no longer actually hungry—but to satisfy one's most fantastic desires. And, like all wish fulfillment, second breakfast comes with a heavy underpinning of impending disappointment.

For some of my patrons, it was that egg, which they told me should be cooked four minutes, even though no one these days really wants a four-minute egg. The perfect four-minute egg—with the white completely cooked and the yolk hot and runny—is a directive from another era, when eggs were smaller. But how do you explain this to someone who speaks another language and who has had that number fixed in his head for a lifetime, ever since his own trusted mother cooked his egg for five full minutes and served it to him as what she called a four-minute egg? At first, I didn't try to explain anything. I simply cooked the egg for the ordered amount of time and then cooked another one for five minutes when the first one came back to the kitchen. Soon I got in the habit of cooking any egg one minute longer than it was ordered, but finally I just ignored the time a patron specified that the waiter dutifully repeated to me and cooked all eggs for five minutes.

I hope I'm not sounding harsh and critical here. How can you argue with an egg, perfectly cooked, familiar from babyhood? With its cheery, bright orange yolk? Its delightful consistency? Like butter. No, like soft buttery cheese. Like nothing else! Even the eggcup it sat in—a fat chicken with a red beak standing on its hillock of grass—is caught and fixed in the memory, like a canned peach deep in a castle-shaped mound of green Jell-O. To get at it, you have to break the whole thing apart. Serving breakfast to foreigners—there, here, anywhere—is like dissecting someone's tongue and stomach in an attempt to find the soul.

I assembled baskets of rolls and sliced bread and plates of sliced meats and sausages and cheeses. Westphalian ham. Aged Gouda. Edam. Camembert. Salami. *Cervelatwurst*, a German bologna. The grim, purple *Blutwurst*—blood-sausage—with its alarming squares of white fat. I formed mounds of *Zwiebelmett*—raw ground pork, seasoned and topped with chopped onions—and the herb-specked cheese spread. All these delicacies were to be eaten on bread. That was one caveat familiar to the child within each patron: Thou shalt not eat more than one slice of meat or cheese per slice of bread, and certainly never—*um Gottes Willen!* (in the name of God!)—meat or cheese with no bread at all. I don't know how many pieces of the raw ham to which I became addicted in my years in Germany I had rolled up in sight of friends and eaten just so before one of them took it upon himself to correct my profligacy.

Many ordered for their *zweite Frühstück* from a handful of standard lunch dishes we always offered in addition to the lunch special. *Bauernomelette*, a farm-style omelet much like a Spanish tortilla containing fried potatoes, onions, and meat of some sort. Meat or herring salad, served in a gigantic ice cream goblet and topped with a sprinkling of capers. And, my favorite, tomato soup, which I made fresh for each customer by sautéing onions in butter, adding a little flour, then half cutting half squishing canned tomatoes into the pan and letting the mixture cook a while before seasoning it, at the last minute, with gin for a hint of juniper. Some patrons wanted it further "refined" with cream, as my cookbooks also recommended, but I preferred it without. Crude, I suppose, but then, I was an American.

And all the while I peeled potatoes and carved out their eyes and said not a word to anyone until the restaurant was almost empty again.

After I got the kitchen cleaned up again and the next day's special planned with Eugen, who did the shopping, I went out to have my own lunch—usually tomato soup—and chat with Eva. Eva was an imposing personage to me at first: a tall, stern-looking woman in black leather with super white skin and short black black hair. I guessed from her coloring and affect that it was probably dyed. She smoked, as most everyone did, almost constantly. Gauloises. She lifted the cigarette fast from the counter she leaned on to her lips and then immediately back, as if she were stealing a puff while no one was looking.

She, alone, of my acquaintances absolutely did not tolerate me substituting a word of English when I needed to. She didn't know any English, perhaps. Or she hated Americans. Or she eschewed small talk and figured, if I had something to say, it was up to me to find the correct word for it. Or else she genuinely wanted me to learn the language and knew that refusing English was the best way to help me. It could have been any or all of these reasons. In any case, we struggled, at first, to talk at all. I felt, much of the time, as I did in love relationships gone suddenly awry: as if I had to create the need for conversation through questions. I asked her everything. What she had done the night before. If she had always lived in Berlin or, like so many Berliners, had come in from one of the *Länder*. If she had ever visited the United States. If she liked to cook. If her lover was coming to eat, as she sometimes did. If she liked Eugen or thought him a jerk. If she had gotten paid yet.

Eugen regularly forgot to pay us.

"*Ach, das nächstes mal,*" he would tell us, striking his head with the meaty part of his small red hand. Next time. But the next time he'd forget again, and the next time, and the next, and I would hear Cecilia telling him she hadn't been paid in a month and was about to be kicked out of her apartment. On occasion he would come in with bills in his fist and dole them out to whoever had last asked, but it was never me, because I was too shy to make demands. Too shy to yell at him, as the waiters did, and then take the money from the till and go my way. Too shy to tell my employer that I, too, was about to be kicked out of my apartment. Eventually, though, I had to do it, and afterward I felt better, and the next time he came in with currency, I was the one who got it.

Over time, Eva and I started to get a bit friendlier with each other. She started offering me her foul cigarettes and even opening conversations from time to time, and she usually came over and sat down at the corner table while I ate my lunch. She herself never ate. She just smoked and drank black coffee and coughed now and then. But I liked her.

Once, when we were standing near each other at the counter, I noticed that one of her black hairs had floated down onto her cheek, and I reach up to brush it off. Eva shrieked and pulled back from me in horror, and I saw that the hair was attached to a small mole on her cheek.

"*Ich lasse sie wachsen*," she explained afterwards, with a winsome smile, "*seit sechs Jahren.*"

"I've been letting her grow since six years," I translated in my head. A moment later, I remembered the grammatical gender issue and corrected *her* to *it*. And some time after that I learned that the word for *hair* was neuter, not feminine, and decided she had either made a mistake or else I had misheard it. Nevertheless, the image of Eva's special hair as quintessentially female remained in my head whenever I talked to her after that, whenever she sat smoking at my little table while I ate my tomato soup and I noticed the barely visible curl of black descending from the beauty mark on her cheek almost down to her jaw.

I cooked a few American meals while I worked at Zartbitter, in defiance of the widespread opinion I was always being confronted with that Americans can't cook and have "*keine eigene Küche*"—no cuisine of their own. I made hamburgers the way I had made them for my family growing up—searing thick patties of ground beef on a dry salted skillet and topping the burgers with sliced onion, tomato, pickle, and ketchup—except that I had to substitute hard German rolls for spongy American hamburger buns. My German customers ate their hamburgers delicately, using their forks and knives, and they told me that my hamburgers were nothing like the hamburgers at the McDonald's on the Ku'damm. I decided to take this as a compliment, even though when they told me that my spaghetti Bolognese was nothing like what they had eaten in Italy I knew *that* was a condemnation. I made jambalaya and gumbo the way friends had taught me back in New Orleans, and Eugen grudgingly said both were good but that New Orleans wasn't really America, in his opinion, and he was sort of right about that. I made the foods of my mother's Arkansas youth: beans and ham-hocks with cornbread, biscuits, and sausage gravy. These truly American dishes met with silence from those of Zartbitter's patrons who ventured to sample them. But, as with every other dish I cooked for the young men who ate at Zartbitter, they ate up every scrap on their plates.

I remember my days as a foreign cook whenever my husband and I go out for Thai food or my children drag me to the Emperor in Tulsa, a buffet-style Chinese restaurant they like for its millions of choices. While my daughters mound their plates with fried meat dishes and Crab Rangoon and skewers of soy-dark chicken and then rush back between the customers in line to fill soup bowls with sweet and sour sauce to dip it all in, a sweaty kitchen worker with an upraised steamer tray pirouettes invisibly past them, gauging their movements to avoid a collision. Twenty minutes later, Lulu returns yet again for another slice of the weird, steamed cake she likes, and Charlotte is working the soft-serve ice cream handle as if it were a joystick. They cover their desserts with sprinkles and sauces and plump back down at the table to eat. Meanwhile, another kitchen worker presses between the customers at the steam tables, dumps the contents of a bowl, and disappears wordlessly through some invisible door back into the kitchen, a tight wet noisy place hidden behind the red velvet walls in the midst of which, according to some personal rhythm unknown to any of the rest of us, some person—perhaps someone with roommates impatient for rent and a degree in the literature of another country— stirs and chops and pours and dips, now dropping a fry-basket into bubbling oil, now shouting orders in a language none of us diners can understand.

SHEPHERD'S PIE

This is Lulu's favorite food in the world. She especially likes the leftovers, reheated in the microwave, for breakfast.

Peel one big potato (or two small potatoes) per person and then add a few extra so that you have leftovers for your kids' breakfast. (Trust me: They will like it even better than cold pizza.) Cut each potato into same-sized chunks. Cover with salted water, bring to a boil, and then simmer until the chunks are easily pierced with a knife point. Drain, but reserve the cooking water. Mash the potatoes with butter and some of the hot potato water or—if you want them richer—milk or cream.

While the potatoes are cooking, sauté a pound of ground lamb (for 4 to 6) with a big chopped onion until the onion is soft. Crumble two cubes of beef bouillon into the meat, sprinkle with two rounded tablespoons of flour, and stir. Stir in enough hot potato water to make a thinnish gravy. (If you get it too thin, just cook it down.) Pour the meat and gravy into a greased casserole. Top with the mashed potatoes, glopping them evenly over the meat mixture, then smearing and smoothing the glops into one another to completely seal in the meat and gravy. Using a fork, make a crisscross pattern on top of the mashed potatoes and speckle with butter. Alternatively, drizzle a little cream over the fork pattern. Bake at 375° until just beginning to brown on the edges—30 to 45 minutes.

SAUERKRAUT WITH PINEAPPLE

If you ordinarily find sauerkraut too acid and assertive, you might like this sweeter, milder version. It's wonderful with ham or pork roast.

Sauté a couple of onions in oil or bacon grease until glassy. Add a big can of pineapple chunks, juice and all, a bay leaf, maybe 1/4 teaspoon caraway seeds (unless your family hates them), and a bag or jar of fresh sauerkraut. Bring to a boil, cover, and simmer for about an hour. Add a little sugar if it's still too sour or salty to suit you.

MY SPAGHETTI BOLOGNESE

This is, admittedly, more tomatoey and less meaty than the traditional meat sauce of Bologna. I also use lots more of the traditional triad of carrots, celery, and onion. It's good, though—as well as less fatty and better for you. My daughters' friends always ask for it.

Mince—or chop fine in a food processor—and sauté in a little olive oil:

1 to 2 carrots
2 to 3 ribs of celery
1 big yellow onion

Add and cook until just beginning to lose its pinkness:

1 pound ground beef

Add and let cook until all the liquid disappears:

1 cup milk
a few gratings of nutmeg (about 1/4 teaspoon)

Add and let cook away:

1/2 **cup wine of any sort** (I use whatever I happen to have open.)

Add:

1 quart canned tomatoes, cut up (I usually use my own tomatoes, which I
can in quart jars. For the kind in tin cans, I use a big—28 ounce—can and a
smaller one.)

a bay leaf

Cook, partly or entirely covered, on low for a long time, ideally an hour and a
half or more. Taste for salt. Serve on any kind of pasta—I like long pasta or penne,
but my daughters' friends get excited about bow ties—accompanied by garlic
bread and a salad.

JAMBALAYA

Brown chunks of smoked sausage—ideally Cajun andouille, but Polish sausage
will do—and chicken or shrimp in a little oil in a Dutch oven. Remove the meat to
a bowl. Sauté coarsely chopped onion, celery, and green pepper and several
minced cloves of garlic in the remaining oil until soft. Return the meat to the Dutch
oven and add a bay leaf and somewhat more rice than you would cook for the number of people you are cooking for. (For my family of four, I use 11/2 cups rice in
jambalaya.) Stir well. Add just under twice as much water as rice—I add about 2
1/2 cups water. Bring to a boil, stir, taste and adjust for salt, and then cover and simmer for 15 minutes. Let sit 5 or 10 minutes (or more). Stir well, scraping the
browned bottom and sides into the rice, before serving.

GUMBO

*Gumbos are like Russian borschts, Chinese hot-and-sour soups, Italian
minestrones, and North African chorbas: They are made with the ingredients you
have on hand. Some gumbos are thickened with roux; others are thickened with the
addition of okra. If I have okra, I use both.*

Make a roux by cooking equal parts oil and flour in a heavy-bottomed pot, stirring with a wooden spoon all the while, until it is the desired color: light caramel
brown for chicken gumbo and very dark chocolate brown (but not burnt) for

shrimp or seafood gumbo. Stir coarsely chopped onions, celery, and green peppers into roux and cook until beginning to soften. Add the meat you are using—I usually add a little sausage or ham, if I have some, to chicken or shrimp—and a bay leaf, parsley, thyme, and water to cover. Cook on low until somewhat thickened. Add salt to taste. Best the next day, reheated. Serve in a bowl over cooked rice.

15

Shame, Part 1:
"Whatever You Do,
Don't Become a Dishwasher"

This morning I read an article in *Time* about a young Jordanian man named Ra'ed al-Banna, who ended up becoming a terrorist. Not long before the suicide car bombing in which he and 132 others died, he had spent two years in the United States, seeing the sights in New York and California and jobbing around. Although outfitted to be a lawyer in his own country, he liked the United States and longed to live here. He told his family before he left Jordan that he wanted to go to law school in the U.S., and his dad reported that, having worked with refugees from the Saddam Hussein regime as a U.N. intern, his son had aspirations to become a leader.

In the U.S., though, he was anything but a leader. He worked here and there for minimum wage—in a factory, at a pizza restaurant, driving a shuttle bus. For a while he had an American girlfriend and wanted to marry her, but it didn't work out. Nevertheless, in photos he sent back to his family, he seems happy. He wears touristy clothes and, in one, poses on a skateboard in a dark cluttered room—the same all-purpose living room/bedroom/dining room of Every-Male of my college years. In another photo, he is on the water outdoors on a cloudy day before a distant city skyline: New York from Governor's Island is my guess. He anchors himself with one arm against a support cropped out of the picture— a boat railing perhaps—and smiles engagingly into the camera. He is handsome and lovable-looking in his tight camouflage T-shirt and black windbreaker: a smart, good-looking young person, seeing a bit of the world before he settles down back home into what will eventually be his real life.

I met many people like Ra'ed al-Banna in my travels abroad. Not exactly tourists—they stayed too long in one place for that. Neither were they true residents, although they knew all the best places to eat and, like me, had apartments and residence permits and work visas. I met them in bars and at friends' houses and in hotel cafés, where their sole occupations seemed to be drinking, smoking, conversing, and reading newspapers. They ranged in age from twenty to forty or so, although some were older. They worked here and there or conducted some desultory course of study at a local university before moving on. Some ended up traveling from land to land their entire lives. A few eventually found the country— or the love or the job—of their dreams and stayed where they found it. Even those who had stayed in one country for decades, though, were still searching, it always seemed to me. Always on the verge of leaving for somewhere else. Glancing up from some task—pulling a beer from the tap, waving a cigarette in the air to make a point, scribbling in a notebook—with a certain ranging look that I knew well because I had felt it on my own face, felt it from within. It was a look of realization, of suddenly remembering that there were other places out there. Other things to do. Other people to meet. Other possibilities.

Like al-Banna, the people I met abroad often left mysterious fragments of a different life behind them. High paying jobs in their fields back home. Prison time under the Shah. Life altering relationships—children sometimes, spouses, lovers— that they mentioned from time to time. Or maybe a vicious anger, learned in some angry household faraway, toward Kurds or Pakistanis or Americans. A drunken Englishman in a bar once spat out what I knew from his sneer and red face and the utter disgust of his tone was the worst possible epithet he could think of to call me: a colonist. I would not have been all that surprised to read an article on one or the other of these acquaintances in a news magazine years later. A draft or tax evader. A chess champion on the lam. A terrorist.

Most, though, suffered more ordinary pains and hates and turmoil. When I lived for a while on an island near Hong Kong, there were two men—one Irish and the other Italian—who seemed to be the best of friends but loved the same woman. She couldn't make up her mind between them. Interacting with the three of them was like playing with snapping turtles. It's funny when you thrust your little twig at them and one of them snaps it in two, but in the back of your mind you see your severed finger in the turtle's maw.

Once I joined the two men in a nighttime swim around a rocky cape separating the island's two main beaches. I am a strong swimmer, but I didn't realize until I was alone, out past the surf in the dark waters, that the two men were racing each other. They often engaged in such competitions, as if they thought in this way to sort out the problem of which one was the better man, which one should have the girl. Soon I couldn't hear their voices anymore or the crash of waves against the rocks or anything but the quiet ocean and the night. There was no moon, no stars, no light, no way to differentiate between land and forever. As I swam, I struggled between terror and embarrassment. Eventually I made it to the other beach, and the two men stood in the surf, waiting.

"We thought you might've drowned," one of them said, laughing. "We were trying to figure out whether to swim out and look for you." I laughed, too, although in my lungs and gut I could yet feel the panic of my aloneness in that black night. They told the story in the bar later. The Italian, they said, had won the race, and their girlfriend, a blithe Australian who reminded me of Lauren Bacall, leaned into him with a lazy smile.

The Scottish bartender on the island repeatedly threw himself from the ferries that carried us to Hong Kong island or Kowloon for jobs or, in my case, the university. He was a skinny man in his fifties with long, widely-spaced teeth stained deep yellow from smoking. His Brazilian wife had recently committed suicide, and he was bent on killing himself, too. He always took the dive in the middle of the forty or fifty minute trip, somehow when no one was looking, although there were always people milling around on both decks, eating the noodles or congee served on board or playing cards or hunching under the awning to keep from getting rained on. I never could figure out how the splash managed to evade notice. In any case, having been a lifeguard in his younger years, the bartender never succeeded in drowning himself, and the ferry crew would find him bobbing in the waves on the way back. They hauled him up and put towels on his shoulders, and we all murmured over him until we docked. That night he'd be back behind the bar, mixing our drinks, telling us his sad stories about a past of which we were not a part.

The majority of the expatriates I knew, though, were, like me, much less interesting. We camped, rather than lived, and skimmed vacant-heartedly around the world, mooching off of people in similar circumstances, finding roommate situations in the cheapest possible housing, working just enough here and there to pay our share of the rent and afford bar food and the next plane ticket. Our real occupation was the pursuit of "experience"—that is, fun, lovers, a few glimpses of the world beyond our own, and maybe a smattering of language or other cultural flot-sam. Enough experience to get by, but not enough to do anything with when we returned home.

Perhaps my fellow expatriates were creating global bonds too subtle for me to notice. Enduring friendships or business connections. Heavy furniture or rugs that reside in their living rooms to this day. Perhaps illegitimate children or vene-real diseases I didn't know about that would link them more indelibly to their past travels than I am linked to mine. If they cooked at all, they likely returned home with international recipes they passed down to their children and grandchildren, recipes that would eventually become essential parts of the family identity.

At the university where I teach, many students come from missionary families who have lived in countries all over the world. In an essay assignment involving food, they often write about such inherited family dishes, usually eaten on holidays. Palacinkas. Persian rice. Or, an assembled dish I have adopted from numerous stu-dents' essays that is especially beloved of my children: chicken curry over rice sur-rounded by bowls of fruits and vegetables and condiments and romantically called Snow on the Mountain, for the shredded coconut you sprinkle on last. I serve it whenever there are lots of students eating with us, and, somehow or another, a game has evolved with it. When I heap the little mountains of rice onto the plates, each person dining has to name theirs. Kilimanjaro. Rushmore. The Matterhorn. Bushyhead. Only when all have named their mountains can we eat.

I think, though, that most expatriates, like me, upon returning home and get-ting their feet again, leave the countries they have visited pretty well behind them. For me, all that remain of my travels in England, Switzerland, Germany, China, and Hong Kong—travels that together comprise over a third of my adult years—are a few Christmas cards and yearly phone calls from people I have largely forgot-ten, a murky passage in my curriculum vitae, and various foreign meals enjoyed by a husband and two children who have never been to the countries where I learned to cook them.

And one other thing: a consciousness that we are all aliens in this world, but for the divine sorting that divides us at birth, not just into countries and cultures but into social classes and families. In a crucial sense, I think, we are all expatriates. *Ex*—out of. *Patria*—fatherland. Separated—as I would later read in the book of Hebrews and eventually come to believe—from our original Father, we are all the same in our foreignness. We spend our lives yearning for love and belonging, for truly fulfilling work, for genuine pleasure. Like the aliens living among us, we all lack—at crucial moments, often in our times of direst need—the language to express ourselves perfectly. All of us, at some point in our lives, feel like outcasts in the world, or tourists perhaps, not really a part of the places we inhabit.

And deep down we all long for home—which is not a place that we have ever been to, exactly, but rather that elusive circumstance in which we are fully known and cherished. Home is a place where all food is good food, where no desire goes unsatisfied, and where enemies, if we have any, are consigned to oubliettes in some well fortified outpost beyond the horizon, forgotten.

Many people have no idea what the life of an alien looks like. Ra'ed al-Banna's father evidently did, though.

"Whatever you do," he told his son before that two-year stint in the Land of Opportunity, "don't become a dishwasher."

For, while many young expatriates—like al-Banna, like me—leave home with marketable degrees or lucrative job prospects, it goes without saying that they will probably spend at least some of their time abroad doing work quite different from their ultimate career goals and often different from any work they would ever have done in their own country, even in part-time jobs as teenagers. They stand at fryers and prep tables and sinks the world over, feeding strangers, fantasizing about the next place they will go, the next job—surely better than this one. And secretly, beneath the fantasy, beneath the work and the grease and the steam in that kitchen, they are, every one of them, hungry for home.

Snow on the Mountain

This is a wonderful meal if you're having lots of guests. Everyone likes at least some part of it, and they can pick and choose. Also, it's really simple to prepare. The chopped accompaniments and the curry itself can be made ahead of time, so all you have to do at the last moment is cook the rice. Children—even picky eaters—love Snow on the Mountain, partly because of the name. And do play the mountain-naming game. You'll find that interesting conversation invariably ensues.

Make ahead a big pot of chicken curry and, when it's near time to eat, a big pot of plain rice. I like Thai fragrant rice: Boil 1 to 11/2 cups rice per 4 people in about 11/2 times as much water and then simmer for 15 minutes. My recipe for chicken curry is the yogurty "Moghul Braised Chicken"—spiced with cardamom, cloves, and coriander—from my favorite Indian cookbook, Julie Sahni's *Classic Indian Cooking*, but any chicken curry recipe will work for this. Also offer a large variety of fresh fruits, vegetables, and condiments: apples, cucumbers, green and/or sweet white onions, green peppers, hot peppers, tomatoes, cilantro, pineapple, raisins, peanuts or almonds, and whatever Indian chutneys and relishes you have. And, of course, coconut for snow. Put everything in pretty bowls and set them on the table as you chop. When it's time to eat, just ladle out the rice and curry and let diners serve themselves from the little bowls.

16

Shame, Part 2: *Abfallfresser*

For a year or so of my six years in Berlin, I worked in the restaurant of a place called the Edinburgh House, a hotel for British officers. I got the job through the job placement center of the *Freie Universität*, where I studied first German literature and later sinology. This was back in the 1980s—before the Wall came down, in case you don't remember, and West Berlin was still divided between the Allies.

I lived in Neukölln, a ratty part of town solidly in the American Sector that I chose not out of any sort of patriotism but because of its cheap housing and proximity to the university. Known locally for the hopsy air of its brewery, Neukölln was inhabited mostly by pensioners and foreigners and had no tourist attractions or museums or artsy bars. The War had pitted and scarred its buildings, which, like all other outdoor surfaces in Berlin, were pinkish and dusty-looking from coal ash. A few blocks from where I lived, people still inhabited a building that a bomb had split completely in half, leaving a pile of rubble beside an inside wall that had become an outside wall and still displayed the remains of what had once been the building's interior: the five floors broken off into jagged ledges, scraps of wallpaper and painted areas where rooms had once begun and ended, brighter colors where furniture and appliances had stood, plumbing sticking out like stray chin hairs.

Students went to Neukölln primarily for its super-cheap thrift stores and decrepit restaurants, some of which had been around since before the Wall. My favorite restaurant there—a dungeon-dark, two-story establishment directly on the Wall—served only *Brathähnchen*: gloriously crispy, spit-roasted chickens, accompanied by a roll. The restaurant lay in an especially bleak, out-of-the-way part of Neukölln, twenty minutes from the farthest subway station, but my friends and I

157

traipsed out there a few times a semester for that uncommon combination of cheap and good. A half chicken cost five marks, about two dollars in those days. For a mark extra, you could get a saucer of watery slaw or potato salad, but every-one—whoever you were eating with and the peevish waitstaff as well—advised against it. Neither waiters nor clientele particularly liked students; so, knowing we were despised became part of the dining experience. My companions and I either ate in uncharacteristic silence or, if it was late at night and the restaurant was our last stop, engaged in deliberately bellicose remarks and overloud laughter.

The Edinburgh House was on the furthest edge of ritzier Charlottenburg in the British Sector, a part of Berlin I seldom had occasion to visit. My subway trip there began before five in the morning and took over an hour. While my German room-mates slept off the night before, rising much later to drag themselves to classes or meet friends at a sidewalk café, I hurtled through the darkness of the real world, a narrow place peopled by those unaccustomed to such leisure. Surly teenagers studying the tabloids. Slumped over and bewhiskered drunks. Lost-looking old people from East Berlin, who upon retirement were allowed to cross over to visit relatives in Free Berlin and returned loaded down with discount canned goods. Tense foreigners on their way to underpaid jobs they feared losing.

I started out as *Küchenhilfe*, kitchen help, a generic term for the lowest job in the restaurant industry all over the world. My fellow kitchen helpers and I not only washed dishes but scrubbed the grey tile floors of the kitchen daily. That was the nastiest part of the job. The tiles were gritty and porous, like stone. We used boiling water and cleaning soda—a caustic lime cleanser used in the U.S. to scour sidewalks—and a hard, short-bristled broom covered with a coarse cloth that we afterwards wrung out by twisting it between us. We also wiped down the cooking surfaces, cleaned the ovens, prepared salad vegetables, pricked dozens of eggs for boiling, washed and chopped and squeezed the juice out of masses of parsley, and peeled onions and potatoes—often ten or twenty kilos at a time. We scrubbed frying pan after frying pan that the cooks deposited on the stainless steel counter of our work area and wanted back spotless, immediately. We did, in short, whatever we were told, whatever was backbreaking or tedious or foul, whatever the German cooks or the British waitresses barked at us to do, whatever we had to do to make our ten marks an hour.

My fellow kitchen helpers were mostly Turkish. Some had worked in that kitchen for years; others were just passing through on their way to other jobs. A stocky middle-aged woman named Irem was my mentor, of sorts. She was the only other female kitchen helper, the oldest of us by far, and certainly the most knowledgeable about the job, having worked at the Edinburgh House much longer than anyone else. She could speak a few words of German and even English, mostly commiserative adjectives like *heavy* and *hungry* and *sick*, enough to get across that I looked tired or to joke that she could lift more than any of the men. The rest of the kitchen help spoke only Turkish, a lush breathy language that I came to find comforting. The cooks spoke only German. The waitresses, mostly British army wives or girlfriends, spoke only English, often with mystifying brogues. The three distinct worlds—Turkish, German, English—intersected only minimally, and I was never fully part of any of them.

The kitchen help always ate together, and I became easy with my peers, although we couldn't speak. Or perhaps *because* we couldn't speak and thus had to rely on more intimate forms of expression—touching, gesturing, raising our eyebrows, laughing. Arriving earlier than the cooks and waitresses, missing out on ordinary leave-takings and breakfasts with those we loved, engaging in strenuous activity before the grouchiness of morning had worn off—these miseries joined us, somehow. Between getting the kitchen in order for the day and filling the tea cooker—an electric urn the size of a garbage can—and setting up the chores we knew would come later, we snatched a breakfast together. This ten-minute meal reminded me of before-school breakfasts in my big family growing up. Everyone reached over everyone else at the same time. Some read newspapers. Nobody said much of anything. Occasionally, one of the men groused comically, in foreign words I nevertheless recognized as the gruff voices of the cooks who would soon be arriving or the whining rage of one of the waitresses, and we all laughed.

We always ate the same breakfast. Plain rolls just arrived from the *Bäkerei* and still warm sometimes and softer inside than they'd be for the officers a couple of hours later. Juice glasses filled to the brim with strong hot tea, into which we stirred so much sugar that it left a yellow sludge at the bottom that we scraped out with our spoons. This was not a meal I would ever have chosen for myself. I preferred coffee—black, unsweetened—to tea, and I would have liked butter and jam with my roll. But somehow, having craved breakfast the whole subway ride there, I found that simple combination of bland, sweet, and hot was just the comfort I wanted.

For lunch—eaten standing around in the kitchen after the tables had been cleared but before we began on the dishes—we saved radish leaves and parsley stems and whatever soft-boiled eggs and hardened rolls were left from the officers' breakfasts. With these we constructed hodgepodge mixtures and one perfect sandwich, a delicacy I still make sometimes when I gather radishes from my garden. We sliced the almost solidified eggs, washed the radish greens several times—they have prickly hairs that catch the dirt—and salted them well, and then layered the greens with the eggs in a torn open roll. Sometimes we pilfered a few tomatoes and an onion to make a salad I especially liked with quartered eggs and minced parsley stems.

"*Abfallfresser*," the German cooks said, pointing to the huddle of us eating. I wasn't sure what that meant. *Fresser*, I knew, came from the verb *to eat*, but it was used only for animals, and I was unsure what *Abfall* was. I took note of the confusing word so that I could ask my roommates when I got home. Trash-eaters, they told me, outraged on behalf of my fellow workers. But it was true. We ate mostly what the cooks and waitresses told us to throw out, although it was perfectly good food. And better for us, in any case, than what the German cooks had been trained to regard as high cuisine: the fussy, fatty food of Old Vienna. Deep-fried breaded cutlets. Bacon dumplings. Sumptuous soups glittering with *Fettaugen*, or "eyes of fat," the yellow fat bubbles that indicate a soup's quality.

Don't get me wrong. Although my fellow kitchen helpers and I were trim and healthy-looking compared to the massive cooks, I have never been what you would call skinny. And I love a Wiener Schnitzel done right: with anchovies and capers and lemon juice to cut the grease and complement the sweetness of the butter-fried veal chop. Also, the cooks' clearly professional culinary techniques impressed me. I frequently snuck up behind them in their work on the pretext of scrubbing an oven not in use or wiping down the prep table with vinegar. I studied what went into the simmering broths that they transformed into rich-colored, sparkling clear bouillons. I watched them mill potatoes; mix in butter, cream, nutmeg; then spritz the yellow paste around the edge of a platter of roast or else work it into a dough with flour and eggs to deep-fry as croquettes or boil as dumplings. The cooks grunted and grumbled and cursed as they worked, lumbering around one another like jumbo jets on a tarmac, but in their work they were delicate and precise. A pinch of parsley in their bulbous fingers sprinkled out like fairy dust, and you never saw a prettier tart crust or zigzagged tomato garnish, with its perfect little crest of mayonnaise in the center. Nevertheless, I found our sandwiches of discarded radish leaves and cold eggs more satisfying than the finest dish that I imagined the cooks had to offer: less fiddled with and healthier.

As soon as the cooks arrived in the morning, we kitchen helpers scattered and did our separate jobs for the day. The most recent hire did the floors. Not long after I was hired, somebody quit, and the replacement—a Romanian who looked fourteen or fifteen at most but somehow made me understand that, like me, he had a completed university degree behind him—took over mopping. I graduated to skillet scrubbing. I wish I had then what I use now—a green scrubber I buy at Wal-Mart that's so heavy-duty I once scratched up the glass of our aquarium when I used one to get the coralline algae off. But, alas, all we had at our disposal at the Edinburgh House were dish rags and, if the cooks weren't looking, the same caustic soda powder we used for scrubbing the floor. Another hire later, the boy took over the skillets. The cooks by then had differentiated him enough from the other male workers to call him *the boy* in German, *der Bube*, which the British waitresses found amusing. After a while they took to calling him the Boob, at which he grinned and nodded devotedly.

I, meanwhile, was promoted once again, to potato peeler, of whom there were several. We worked in groups of two or three, kneeling around the burlap bag in a cool, unlit workroom where we kept fresh vegetables and eggs. German potato peelers peel toward you, instead of away from you, and have a sharpened protruding part for gouging out eyes and rotten spots. I kept stabbing myself with the eye-gouging part at first and found the backwards peeling so awkward I decided to use a paring knife instead, but Irem, returning to check on me, wedged the peeler back into my fist and said, "*Besser! Besser!*" until I finally gave in. She was right. Once I got the hang of it, peeling potatoes *was* better using the German peeler, and now it's the only kind I use.

I alone probably peeled over a thousand pounds of potatoes that year at the Edinburgh House. We tossed the peeled potatoes into a pot like the one the old woman stirs in that Grimm Brothers' story "The Robber Bridegroom"—big enough to boil a person in. When the potato pot was full, it took two people to lug it out to the sink, where we rinsed the potatoes and covered them with water to keep them from turning pink before they were cooked. If the cooks shouted something, one of us stopped peeling to run and do whatever it was they wanted. The Turkish men always sent me, because I spoke the most German. Nevertheless, I usually didn't understand the cooks' orders, which were garbled by regional dialects and impatience and a culinary vocabulary beyond what I had learned from my earlier restaurant job in Berlin. My incomprehension infuriated the cooks and embarrassed me, even more so when Irem had to run over and dance me through some simple task.

Even without German or English, kitchen helpers who had been there a while usually knew what to do before they were asked. When Irem was busy somewhere else, the nearest one gave me—or the boy, or any newer kitchen helper who didn't get it—frantic instructions for how to do whatever it was, using the universal sign language of the alien and slave: thrusting a tool into my hands and shoving me in the direction of some unknown task, grabbing my forearms and positioning them correctly, yanking and pointing, slapping their foreheads in frustration, and chasing after me when I did it wrong. Sometimes my ad hoc instructor said a word over and over again, as if he believed this incantation could make me understand Turkish, and then later I would realize it was a German word he had picked up from Irem that I hadn't recognized.

I could tell from their zeal that my fellow workers were worried that at any moment I—and they—might be fired for doing some job wrong, although I remember no angry dismissals. Usually the people who left seemed to just disappear and never return, and the rest of us absorbed that person's work until Irem went to the hotel manager to request a replacement. In any case, although the more experienced kitchen workers did their work better than I did, I knew from what I overheard in the cooking area that I would never be fired. Distinct from the others, I was *die Amerikanerin, die Studentin, das Mädel*—the American, the student, the girl—and, as such, I had special status. The hotel manager himself— a German who spoke accentless *Hochdeutsch* and perfect English, in a clipped British accent, and even a few words of Turkish and was universally despised— came to the kitchen from time to time to ask me how I was doing. He didn't check on any of the other kitchen help or stop and chat with the cooks or the waitresses. Somehow, as an English speaker studying German but working and eating trash like a Turk, I spanned the cultures of the restaurant.

The waitresses didn't know what to make of me. *Why would an American want to work in that kind of job?* I imagined them musing whenever I caught one staring at me and my co-workers goofing around as we peeled potatoes. The cooks speculated about me more openly. My interest in their cooking clearly excited them. Occasionally one of them offered an exaggeratedly simple explanation of some technique. Mostly, though, they didn't speak to me much but made their thoughts clear through whispered remarks to one another. They never could quite believe that I understood anything at all of what they said. Or perhaps they forgot. Or maybe they intended me to understand their comments as I gathered pots and watched in surreptitious admiration as one of them plunged his bare fingers into boiling oil to retrieve a croquette that had escaped the slotted ladle. I have never been as aware of being a sex object as during those days. They mentioned every part of my body, and I felt naked despite my grease-flecked T-shirts and baggy pants.

The work was unbelievably dirty. The potatoes came caked in dried black mud. When I ran over to help a co-worker wring the mop rag, the burning water was purplish-grey with grime and left my knuckles and cuticles indelibly dark.

The soft-boiled eggs the British officers ate for breakfast left dribbles of yolk down the dainty egg cups they were served in that the dishwasher never got clean, so we had to scrape them with our fingernails before putting them in the machine. By the end of the day—at four in the afternoon if I had the early shift or at four in the morning if I worked late—I smelled like a pot of leftover soup forgotten in the back of the refrigerator for weeks.

Everyone but the kitchen helpers somehow stayed spotless in their uniforms, the cooks in their pristine white coats, hounds-tooth trousers, and white clogs; the waitresses in blue button-down dresses with little white aprons. Evaluating them all from the bleak perspective of the kitchen corner where I worked, I liked my Turkish co-workers better than the German men and the British women, but I envied the cooks and waitresses the relative cleanliness of their jobs. So, when the hotel manager sent the head waitress to ask if I wanted to replace one of the waitresses going on maternity leave, I was reluctantly interested. The promotion meant more money, Jane told me. And time off between the officers' meals to eat our own meal out in the dining room. And tax-exempt liquor and cigarettes from the commissary upstairs. Jane smiled enticingly as she detailed these amenities, as if I were a child or a pet she was trying to wheedle. When I agreed, she told me I would need a uniform, and, as I didn't know my European size, she took my measurements, trying, I could tell, not to touch me in my moist, dirty clothes. Jane was a shapely woman with brown hair and pretty skin. The fitted blue dress, I reflected as she rolled up her tape measure, became her.

"Now," she said, after she had located a uniform the right size and had me try it on in the staff lavatory, "about that hair on your arms. Our officers are not accustomed to hairy arms. You'll want to shave it off."

I have always been a bit hairy, as women go. The hair on my legs grows in dark, but, like the German women I knew in those days, I didn't shave. With the limited bathing facilities of my Berlin apartment, it was too much trouble, and Europeans, I had found, didn't seem bothered by hair. Some even found it enticing.

In fact, I had only ever found my hairiness to be an impediment in the United States. In the mall bookstore where I had worked as a teenager, numerous strangers—always middle-aged women, for some reason—noticed the dark down mashed beneath my nylons and asked me why I didn't shave my legs. And once, during my college years, I was wearing a sun dress on my way to Sunday dinner at my parents' house and a passel of mean-spirited teenagers in bathing suits barked me off the public bus.

Nevertheless, Jane's comment took me by surprise. When she held out her pale slick arm next to mine to highlight the problem, I recited in my mind a funny Robert Herrick poem I had memorized in college:

> Fain would I kiss my Julia's dainty leg,
> Which is as white and hairless as an egg.

Evidently Jane and the British officers were not the only ones who loathed body hair.

Of course, I refused to shave my arms, and there was a skirmish of uncertainty about what to do. Jane conferred with the other waitresses, spoke to me again, and eventually threatened to bring the hotel manager in to arbitrate. She referred to him derisively as Herr Chef, which means Mr. Boss in German, but the conflation of languages threw me. I thought she was going to bring in one of the German cooks to examine my arms and settle the matter.

"Do what you want," I told her. "I'm not shaving my arms."

I almost said I'd stay in the kitchen rather than comply, but by this time, it shames me to say, as critical as I was by then of the racism and sexism and general benightedness I observed among the higher paid workers, I wanted the better job. I wanted not only out of the filth and drudgery of the kitchen but into the world of the dining room, where officers lounged with their egg cups and tea, waitresses primped and cooed, and diners enjoyed foods as yet unknown to me beyond the raw ingredients that went into them and their mucky remains on dishes and cutlery. I wanted to go to that strange land, to know those people, to eat their delicacies.

So, before long, Jane took me in to see the hotel manager in his office behind the reception desk of the hotel proper. I felt exactly as I had felt in an earlier decade of my life, when Sister Agatha took me to the high school principal, Father McGrath, for wearing ankle-high boots with my school uniform instead of the requisite loafers. That time I lied and said I had weak ankles, but to Herr Chef I said nothing at all. While Jane explained the problem, mentioning once again the officers and their fragile sensibilities, the poor man looked anywhere but at me, and I held my arms behind my back to keep him from having to concentrate on not staring at them. When she was finished with her complaint, he looked pained and angry simultaneously—not just at this woman with her embarrassing complaints but at me, too, for not simply conforming and leaving him out of it. He looked just exactly as Father McGrath had looked about the shoe problem, and his response was the same.

"This is ridiculous," Herr Chef told us both, casting his vote in my favor. But from that moment he treated me differently. I was a troublemaker.

So, that afternoon Jane gave me instruction on the new work I would be doing the next morning, and I became a waitress, as inescapably one of them as I had not been one of them before.

Hotels are strangely stratifying work places, in my experience. In addition to working and more or less living at a resort in Connecticut during the summers of my early teenage years and much later spending considerable time hanging out with other expatriates in hotels abroad, I have worked in two hotels—the Edinburgh House and the St. Charles Hotel in New Orleans—and I have found all hotels to be the same in this regard. At the bookstores and libraries and tailor shop where I had also worked back in the United States, every employee could do just about every job, if needed. In hotels, though, duties are sharply delineated one from the other by titles, uniforms, gender roles, and habits of comportment. Never does the bellhop stand in for the desk clerk in a rush, or the concierge for the doorman or the valet. Bellhops are always male. Chambermaids always female. And even within a single job description, workers are further defined and separated from one another by rank, seniority, uniforms, and strictly defined workstations.

Perhaps this propensity to create borders derives from the very borderlessness of hotels, where foreigners and passers-through are welcomed as nowhere else, leaving those who work there defenseless against the outside. Hotels do not exist, in a certain sense, in the familiar world of "us and them"; so, for protection, workers manufacture artificial boundaries. Thus, in the fairytale land of the hotel, workstations become countries, each with its own language and visas and rules of engagement, and each job description embodies a culture and a point of view. No amount of magic can fully fuse them. From the vantage point of the hearth, Cinderella can see only the work to be done—the peas and lentils that her step-sisters, out of meanness, have tossed into the ashes for her to gather up again and sort. But from the point of view of the ballroom, she can no longer see the ashes or the meanness or the work—or even, I suspect, the friendly little birds who helped her out of her misery by picking the lentils and peas from the ash. In any case, after becoming a waitress at the Edinburgh House, I never entered the kitchen again, except to fill tea pots from the big cooker or load up on salt shakers and mustard pots or roll in carts of dirty dishes to be washed. When I did have to go there, Irem and the others and I nodded at one another politely, and then we scurried about our business, and I didn't think much about it. I had crossed over.

I can still taste the inescapable shames of that year. I was ashamed to be an *Abfallfresser*, but also ashamed not to be one, to sit out in the dining room with the waitresses playing cards and, while the kitchen helpers toiled, enjoying that day's special—lamb, maybe, or roast chicken with bread sauce—or else the waitresses' ritual teatime meal of bread, cheese, and funny British pickles and relishes. And even now I am ashamed to be so categorically critical of those women, most of whom were kind to me and, in the end, quite likeable. I wonder if such sentiments could have been part of what motivated Raed al-Banna? The shame of belonging, of not belonging? The mixed up longing that drove me to seek home in lands utterly alien to me, where I would inevitably end up alone?

Even so, it is no excuse for killing 132 others, you may argue, and I agree. Still, when I read about al-Banna's jobs and consider his failed relationship with the American woman he loved, when I see the photographs of his temporary joys, I see myself in that restaurant. Twisting the mop rag. Positioning an egg cup on its saucer behind an officer's upraised newspaper. Dreaming about the salty radish greens I would have for lunch, the sandwich of cheese and dark, clovey Branston pickle. Hungry for it.

ROAST CHICKEN (*Brathähnchen*)

There is no simpler, more impressive, and more delicious meal to serve to guests. Roast your chicken on a spit for crispiness all over. If you don't have a spit—and I don't, although I've always wanted one—a roasting pan works almost as well, although you do lose the crispiness on one side, unless you stand the chicken up on a can, which I have never tried. I do roast breast side up, though, so that the wasted side is the back.

Wash a chicken and pat it dry with paper towels. Put it in a large roasting pan. You may salt it, if you like, or sprinkle it with herbs. I either don't season it at all— I love just the intense chicken taste of roast chicken—or else I stuff it with lots of minced garlic and sprigs of rosemary and sprinkle a little of both on the outside to brown. Roast the chicken for 1 hour or so in a hot oven—450°— until it is brown and crispy. Carve it at the table. Serve with salad, bread, and cranberry sauce or some sort of good jelly, like crabapple or red currant or jalapeño. If my guests are intimate enough to be this casual, I put the roasting pan on the table so we can scrape at and sop up the savory drippings with our bread.

REAL GERMAN POTATO SALAD

In contrast to our American recipes for potato salad and especially to the sweet, bacony salad we call "German potato salad," (see page 54), real German potato salad is delicate and relatively low in fat. You need what the Germans call waxy potatoes—potatoes with less starch that hold up when boiled. Yukon golds and red potatoes work well. As always when boiling or baking potatoes whole, choose potatoes that are approximately the same size so they all get done at once, and for this recipe select, if possible, potatoes that are long and skinny so that, when you slice them, you end up with smallish rounds. Also, no German I know leaves the potatoes unpeeled, but I often do—for the nutrients as much as for the taste and texture.

Boil potatoes in their skins until just barely done. Check on them with the point of a knife while they're cooking. Drain and cool just enough to handle. Meanwhile, in a big serving bowl, make a vinaigrette out of a little oil, some minced onion and parsley and/or chives, salt, pepper, a little vinegar, and—this is the most important ingredient—warm broth. (Use bouillon in hot water if you have no broth). You need about twice as much broth as oil and vinegar combined, but don't worry: I never measure any of this when I make it, and it always comes out good. As soon as the potatoes are cool enough to peel, do so (if you feel you must) and slice them into thickish rounds—between a 1/4 and 1/2 inch thick—into the vinaigrette. Toss lightly, trying not to break up the rounds. Serve warm or at room temperature.

CHICKEN AND LEEK SOUP

My friend Susanne made this soup a lot. Like all simple chicken soups, it is profoundly comforting, whether you are sick or just need encouragement. It's also pretty. I make it when someone in my family is sick or when I feel sad for some reason.

Wash and cut up a chicken. Put it in a big pot, well covered with water. Cook until the chicken is tender. Remove the chicken to a plate and let it cool enough to handle. Then remove the bones and skin and return the chicken—you can cut it up or leave it in big pieces—to the pot. (Refrigerate at this point if you want to solidify the fat for easy removal.) Slice several leeks into thick cylinders—use the white part and the lighter green part—and wash them well in a colander. Add them to the soup along with, if you like, peeled and thinly sliced carrots and large chunks of peeled potatoes. Often I leave out the carrots and potatoes. Cook until the vegetables are done. Salt well.

17

The Hunger Voyages

Possibly my favorite book in the whole world is Pearl Buck's *The Good Earth*. It was my mom's favorite book, too: one of a handful of books—from my parents' mysterious past lives as teenagers and unmarried adults—that followed us from house to house when we moved from California to Connecticut and back to California, books that became the private library of my childhood.

The Good Earth opens with Wang Lung's hunger. He is making tea for his crotchety father, who scolds him for using actual tea leaves instead of his usual hot water. But Wang Lung is celebrating. He is about to marry a slave from the local rich man's house, a woman who—in my mother's favorite passage—will soon squat in the field to give birth to their first child and then return to her farm-work. O-lan is a plain woman with unfashionably big feet and a simple, hard-working scope on life. She has known hunger and abuse and will know wealth but will never wield the sort of power that was once wielded over her. She and Wang Lung work hard, raise children, suffer, and come to value what's important to them only after a lifetime of failure.

They live, in short, the life most of us have lived, or will live. Except for one governing event. Like other poor people all over the world since the beginning of time, Wang Lung and his family become hunger emigrants. They live in a place and time when drought and famine are so profound and the distribution of wealth so inequitable that many poor die, all suffer, and not a few are reduced to villainy. Friends and relations fight over food. Neighbors pillage one another's houses. Daughters are sold as prostitutes and slaves. During one famine, O-Lan murders her newborn baby rather than watch the child starve.

At several points in the saga of their life together, Wang Lung and O-lan leave

169

home in search of food. Wang Lung builds the family a shelter of mats along the roadside and gets work as a rickshaw driver. O-lan, with her children, begs. They move from place to place, propelled by hunger.

Migrations have always fascinated me. I like to read about mass hunger migrations, like the ones caused by the potato famine and the weather disasters of the nineteenth century that brought my Irish and German ancestors to this country's shores. And I am intrigued by the emotional famines—lack of community, a shared heritage, happiness—that triggered my own family's moves during my childhood and possibly fostered my parents' earlier migrations from New York and Arkansas to golden California, the promised land of their growing up years. They suffered the same sort of hunger, I'm guessing, that drove the travels of the many expatriates I met in my years abroad.

The small miseries that drove *me* to flee family and home to live among strangers can hardly compare to those of the hunger emigrant or war refugee. Nevertheless, the part of me that fled in my twenties still struggles to understand the moment of leaving. Where does the confidence come from that says, "Leave this place. Leave your home. Find a better place"? What fragile catalyst motivates the emigrant to abandon all for an unknown, unseen something better? Mere unsubstantiated hope? Hope that somewhere else there must be food, shelter, a welcoming community, or at least respite from war, abuse, loneliness? If it's true, as scholars of family dysfunction claim, that what we already know is what we expect to find in life, then where does this idea come from, in a person who has long suffered, that somewhere else will be any better? Is it hunger itself that conjures the promise of abundance elsewhere and motivates the fleer to take the first step away from home into the unknown?

In Buck's novel, hunger seems a live creature, a character whose exploits are as important to the plot as those of Wang Lung's no-good uncle and prissy concubine. Again and again in the couple's struggles, hunger confronts them, follows them, settles in with them. Hunger is especially present when they are in transit— fleeing, seeking, setting up yet another temporary shelter. Hunger is the emigrant's traveling companion.

Wang Lung and O-lan eventually return home, but frequently emigrants don't. Once they find what they are looking for, they stay put, and "home"—not the place they left, exactly, but a fantasy version of that place without drought or war or famine—becomes first a story they tell to their children, then a vague memory, and finally a dream, encountered only in sleep.

Or, in the foods of home that they increasingly think about and often try to recreate. Scientists list obsession with food as a key symptom of starvation, and I know from reading the essays of international students studying abroad—as well as from my own experience as an expatriate—that emigrants often seek to recapture their lost homes by talking about, cooking, and eating the foods of their pasts. Consider the dreamlike recipes assembled by those starving women of the Terezin Ghetto. Seeing others—their own children, perhaps—die from hunger daily and surely uncertain of their own survival, they recorded recipe after complicated recipe for delicacies they had cooked before their imprisonment in the concentration camp, recipes using ingredients long since unavailable and displaying a culinary largesse they would never again enjoy. The resulting cookbook is frustratingly elliptical. You can't really cook from it. It documents not the cuisine of the women's past lives but the hunger of their present.

I remember coming upon a hotdog stand once after getting off the subway in Hong Kong. The hotdogs were crazily expensive, and, having lived in Hong Kong for almost a year, I was at the end of my money. Nevertheless, I had to buy one.

The man in the booth nestled the hotdog in a split bun with his tongs and then started to squirt mayonnaise from a squeeze bottle onto the pink meat.

"No, not mayonnaise!" I cried out, clearly scaring the man. "Mustard! Don't you have mustard?"

"Hah-dog? Want hah-dog? Fi-dollars," he said, the mayonnaise container still suspended upside down, like an IV bottle, above the hotdog in its bun.

It turns out there was no mustard. And no relish or chopped onions. Not even ketchup, which I normally consider scandalous on a hotdog but, in that moment, would have eaten with gratitude. Instead, after considering the man's sign language offerings, I let him dress the hotdog with the only condiments he had: mayonnaise and sliced tomatoes. Needless to say, it wasn't the same. I left the stand hungrier than ever and traveled to my classes that day crippled by a homesickness that didn't leave me for weeks. For it is not merely a dish itself that one longs for in absentia but the context as well. Suitable accompaniments. The right eating companions. The traditional sounds and smells and habits of a season. The same jollity of sharing.

On the fourth Thursday of November every one of the six years I lived in Berlin, I spent considerable time and effort and more money than I could afford to reproduce Thanksgiving—ostensibly for my German friends, but in reality for myself. To give you a sense of what this mission entailed for me in those days, let me say that I was the quintessential expatriate. In the bank, I kept just enough money for a plane ticket to some other place, and I lived day to day by working, often under the table, in low-paying jobs as kitchen helper or language teacher, waitress, cook. I lived frugally. In Berlin, I had a no frills apartment built before the wars in a remote district of the city. It had one large room, high ceilings, and enormous, open-in windows overlooking the street with two tiny alcoves to cook and sleep in and neither bathtub nor shower. I heated, just barely, with gigantic coal briquettes that I hauled in a tin bucket from the unlit cellar.

My American students are always amazed that my apartment provided no way of bathing the whole body.

"How can they live without showering?" they always want to know.

And I tell them about a grey plastic tub that I crouched in to shave my legs on occasion. I filled it about halfway, using a pot to transport warm water from the one-gallon water heater above my kitchen sink. It took a long time to fill the tub, even though it was not very big. Once, I got stuck in it and drenched the kitchen floor with soapy water when I finally managed to plop myself out. I worried for weeks that water might have seeped through the cracks in the wood floor to the apartment below and I'd have to pay for repairs. I remembered something to that effect, in German officialese, in my rental agreement. Fortunately, my downstairs neighbors, a hippie couple from Swabia, were not the sort of people who cared about such things. They baked their own bread and told of how, as children, they were made to stomp barefooted on the cabbage their grandparents had shredded for sauerkraut so that the natural fungi on their feet would cause it to ferment. Evidently, they didn't notice any spots on their ceiling. Or, in any case, they never mentioned it.

For me, though, it was not the lack of a bathroom but the coal cellar that most clearly said I was in an utterly foreign place. If it hadn't been so unbelievably cold in winter, I would have forgone heating altogether. I layered myself in sweaters throughout the fall and early winter, but eventually the cold overwhelmed me and drove me down the five flights of stairs with my pail and oversized keys, across the dirty cobbled courtyard where we kept our garbage and ash cans, to the low doorway of the *Hinterhaus* cellar.

Inside, the air was close and earthy smelling, like old potatoes and beer and dirt. I had to stand a full five minutes in the dark before my eyes were acclimated enough for me to make my way past the broken furniture and bloated cardboard boxes full of forgotten junk and a creepy tree stump about thigh-high with an ax driven into it to the padlocked stall designated for my apartment. The ax was for chopping wood, I speculated, although I never saw anyone do it and couldn't imagine undertaking such a task with any precision in the dark. Stumbling in the blackness, my pail clanking in one hand and the stall key extended before me in the other, I expected every moment to come upon some worse horror lurking in the shadows than merely that ax handle jutting out at me. A person with questionable intentions, perhaps. A decapitated body. Or some other object foul and rotting. Something that had, as Dickens writes in a favorite line of mine from *A Christmas Carol*, "a dismal light about it, like a bad lobster in a dark cellar." That was my cellar. After I finally got my stall open, I had to fish around in the even blacker dark for eleven briquettes from the pile—the most I could carry—and then lock the stall back up. When I reemerged into the grey Berlin sunlight, I felt as if I had returned from hell itself and entered a new world.

My refrigerator in Berlin was just big enough for essentials—milk, butter, cheese—so the cellar is where I kept my yearly Thanksgiving turkey, well wrapped in layers of newspaper and nestled among the briquettes. I had to buy it over a week in advance. In those days—the early 1980s—turkeys were just about nonexistent in West Berlin, available only at the PX, and then only in November and only if you had connections to the American Armed Forces stationed in the city. I had no military acquaintances. So, the only way to get a turkey was to special order one from Ka-De-We, a super-fancy department store, akin to Harrods of London, located on the Ku'damm, the fanciest street in Berlin. Each year, that turkey alone cost me a month's wages.

Add to that cranberries for my family's traditional relish, in which they are ground up with unpeeled oranges, apples, walnuts, and sugar. The cranberry relish was always a big hit at my Thanksgiving dinners in Berlin, so I made a lot. My German friends referred to it as *"das Rote"* (the red)—as in, "Give me some more of that red stuff." The only cranberries I could get were wild ones, imported, handpicked, from the woods of Poland—and correspondingly expensive. It would have been less expensive to buy preserved wild cranberry compote, which Germans eat with game, but for my relish I had to have fresh ones—another quarter of a month's wages.

And then there were the teeny onions, available in Germany only pickled. And pecans and Karo syrup for the pie. And real celery ribs for the stuffing. (Germans eat only the pithy celery roots.) And finally such readily available essentials for the meal as mushrooms, potatoes, cream, butter, and sweet German wine.

But even with this outlay of money and effort, the meal always tasted foreign, somehow, and my guests were always less appreciative of the results than I would have liked. To my German friends, Thanksgiving was just another meal. Meat and potatoes. No one knew or seemed to care about the historical event on which Thanksgiving was predicated or even the fictions I was taught in grade school, much less understood the mythic value of the meal for us Americans. No one gave thanks, that I could tell. Certainly no one prayed. And even though I was an atheist myself in those days, a thankless Thanksgiving rankled, somehow. In short, serving up Thanksgiving dinner to a dozen or so Berliners depleted me—financially, emotionally, spiritually. And yet I did it year after year.

Earlier, as a graduate student in New Orleans, I knew a French woman who suffered from severe culture shock. Having experienced culture shock myself, I think it's just plain old depression resultant from whatever want or misery drove one from home in the first place, a conflation of rage and longing that we all suffer from time to time and that some people suffer all the time unless they take drugs to control it. The condition does tend to get worse the farther and the longer one is away from home. I suffered from it on and off for the entire ten years I lived abroad.

My French acquaintance, in any case, had culture shock about as bad as I've seen anyone have it. She kept to herself, wore the same clothes every day, barely spoke, and, when she did, spoke in a monotone, as if she were reading what she said from the side of a box. She had no friends that I knew of. Or boyfriends, even though she was pretty and smart and, of course, French.

Every once in a while, though, she'd throw a big party and invite everyone in her classes and all the international students who sat, as I often did, at two long tables in the cafeteria. She'd spend an entire day making crêpes. She bought dozens of eggs and made the crêpes one by one in a little fry-pan, stacking them up in columns so tall that one more crêpe would make them all fall over. Then she'd start on the next column. By evening, she had hundreds of crêpes ready as well as big bowls of raspberry jam and apricot preserves and slivers of ham and grated cheeses, and she assembled crêpes for us tirelessly, all night long, warming the crêpes first in the same little pan, sautéing some longer to heat the filling, one after the next, until we had eaten them all up. It was an arduous undertaking—if you've ever made even a dozen crêpes, you know this—but at no other time did I ever see this woman smile.

"*Je suis 'appy*," she sang out, as she folded yet another crêpe into thirds around the mound of filling in her fry-pan, shaping my only memories of her with the edge of her spatula: I can't remember this woman's name or field of study or anything else but her dark homesickness and those rare moments of release from it.

Imagine hunger. It is difficult to do, in our time, in this rich country. You may have to starve yourself a few days to get there. That, too, is difficult. I have never managed it for longer than two days, for a colonoscopy. But you are perhaps stronger than I am.

In any case, imagine, try, a hunger with no end in sight. A hunger that consumes your consciousness of everything else, that separates you, as if you had a terminal disease, from those around you. A hunger so great that you trade in everything you have—your house, your bed, all your clothes but the ones you're wearing—for passage to another country. On the way there, you continue to starve. Slowly. In the dark, smelly hold of a ship, perhaps. Or up on deck, freezing, huddled into yourself for warmth, staring down into the sea with longing. You are so hungry, you want to die, and many of your fellow travelers do die.

But then, finally, you arrive. But you are still alone. Still cold.

And still hungry. You remember the cod pies your mother once made. The potatoes mashed with cabbage and leeks. You remember sausages and bacon and hard, chewy bread. You remember the first vegetables of summer. A salad of cucumbers and sweet onions. A bowl of green peas with mint.

Your memories feed your hunger, intensifying it past bearing, until you are overcome. Seeing before you those peas, that ham simmered in milk, and weeping from hunger and fear and hope, you take a step.

CRANBERRY RELISH

Begin at least a couple of hours and as long as a day before serving. Working one item at a time, coarsely grind in a meat grinder or process in a food processor until well chopped (but NOT pureed):

12 ounces fresh cranberries, washed and picked through to get rid of any
  soft ones
1 or 2 navel oranges
1 or 2 green-skinned apples
1 1/2 cups walnuts

Stir in:

1 cup sugar (or less or more, according to taste)

Let sit, covered and refrigerated, until the sugar is no longer gritty. Serve in a pretty, clear glass bowl.

Turkey Stuffing

Sauté together until glassy, then put in large bowl:

1/2 cup butter
1 or 2 onions, chopped
6 ribs of celery
1/2 pound mushrooms, sliced

Toss with:

6 to 8 cups of cubed good bread, toasted in a 250° oven until dry, OR
    1 large bag of unseasoned stuffing cubes
1 to 2 eggs
11/2 teaspoons salt
pepper

Add and mix well:

enough turkey broth to moisten the bread cubes slightly: 1–11/2 cups—
    make the broth by boiling the neck, giblets, and trimmings with a bay leaf.
chopped neck meat and any giblets you don't want to chop and put
    in the gravy

Stuff both the turkey's cavities and sew or skewer shut. Preheat the oven to 350°. Roast the buttered turkey breast down on a rack in a large roasting pan tented under brown paper (a grocery bag) until you can wiggle a leg easily. Plan for about for 15 minutes per pound. Remove the turkey to a platter and let it sit while you make the gravy. Then spoon out the stuffing into a big bowl and carve the turkey.

Note: About that giblet gravy: Do make it; it's so good. The giblets sink to the bottom of the gravy boat, so only those who fish for them will know they're there. Use the turkey broth for liquid and add the chopped giblets as soon as the gravy's thick. (See page 20 for more details.)

Ham in Milk

A simple invention of mine and one of my girls' most dependably beloved meals. A perfect quick meal with potatoes boiled in their skins and a salad.

Put 2 or 3 slices of ham per person in a frying pan and cover 1/2 to 3/4-inch deep in milk. Cook on medium until about half of the milk boils away, leaving curds and a wonderfully flavored, unthickened "gravy." Spoon the "gravy" over a boiled potato that has been lightly mashed with a fork.

18

The Oven

The first year I voted, I registered as a Communist, which, at eighteen, I understood to be a person who believed in sharing resources equally for the benefit of all. It was 1977. I registered at the shopping mall. Having grown up in wealthy suburbs and nice houses with a mom who had experienced inconceivable poverty as an Arkansas migrant worker but nevertheless always insisted we were poor, my earliest political feelings were about sorting out my economic confusion. Sharing, I believed, would be the best solution to worldwide economic inequality, but what I heard the Republicans and Democrats saying through the mouths of my parents and teachers and friends didn't seem to promote it.

My convictions about the equal distribution of resources deepened throughout college and graduate school. While I lived in West Berlin, I made numerous trips to East Berlin, not to buy cheap books as my friends did or even to see the sights—the ruined Jewish synagogue, the dilapidated museums and overgrown cemeteries, the piles of building materials everywhere—but to feel, if I could, what communism was really like. All I felt, though, was depressed. Although East Berlin was just a few subway stations away from where I lived in vibrant West Berlin, everything there seemed broken, dead, grey. Even the food was grey. Salads of canned vegetables thick with mayonnaise. A wet-looking mess called *Altberliner Schlachteplatte*—Old Berlin-Style Butcher's Platter—comprising boiled pork kidneys, blubbery pork belly, and mushy liverwursts and blood sausages in their casings of intestines that usually arrived burst open in glistening gray and black piles. Served with potatoes on a bed of grey-yellow sauerkraut, the whole visceral assemblage reminded me of the ghastly murderers' basin in the Grimm story "Fitcher's Bird."

My Berlin roommate Susanne was a delegate of the *Alternative Liste*, a democracy-obsessed composite political party that had just acquired its first seat in the City Parliament. It represented all of the city's smaller parties—Greens, Communists, Socialists, Maoists, Marxists, Anarchists, right-wing skinheads in camouflage who weren't allowed to call themselves Neo-Nazis but were, and even tinier splinter groups. The *AL*, as it was called, sponsored demonstrations and political *Aktions* almost every week. At one point, *AL* members organized to buy up special government food stamps designated for refugees seeking political asylum in Berlin so that these people's limited resources would not be unfairly restricted to food but could be used for tobacco and liquor and going to the movies. The city was overflowing in those days with Turks, Kurds, Romanians, Iranians, Poles, and others fleeing poverty and oppression in their countries, and *AL* members approached asylum-seekers exiting government offices and asked to exchange their food stamps for real money, *Deutsche Mark* for *Deutsche Mark*. Within days the stores were requiring IDs for food stamps, and my *AL* friends had to sell the stamps back to the immigrants at a discount. And the policy didn't change.

Susanne and her friends laughed at me when I said I was a communist. At thirteen or fourteen, entirely unassociated with school or any adult influence, they had all been in Socialist "work groups" in which they had studied the entire opus of Marx and Engels. I—like all Americans, they told me—was utterly ignorant of history and international politics, unable to differentiate between a Maoist and a Marxist. Also, as an American, I was inescapably capitalist. All over the bomb-scarred walls of the worker ghetto where we lived I saw the graffiti imperative of young Berliners of those times: "Ami go home!"

Still, I liked Berlin. The motto of the *AL* was "*Tu wat!*"—"Do Something!" in the Berlin dialect—and most of my aquaintances lived it out. You never knew when the people around you might start poking the ends of their umbrellas between the cracks in the cobbled street to prize up stones to throw at the police—referred to as *Bullen*, bulls, rather than *Polizei*—who would mysteriously appear at every corner with helmets and see-through shields. It was an exciting time.

But excitement wasn't what I was after in those days. I wanted to live in a communist country, cook simple food and share it with others, experience equal distribution firsthand, and find out if it could resolve the economic confusion of the world I saw around me: my parents' world and the refugees' world and my own.

Toward that end I kept trying to get a job in East Germany, just on the other side of the graffitied Wall. After getting nowhere with correspondence to ministries and applications for jobs I found advertised in East German newspapers, I went in person to Humboldt University and applied directly for a position teaching English. They were perplexed and ended up escorting me, with grim bemusement, to the dingy subway that would take me back to Free Berlin.

In 1985 I gave up on German Communism altogether and applied for a job I saw advertised in a magazine for teachers of English to speakers of other languages. The job was in the People's Republic of China, which had newly opened itself up to foreigners after a brief period of economic and political convalescence following the Cultural Revolution. Hardly a month later, I was teaching English at an elite Beijing university where members of China's government were educated. Unlike most foreigners in Beijing at the time, I did not live at the Friendship Hotel—a partly live-in hotel exclusively for foreigners—but instead on campus, among my students and Chinese colleagues.

My apartment was spare but more than satisfactory, featuring a kitchen, a sitting room, a bedroom, a bathroom, and even a little balcony overlooking the campus's muddy quad. The rooms were entirely concrete—floors, walls, ceiling. The bathroom had not only a toilet but also a rudimentary shower, rare in those days in China: an electrically heated box of water that hung from the wall and drizzled a weak stream into the room. The water drained slowly out of the soaked room through a grate in the floor. To take a shower, I plugged the box into the wall outlet just below it, waited half an hour for it to heat up, and then crossed my fingers that when I got in and turned the knob to let the water flow out, it wouldn't shock me. It always did, either then or as I was showering, so I reluctantly quit using it and showered instead at the public bath down the road or else in my downstairs neighbor's shower, which he had rigged up with extension cords to plug in outside the bathroom. I had a bed, a desk, a table, some wooden chairs, a couch, and two armchairs. The upholstered furniture was covered in khaki slipcovers. It was not okay, I soon learned, to take the slipcovers off to expose the pretty green silk damask beneath or to tape a picture to the wall. Still, the rooms were airy and nice, pleasantly cool in the humid summer heat of my arrival.

An envoy of the university told me I could eat in the cafeteria or else buy food and cook for myself. For shopping I would be bused across town to the Friendship Store once a week with my ten foreign colleagues. There I could buy bread and Beijing beer and other necessities for foreigners and would have to use the special foreigner money that constituted half of my salary. Alternatively, I could shop in the roadside market outside my apartment that was called a "free market," where I had to use the people's money, *renminbi*.

Free markets were new in 1985. Government-run stores required ration tickets and, my students whispered, sold only low-quality products: bad rice, weevily flour, old meat, limp cabbages and onions, big chunks of soap that hurt your skin. In the increasingly popular free markets of China's "new wave" of economic freedom, however, licensed venders from the provinces could sell specialty items like seasonal produce, better quality dry goods, and even small appliances. So, although I went to the university cafeteria whenever they served meals that everyone loved—like cold, red-cooked tripe and *mantou*, or steamed bread—for the most part, I shopped at the local free market and cooked in my little kitchen, which had a stove, a deep sink with a narrow metal ledge that was my only counter space, a miniature refrigerator, a cupboard, and a window.

The free market near my apartment was one of the biggest and oldest, so it had more variety than most. Greens of all sorts. Yard-long beans. Melons. *Da cong*, the long, leek-like onions, sliced into curled strips and served in most stir-fried dishes. Flat pink tomatoes, which were typically served piled in wedges on a plate and then heaped with white sugar. Thick romaine stems—called *wo sun*, or stem lettuce—whose jade green cores stayed crunchy and kept their beautiful color even when cooked. Occasionally I found some contraband jasmine rice. It was much more expensive than the gritty broken rice in the government stores that everyone complained about, but there was always a long line of people waiting with their bowls to buy it, all of them looking around anxiously, as if they were afraid of being caught. There were vendors of nuts and dried fruits—persimmons and apricots and fruits that I had no name for—and of artificial meat products for Buddhists: little slices and nuggets made of soybean in various colors and flavors. Yogurt, the only milk product I ever saw for sale in the free market, came sweetened in a reusable ceramic bottle decorated with a blue cow. At night, I bought candied crabapples and haws, five to a stick, and popcorn from an old woman who popped dried corn still on the cob by roasting it in a canister—the foreigners called it a cannon—until it exploded, just once, whereupon she shook the popcorn out into a burlap sack and sold it in little bags.

In wintertime there was a man who sold yams and sometimes white potatoes and had a big steel drum to roast them in. You chose your yam, paid him, then came back at the end of your shopping to pick it up, blackened and wrapped in a piece of newspaper. Once I saw a huge line of old women standing around stamping in the cold, each with a bowl, waiting to buy something. I ran back to my apartment for a bowl of my own so that I wouldn't miss out. Whatever it was smelled really bad, but no one else seemed to think so. Every once in a while, the women stopped chattering and sniffed meaningfully toward the head of the line and then nodded excitedly. When I finally got there, everyone crowded in around me, laughing and pointing as a tiny, bent over woman ladled out some of the positively foul smelling delicacy into my bowl. It was a thick, reddish-brown liquid with grey lumps in it. I paid for it, went home, and flushed it down the toilet without tasting it. I couldn't stand to have the smell in my apartment. Later, a Chinese friend told me it must have been *Beijing furu*—the local version of *choudoufu*, or "stinky tofu," a fermented tofu used mostly for seasoning. Everything else I bought in the free market was good, though, if in limited supply, sometimes just a few items arranged on a flimsy folding table. I bought whatever I wanted with no other language than pointing and carried it home in a plastic tote-basket just like the ones everyone else carried.

My stove in Beijing had just one burner, fitted out with little arms specially designed to hold a wok. Whenever my Chinese colleagues or students came to dinner, they always stepped into my narrow kitchen to marvel over the stove, crouching to look at the propane bottle underneath the burner. They looked at each other and pointed at it and even patted it familiarly, as the women in the public bath always did the hair on my arms and legs. Since every Chinese apartment I entered had precisely the same cooking facilities—the same tiny concrete kitchen, the same deep work sink and ledge, the same one-burner stove holding the same steel wok or gigantic aluminum kettle—it took me a while to finally figure out it was the bright new bottle of propane that impressed them. Most of my guests, if they had a stove at all, had to strap a rusted bottle onto their bicycle when it got empty and travel five or ten miles to buy propane, if propane was available, which it often wasn't. When there was none for sale, they forwent home-cooking altogether—a hardship for them as it would be for me—and bought every meal from the cafeteria, carrying it back to their rooms in tiered aluminum lunch boxes.

My propane was supplied in a brand new bottle by the same invisible forces that mopped my floors, made up my bed with clean linens once a week, and left two big thermoses of hot water outside my door every morning. I felt coddled, uncomfortably so. On my first day of teaching, a cadre student asked me, on behalf of the whole class, how much money I was earning. It was laughably small, a fraction of what I had made even as a teenager working in a bookstore at minimum wage, but when I told them, I could sense resentment beneath their congratulatory smiles. Their envy of my advantages as a foreigner—the shower, the propane, the bottles of beer in my refrigerator, the big apartment that I shared with no one else, the fact that I could come and go as I pleased and that half of my salary was in a special currency they had no access to—made me value what I had there more than I might have, and it wasn't long before I forgot all about American bathrooms and grocery bags and pretty furniture and the masses of money I had earned so effortlessly in the past.

There were only two lacks I couldn't get used to. One was morning coffee. I can't act nice without a big cup of coffee drunk in relative silence as soon as I get up in the morning. It doesn't have to be particularly good coffee. I am not a coffee weirdo. The coffee I snuck as a child from the aluminum pot on the stove—my parents forbade coffee for us kids because it would "stunt our growth"—had percolated all morning long and tasted like metal, but I loved it. In New Orleans, I got accustomed to the thick, milky chicory/coffee mixture people drink there. But Chinese coffee, which was only available at the Friendship Store, was undrinkable—sour and weak. Unlike the jasmine tea everyone drank in Beijing, the coffee never seemed to get darker than a brownish yellow, like diseased urine, no matter how much of it I brewed or how long I brewed it.

My downstairs neighbor, Jean-Pierre—the one with the extension cords for his shower—was a French priest in hiding. Almost every foreigner I met in China was some sort of missionary using teaching as a front. In any case, the nuns of Jean-Pierre's parish back in Alsace sent him care packages of excellent coffee, which he shared with me, but to get it I had to go down to his apartment early in the morning, just after he had said 4 a.m. mass and swept out the stairwells—his secret ministry to the women called *ayis*, aunties, who did the rest of the cleaning—but before he left for his morning session of *tai qi chuan* at the park. And, I had to drink it in his sitting room and be sociable, as if at a formal tea, chatting with him in my strained high school French, our only common language, and effectively eliminating the relaxing silence part of my morning coffee routine. Not only that, but the *ayis* noticed me coming out of Jean-Pierre's apartment in the morning and spread the word that he and I were having an affair, which was hugely scandalous. Although he seemed to enjoy the scandal, I was embarrassed. So, I took to drinking hot water—the popular alternative to tea—but I never did like it.

The other hardship besides giving up coffee was cooking everything in a wok. I have always liked constraints in the kitchen. I like to cook for vegetarian friends and people with allergies and illnesses that prevent them from eating certain types of food and even for picky eaters, if they are especially lovable, which they're generally not. Cooking with restrictions is fun, like writing sonnets or villanelles or sestinas instead of free verse. And I often find out things that I wouldn't have found out otherwise. I discovered my favorite bread grain, spelt, while trying to bake a white loaf for a friend with violent skin reactions to wheat. And, for a weight-watching vegetarian friend who complains that all meatless recipes are loaded with fat, I invented a nearly fat-free version of eggplant Parmesan that I much prefer to the deep-fried versions in my Italian cookbooks. So, limiting my cooking to a wok was easy at first. I stir-fried every vegetable I could buy, singly and in combination. I steamed yard-long beans in a little water under a plate, then made them into salad. A student gave me a lesson in what I now regard as the best way to cook bitter greens: flash-frying them with garlic, sugar, and salt. A friend taught me to season ground pork with ginger, garlic, green onion, and soy sauce and then sandwich gobs of it between slices of peeled lotus root and panfry them to make *zha ou he*. Another friend brought me a big fish and showed me how to red-cook it whole, head and all, with ginger, the leek-like onions, sugar, and soy sauce.

As the weather grew colder, fresh vegetables grew more limited, and locals bought up winter stores of cabbage and onions and stacked them in triangular piles in their stairwells. I bought what I could get and combined it with pork: pork with onions, pork with cabbage, pork with yams. Someone taught me to make a winter salad by shredding a huge green-and-white radish—called *shinrimei*, beauty-heart, for its magenta center—and combining it with canned oysters and straw mushrooms and dressing it with sugar and pungent, black Chinese vinegar made of wheat.

Whenever I went to a banquet or to someone's apartment, we made and ate *jiaozi*, boiled dumplings, the party food of northern China. *Jiaozi* are popular winter dish because they are made of pork, cabbage, onions, and flour, all staples of China's north and available year-round. *Jiaozi* production is typically a group project and usually competitive in nature. The person who makes the prettiest *jiaozi* and the person who makes the most the fastest are identified from the outset, and everyone else strives to outdo them. Any foreigners present are mocked in their attempts to make a dumpling that even stays together. Dumplings are actually simple to make, and I occasionally made them all alone in my apartment and boiled them in my wok, but it was always a sad meal—like making and drinking all by yourself that wonderful ginger ale and sherbet punch that they serve in a crystal bowl at weddings.

Eventually the constraint of cooking everything in the wok grew to be a burden, though. I longed for baked things—not just the sorry bread from the Friendship Store that my foreign colleagues subsisted on but the grainy breads I had left behind me in Germany and the rich braided bread called *Zöpfli* I had learned to make in Switzerland and even the smushy white Wonder bread I had toasted and dunked in coffee as a child. Although I'm not much of a sweets eater, I fantasized about the soft, slightly sour snickerdoodles my sisters and I had baked growing up, the Apple Brown Betty and gingerbread my college friend Donald and I had made in the toaster oven in his Airstream trailer, the chocolate-and-cherry-studded brown cake that my Berlin roommate Susanne and I would make some Sundays and invite the whole apartment building in to share. I even dreamed about the ingredients of baking: familiar foods with familiar smells that came in familiar sizes and packages. Sugar: white and brown. Sticks of butter marked neatly into eight tablespoons. White, five-pound bags labeled, in words that I knew how to read, "UNBLEACHED ALL PURPOSE FLOUR."

I started to get this idea of building an oven. An oven is simply a metal box with a heat source, I reasoned, with a door and a rack to put things on. If I could get a metal box with a hole in the bottom and put it over my burner, I could at least bake cookies or something. So I had Jean-Pierre, who had lived in China for many years and spoke serviceable Chinese, help me negotiate the building of such a box with a man with welding equipment that I had seen at the free market. I made diagrams of what I wanted the box to look like, and the man sketched modifications. We eventually agreed upon what looked like a doghouse made out of bent sheet metal with a door and a stretched wire shelf inside. It took the man about a month to get it done.

After filling my apartment with smoke by immediately trying to roast a piece of pork in my new oven, I learned to set the burner as low as it would go and figured out that I would need to have the welder make me a flat pan of some sort, too, before I could bake anything. While I waited, I set about collecting ingredients. I could smell the yeast in the steamed bread from the school cafeteria, but I couldn't find it anywhere for sale, so I finally gave up trying to find any other leavening besides a gigantic bag of what I decided was baking soda. With my students' help, I was able to find everything else I would need for cookies: flour, some strong smelling butter, eggs, salt, chocolate, cinnamon, nuts, and, in addition to white sugar, a hard loaf of brown sugar—called red sugar in Chinese, *hong tang*—which my students told me, tittering into their hands, was only ever eaten by women who have just delivered a baby, to enrich their blood. To use the brown sugar in baking, I had to smash it apart with the heavy handle of my chopper-knife.

I invented approximations from memory of every recipe I could think of—plain sugar cookies, chocolate chip cookies, snickerdoodles, brown-sugar brownies. But my most successful baked creation was peanut butter cookies, for which I had to roast the raw peanuts first and then grind them into butter with a mortar and pestle I had found in a government store. It took me a number of tries before I got the recipe just right, but, when I did, I cried. The cookies filled my whole apartment building with such a wonderful smell that students utterly strange to me came by my apartment to try one. Among the Chinese people I knew, the whole notion of baking was foreign. They had never tasted the fortune cookies or almond cookies of Chinese restaurants in America, and no one actually baked the mooncakes they ate for holidays: They bought them from a special vendor. But they loved my cookies immediately. It became a tradition for me to bake a huge batch once a week and share them with my students and colleagues and anyone who showed up at my door.

I also made pies. Jean-Pierre missed the German/French food of Alsace—the *choucroute* with sausages, the beer, the fruit tarts. He often cooked for me. Once he made an Alsatian tripe salad—finely sliced pork tripe in a garlicky homemade mayonnaise—that was one of the better things I have eaten in my life. But most of the Alsatian foods he missed he didn't know how to cook. His mother had died when he was six—he had vowed to become a priest standing before her coffin—and, although he remembered her apple pie, or *tarte au pommes*, he had never been taught how to make a crust. When I got my oven, we decided to make a pie using the crispy pear-apples we could still find in the free market.

I amazed him by making, from his guesses about what might have gone into her crust, what he said was the perfect *pâte brisée*—otherwise known as a plain old American pie crust with a bit of sugar in it. Once I got the dough to just barely stick together, I batted his sweaty hands out of my way and rolled it out on his table using a big Beijing beer bottle and laid it into a deep ceramic platter he insisted would not blow up when we baked it in my oven. We filled the dough with slices of pear-apples, which we had cooked slightly in a little sugar and water first and then cooled, the way Germans do their apple pie fillings. Then we topped the pie with a crumb topping— the same ingredients as the crust but with more sugar and no water—and took it upstairs to my oven to bake it. It got somewhat burnt on one edge but was otherwise pretty good, although I missed the tart apple-y flavor of ordinary apples. "*Parfait!*" Jean-Pierre pronounced it, using his favorite word that day. Perfect. Just as he remembered it. He had a new respect for me after that. He had always heard that Americans were incapable of cooking anything but hamburgers.

It's strange how profoundly dependent we are not only on familiar foods but even our way of cooking them. If you have ever gone from a gas stove to an electric one—or vice versa, I'm told—you will know what I mean. I have searched all of Berlin for a real pie plate with slanted sides to use instead of the straight-sided cake pan Germans use for their equivalent of apple pie, and I have seen Asian friends in the U.S. in true despair about not being able to find a decent wok to cook in. Recently, a friend of mine whose oven was being fixed told me she just couldn't do without it in the meantime and had taken a cheesecake over to a neighbor's house to bake.

I sometimes wonder how it would be if we ever had some sort of apocalyptic disaster, something worse and less locally concentrated than a tornado, something that eliminated sources of electricity and gasoline and made us have to live off the land itself, as people did in the past. My family could boil pond water to drink, but eventually our big tank of propane would run out. How would we survive? There would be a scramble for what was in the grocery stores for those who could get there—canned goods, cereals, root vegetables that are filling and will keep. But here, out in the Oklahoma countryside, we are far from stores. We would at first have my minimal garden and the rotting meat from our deep freezer, but then it would be the cattle in our fields that we would have to somehow kill and slaughter, and finally dandelion and dock leaves and such animals as we could trap, maybe even our own starving dogs. And how would we cook? For how long would we be happy, even in such extreme circumstances, to either roast what we had on a spit or boil it over a fire out in our yard?

What would we do? Would my neighbors and I bond together? I hardly ever see them now. Would we, in the end, pool our last matches and lighters? Or take turns tending a communal fire that we kept continuously going? Would we raid the local feed mill for the grain that now goes to livestock all over the world and divvy it up between us? And how many of us would be satisfied to eat our share of the whole grains, boiled in water, as a simple and nutritious cooked cereal, and for how long?

I have an old Hopi *matate* for grinding corn, left behind a long time ago by some nomadic family in their travels. A relative of mine stole it from an Arizona desert long ago—it is illegal to take them—and gave to me. I keep it out on my front porch, where it collects bugs and dirt. Occasionally I use the heavy *mano*— the part you hold in your hand to grind with—to crack black walnuts the girls bring in from the woods or the apricot pits I put in jam. Would my neighbors be lining up to borrow this ancient tool, once strategically left behind, too heavy to carry, but now, in the absence of milled flour or meal, more precious than any money? Would we take turns grinding our flour and then relearn from our collective memory how to ferment it to make a risen dough? Would we build a public wood-fired oven, like the ones people shared in medieval times—and would we know how?—an oven big enough, as they were in those days, to hold each family's bread for the week? And would we bake collectively, to conserve our resources, the steadily dwindling supply of brush and wood from the edges of our pastures? Or would we simply go without bread, allowing, finally, all memory of what we used to eat to fade, as such memories do, into first a real remembered scent—the smell of new-baked bread just out of the oven—and then a forgotten one, an illusory fragrance like a charm, recreated in vain and embroidered upon in stories for our children, the faintest whiff of what had been and would not ever be again?

CANDIED CRABAPPLES OR HAWS ON A STICK

Crabapples grow all over the place in the U.S. as ornamental trees, but for some reason we rarely eat their wonderful fruit. Look for miniature apples on an apple-looking tree. Their fruit is usually bitter, but it makes an excellent pink jelly, my daughters' favorite, and tastes wonderful cooked with a little sugar and water and then pureed to make crabapple sauce, a fantastic accompaniment to roasted meat or filling for turnovers. Some varieties even taste good raw, and these are the ones you use for candied crabapples. Haws are a relative of roses that bear crabapple-sized fruits that taste like rosehips but are somewhat fleshier. The Chinese eat a variety of haw called a Chinese hawthorn, Crataegus pinnatifida, *but in the U.S. look for the mayhaw or downy hawthorn,* Crataegus opaca *and* Crataegus mollis *respectively. Haws have the same rather hairy seeds as hips. The Chinese make many candies and sweets out of them, and people say they make wonderful jelly. Candied, they are even better than the crabapples—tart, caramely-tasting, and full of vitamin C. I have read that tangerine sections are also strung on sticks and candied in this way, and that sounds good to me. The concept is tart fruit covered with crunchy, caramelized sugar.*

Thread fruits on pointed wooden skewers, five to a stick. Combine and stir to dissolve:

> **3 3/4 cups sugar**
> **11/4 cups light Karo syrup**
> **1 cup water**

Bring to a boil and cook without stirring over medium heat to hard crack stage: 300° on a candy thermometer or until a bit of the syrup dropped into cold water makes brittle—not malleable—threads. Add a squirt of red food coloring to the syrup if you want the resulting candy-coating to be red. Dip the fruit into the syrup; then poke the skewers through the cardboard bottom of an upturned shoe box to let harden. Don't get any syrup on you; it burns.

Roasted Yams

This is the best way to eat yams: Set your oven at its highest temperature. Wash and prick as many yams as you want to roast and put them on a cookie sheet. Roast them until they are very soft and beginning to ooze a black, sugary goo—which, by the way, will burn on your cookie sheet but comes off easily if you soak it awhile in cold water. Eat the yams just like that, skin and all. They are also magnificent sliced open like baked potatoes and filled with butter, salt, and lots of pepper. Either way, eating the skin is very important: Not only is it full of vitamins, but it has a chewy consistency that perfectly complements the soft, sweet yam flesh. My girls have learned (from their father and grandmother) to fill their roasted yams with butter and brown sugar and eat them as dessert, but they are wrongheaded in this, just as all those people are who bake yams with syrups and sugars and marshmallows and sweetened coconut. Yams are sweet and flavorful enough all on their own.

Stir-Fried Tomatoes with Ginger and Onions

An unlikely sounding recipe that's surprisingly good, from a homeless, vegetarian drug addict I was briefly acquainted with in New Orleans.

Cut into wedges:

2 or 3 big tomatoes
1 sweet onion

Combine in a small bowl:

1 tablespoon soy sauce
1 tablespoon powdered ginger

Stir-fry the vegetables in a little oil. When the onions are still crunchy but hot all the way through, remove them from the heat and add the ginger–soy sauce mixture. Stir. The ginger thickens the vegetable juices up very quickly, so be sure you have taken the pan from the heat. Serve with rice and some other dish that is green.

Chinese Green Bean Cold Dish

These are reminiscent of Salade Niçoise–*the creamy egg yolks with something sour and the bright green beans. I can offer only this approximation from my imperfect and possibly entirely false memory of the dish. It's not quite right, but I do like it.*

Boil a pound of whole green beans until bright green but still crunchy. Cool in cold water. Drain. Meanwhile, combine:

3 hard-boiled egg yolks, mashed
1 clove of garlic, mashed or minced
1 teaspoon salt
1 to 2 teaspoons sugar
the juice of a lime or 1/2 **a lemon or 1 to 2 tablespoons of rice vinegar**
a drizzle of sesame oil
2 to 3 tablespoons vegetable oil

Add the dressing to the beans, stir well to coat, and serve at room temperature.

STIR-FRIED GREENS *(Chao Cai)*

This recipe is good not only for Chinese cabbage but for any sort of green leafy vegetable. Some of my favorites are beet greens or chard (for either of which I substitute thinly sliced onion for the garlic and double the sugar), mustard or turnip greens, kale, spinach, and even radish greens.

Stir-fry in a wok in a little oil over a high flame:

1/2 **to 1 pound washed greens** (a huge pile of greens)

As the greens begin to cook down, season them with:

2 cloves garlic, mashed
1 teaspoon sugar
1 teaspoon salt

Continue to cook. The sugar and salt create a surprising amount of a wonderfully flavored, clear, green sauce. As soon as you see it forming, serve the greens immediately or turn off the flame, clap a lid over the pan, and serve them very soon.

RED-COOKED FISH

The combination of flavors in this dish—ginger, Chinese leek-like onions, sugar, and soy sauce—is so closely associated with fish in China that when you cook other things with those flavors—such as chicken or vegetables or bean curd—it's called yuxiang, *or fish-tasting, in reference to the flavor combination, not a fishy taste.*

You need a very fresh whole fish for this—cleaned but with the head and skin intact. Buwei Yang Chao, in her classic How to Cook and Eat in Chinese, *comments, "Clean the fish but leave its tongue in its cheek." The fish my friend Kaige cooked with me was a slick-skinned, freshwater fish like a trout, about a foot long. Also, he was very particular that one should use peanut oil for cooking, so I specify that here, but any neutral vegetable oil will do. I like canola. Kaige considered this dish the shining star of Chinese cooking. Cook rice and maybe one other dish in addition to it: something light that goes quickly, like greens sautéed with garlic. (See page 189.)*

Combine in a small bowl:

1/2 cup soy sauce
2 tablespoons sugar
1/2 cup water

Wash the fish well and make several long gashes into its sides to soak up the juices. On high in a wok or skillet big enough to hold the fish, heat a good amount—at least 1/3 cup—of peanut oil to smoking. Swirl it around once and then immediately—and carefully—lower the slippery fish into the hot oil. Let it fry on one side until you can smell that it's getting brown; then, carefully turn it over. This is hard to do, and it is essential that you don't wreck the fish or its skin: Use every hand and tool you have and be patient and gentle.

While the fish is frying on the other side, slice a bunch of green onions (or a leek or, best of all, a long Chinese onion, if you can get one) lengthwise into long threads that curl up as you cut them. (Don't think about this too hard. It explains itself as you cut.) Also thinly slice about an inch of peeled ginger and cut the slices into thin strips. Some recipes call for chopped garlic as well, and it's good that way, too, but we didn't use any.

By now you smell the fish getting brown on the other side. Throw in the curls of onion and the ginger strips, completely covering the fish and being sure to let some get down in the hot oil. Fry a minute or so, until the onions in the pan get a little wilted looking. Then pour in the soy sauce mixture and clap on the lid of the wok. Cook on high for 5 to 10 minutes, depending on the size of the fish. Our fish was, I'm guessing, three pounds, and it took about 8 or 9 minutes to cook. You want the finished fish to be cooked through but not mushy. Slide it carefully out of the wok into a big serving platter, and provide a spoon for the sauce. Unless you are married to my husband, who is finicky about germs, you should eat it Chinese-style: everyone picking from the common dish with their chopsticks onto small individual bowls of plain rice, held in one hand. This is so good. The sauce is the best. You will want to pick the carcass bare—and from Buwei Chao's specification about the tongue, I'm guessing the tongue may be the best part.

BOILED DUMPLINGS (*Jiaozi*)

This is so much easier in a food processor than it ever was without one, so, if you have one, use it. One special tool that I find indispensable for jiaozi is a Chinese rolling pin, which is just like a French rolling pin—a wooden dowel fatter in the middle than it is on the ends—but much shorter and narrower. Its size and shape enable you to maneuver it more easily to make little rounds of dough that are fatter in the middle than they are on the edges. My Chinese rolling pin is 91/2 inches long, an inch in diameter in the very middle, and slightly more than 1/2 inch in diameter at the ends. Look for one in a big Asian store that carries cooking tools. (You can get the Chinese black vinegar for the sauce there as well.) Otherwise, you might whittle down the ends of a 1-inch wood dowel. Other tools you will need for jiaozi are a piece of cheesecloth or a thin dish towel for squeezing the cabbage dry and a big, flat, textured surface to put the finished jiaozi on. I have a stiff mat of sewn-together reeds that I brought home from China, but I have also used a flat basket. Your goal is to minimize the area of each dumpling that is in contact with a surface that will cause the dumpling to sweat and stick. A cooling rack for cookies might work, although you will not be able to coat it with flour, so dip the bottom of each jiaozi in flour before setting it on the rack.

Dough

Put 4 cups of flour in a food processor and add water (probably about 2 cups) slowly, while processing, until a soft dough comes together. Continue processing for about a minute. Remove the dough to a bowl, cover with it plastic wrap, and allow it to rest while you make the filling. Alternatively, mix water into the flour by hand in a bowl and knead the dough until it is very soft and smooth, probably a good ten minutes, before you let it rest.

Filling

Grate or chop in the food processor:

1 small head of Chinese cabbage

Add:

1 teaspoon salt

Let the salted cabbage sit until juicy; then dump it into a piece of cheesecloth or a thin towel, twist closed at the top, and squeeze hard into the sink to extract the juice. Put the squeezed cabbage back in the bowl. Add and mix well:

1 pound ground pork

2 or 3 green onions, finely chopped

1/2-inch piece of peeled ginger, finely chopped

2 tablespoons soy sauce

1 tablespoon vegetable oil

1 teaspoon salt

1 teaspoon sugar

Assembly

Cut the dough into six equal lengths and roll each into a log about an inch in diameter. Cover five of the logs with plastic wrap and cut the remaining log into pieces about an inch long. Flatten one piece into a circle; then, on a floured surface, roll its edges out, turning it to make a 3-inch circle that's fatter in the middle than it is on the edges. Holding the piece of dough in the fingers of one hand, spoon a bit of meat filling in the middle with your other hand, being careful not to get any on the edges (in which case it won't stick together and will fall apart when you cook it). Using both hands, pinch your thumbs up over the filling against the sides of your index fingers and squeeze them together at the top to seal; then pleat the edges all the way around. It will take a few *jiaozi* to get the hang of this. Ideally, you want the finished *jiaozi* to look like a little purse, pleated and bulging along one side and pretty much flat on the other. Set the finished *jiaozi* on your floured basket. (Remember to flour the bottom of the *jiaozi* if you are using a cookie rack.) Repeat with the other pieces of dough and then with each log until you finish. Be careful not to leave the unused dough uncovered, or it will dry out, and don't let the *jiaozi* touch one another because, where you pull them apart, there will be a hole, and the *jiaozi* will fall apart when you cook them.

Cooking

Bring to a boil a big pot half-full of water. Keeping the fire on high, drop 15 or 20 *jiaozi* in at a time and stir to separate them. When the water comes back to a rolling boil, add one cup of cold water and bring to a boil again. Repeat with an additional cup of water and a second boil; then remove *jiaozi* with a slotted spoon to a bowl. I don't usually trust that they are done and have to test one to make sure. Once you are sure that the dumplings have cooked the right amount of time, repeat the cooking process until you have used up all the *jiaozi*.

Dipping Sauce

Provide each person a little bowl to make a sauce in and the following condiments to choose from: soy sauce, Chinese black vinegar, sesame oil, and hot chili oil. A few people I have met like to use just soy sauce or just vinegar, but most like *jiaozi* dipping sauce to have a little of both (I use equal proportions) with a drizzle of sesame oil or, if they like hot, chili oil. I have also found that some people put Chinese pickled garlic on the table. Some people eat the garlic with their *jiaozi*; others use the garlicky vinegar in their sauce. You can also preempt your guests' preferences and inevitable ignorance of what the sauce should taste like and mix it up the way you like it in a little pitcher for them to pour out in their little bowls.

Serving

Put the *jiaozi* out in big bowls on the table as they come out of the water so that people can eat them hot. Stir them as they cool to keep them from sticking together. If you have leftovers, panfry them the next day as potstickers: Heat a little oil in a big skillet or wok, arrange the *jiaozi* in one layer, cover, and fry on medium until browned on the bottom and hot. Serve with the same sauce.

MY NEIGHBOR KATIE'S FAMOUS PUNCH

This is one of those recipes everyone in my little Oklahoma town wants. As the local school treasurer and a member of a Baptist church, Katie is often called upon to make this punch for all sorts of receptions in town: weddings, showers, school board dinners, and the high school prom, which is held in the school cafeteria. The recipe, she says, will fill two "regular-sized punch bowls." For a wedding—"200 or 300 people who will probably drink one cup each"—you will need to make four recipes' worth. The junior-senior prom is about the same size as a wedding, but Katie says, "Those kids'll be drinking that punch all night long" and you need to make six to eight recipes' worth.

Mix together in a one-gallon container and refrigerate until ready to serve:

2 small packages of Jell-O in two cups of boiling water
1 12-ounce can of frozen lemonade
4 cups (one large can) **of pineapple juice**

41/2 **cups of cold water**—or enough to fill a one-gallon container with punch mixture.

When ready to serve, soften a half gallon of pineapple sherbet briefly and divide it between two punch bowls. Add one two-liter bottle of ginger ale and stir until foamy. Then add the punch mixture, stir, and start ladling it up.

Katie uses sherbet from a regional ice cream parlor chain called Braum's, whose sherbets, she says, are not as sticky as other brands. When I asked her what flavor of Jell-O, she told me, "For red punch, use red Jell-O. For yellow punch, use yellow Jell-O. For green punch, use green Jell-O." You can also experiment, she told me. Black cherry Jell-O, for example, makes a beautiful mauve punch.

SNICKERDOODLES

I have collected recipes for snickerdoodles over the years, none of which tastes exactly like my memory of these cookies. The family recipe box of my childhood no longer exists, alas. The cookies were like none other: soft and puffy and discernibly sour from the cream of tartar beneath their gritty, cinnamon-sugar outsides. All the recipes I have tried flatten out, get brittle, and are not as sour and cakey. I have several theories about why: (1) The weather is different here in Oklahoma than in Southern California and Connecticut, where I made them. (2) I may have used margarine—or a mixture of butter and margarine—and margarine's so different nowadays. I know I did not use Crisco, which I have always found disgusting as well as flavorless, bad for you, and visually evocative of cholesterol buildup in arteries. Everyone should boycott it, in my opinion. (3) Possibly I just haven't found the right recipe. The closest I can get is this evolving recipe and two important cookie directives: Always cool your cookie sheet before baking more cookies on it and take care not to overbake or underbake. Snickerdoodles should remain puffy and light colored, except for the outer edges.

Preheat oven to 375°. Cream together:

1/2 **cup cheap margarine** (that is, with high vegetable oil content)
3/4 **cup sugar**

Add:

1 **large egg**
1 **tablespoon heavy cream**

Sift together:

1 1/2 cups all-purpose flour
1/2 teaspoon baking soda
1 1/4 teaspoons cream of tartar
1/2 teaspoon salt

Add the flour mixture to the butter mixture to form a soft dough. Chill for half an hour. Meanwhile, combine in a bowl:

2 tablespoons sugar
2 teaspoons cinnamon

Make walnut-sized balls (a heaping tablespoon) of dough and roll them in sugar-cinnamon mixture. Place on cookie sheets—either ungreased or covered with baking parchment—about 2 inches apart. Bake around 13 minutes or until very lightly colored around the edge and just firm to touch. Do not overbake. Transfer to wire racks to cool.

Apple Brown Betty

This is an approximation of my friend Donald's recipe, which we made up together as we went along. We baked it in the toaster oven of the trailer he lived in when we were in college. The toaster oven was hard to regulate, and we always burned it a little, but it was still good. Apple Brown Betty is about warmth in cold weather and the pleasant, old-world syntax of its name.

Brown Betty is simply a layered casserole of homemade bread crumbs mixed with melted butter alternating with sliced sour apples mixed with brown sugar and cinnamon. Start and end with the buttery bread crumbs in a buttered baking dish. Drizzle the top layer of crumbs with a little hot water and bake until brown. Most recipes say to cover it while baking, but we didn't.

Gingerbread

Another recipe my friend Donald and I used to make together. The key things that make it special are the hot orange juice and the iron skillet, both of which are essential.

Preheat oven to 350°. Melt in an iron skillet:

1/2 cup butter

Pour it into a bowl—don't clean the skillet, as you'll be using it—and combine but don't overmix with:

1 cup brown sugar
2 eggs
3/4 cup boiling orange juice
3/4 cup molasses
21/2 cups flour
2 teaspoons baking soda
1/2 teaspoon salt
11/2 teaspoons powdered ginger
1/2 teaspoon cinnamon

Heat the buttery skillet and pour in the batter. Bake until holey looking on top but firm to the touch. Serve with unsweetened whipped cream.

BROWN CHERRY-CHOCOLATE CAKE *(Brauner Kirschkuchen)*

This is another of those German cakes that use grated nuts and bread crumbs instead of flour. A variety of nuts are available pre-grated in German grocery stores, but in the U.S. you will need a tool: a hand-cranked nut grater, which can be difficult to find. (See page 135 for details.) The goal is feathery particles of finely grated nuts about the consistency of fine bread crumbs. My friend Susanne used hazelnuts (aka filberts), not almonds, and they are definitely better, but I can't find them hulled where I live, and they are such a pain to crack. If you can get hulled filberts or have an afternoon to spend cracking whole ones open, use them, by all means.

This recipe is very particular, and I am sorry for that. I have tried in the past to make a true-blue American cake out of this recipe by substituting chocolate chips and using a food processor and so forth, but it just does not look or taste right that way. To get anything like the cake I'm talking about, you'll have to follow the directions pretty much exactly—which is ironic, as Susanne never followed recipes herself, and I had to record this one purely by observing and guessing amounts. I recommend readying the various special ingredients—the pan, the grated nuts, the bread crumbs, the cherries, the hacked chocolate bar—then proceeding with the mixing of the batter, so I have arranged the recipe that way.

Preheat oven to 350°. Prepare and set aside:

Cake pan: Butter a 10-inch cake pan with a removable bottom and coat it well with dry bread crumbs. If you don't have such a pan, you can use a regular cake pan, but the timing of the baking may be a bit off and you'll want to cut a piece of parchment paper for the bottom so that you can get the cake out more easily. I'm guessing a 9-inch cake pan would take five or ten minutes longer to bake, as it would be a deeper cake.

Nuts: Use a hand-cranked nut grinder or Parmesan grinder to grate whole, unblanched almonds or filberts. You will need 5.5 ounces (approximately a cup) of nuts, which, when grated, will amount to $2^1/4$ to $2^1/2$ cups.

Bread crumbs: Use store-bought plain bread crumbs or make your own by smashing zwieback (or unseasoned croutons or stout white bread that has been toasted in a low oven until golden and very dry) in a plastic bag or by grinding them in a food processor. You will need $1/2$ cup for the batter and a few tablespoons more for the pan.

Cherries: Drain a large can or two smaller cans of sour or sweet cherries. If you can't find them, use 2 cups of frozen sour cherries but don't thaw them. Germans also make this sort of cake with fresh cherries, but you'll have to pit them or else be okay, as Germans are, with people spitting them out as they eat.

Chocolate: Roughly hack 2 3-ounce bars of *good quality* dark chocolate (preferably European chocolate, such as Lindt) into uneven chunks. Do *not* use chocolate chips and do not chop the chocolate too fine. You want it uneven, with mostly pretty big chunks, the size of nickels and quarters.

Combine and set aside:

$2^1/4$ to $2^1/2$ cups grated almonds or hazelnuts
$2/3$ cup dry toasted bread crumbs, finely ground

Using an electric beater on the highest setting (or a food processor), mix until fluffy:

$1/2$ cup plus 2 tablespoons butter
$2/3$ cup sugar

Add, one ingredient at a time, beating after each addition:

4 egg yolks
the juice of $1/2$ lemon
2 to 3 drops of almond flavoring

Beat for a long time, at least five minutes, until you can no longer hear the grains of sugar against the bowl or feel them when you rub a bit of the batter between your fingers. Then add the nut mixture to the butter/egg mixture and combine well. Set aside. Beat until stiff but still glossy:

4 egg whites

Lay the beaten egg whites on top of the nut batter and use a rubber spatula to fold—that is, scoop up from the bottom of the bowl and back into the batter from the top—the egg whites into the batter. Keep folding until the batter is homogenous and you can no longer see any whites. Be gentle! Your goal is to retain all those bubbles that turned the slick egg white into froth. These will make the cake rise.

Spread the batter in the pan and scatter first the chocolate, then the cherries, on top. Don't worry about getting them too even. They will drop down into the batter as the cake bakes, and their unevenness makes the cake interesting. Bake for 60 minutes in the middle of the oven. This is one of those cakes that might fall if you open the oven before it's done or close to done, so don't worry over it. Let it cook and, if you have to check on it, use the oven window, if you have one, or at least wait until 50 minutes have passed. The cake should be a pretty brown color, with the cherries and chocolate partly sunken into the top.

MY BROWN SUGAR BROWNIES

These are quick quick to make and use only one bowl, and everyone loves them, even people who, like me, are not big chocolate lovers. Numerous people who say they hate brownies have told me these are the only ones they've ever tasted that they like. I invented them by messing over the years with the butterscotch brownie recipe in the Fannie Farmer *cookbook.*

Preheat oven to 375°. Grease and flour two 8-inch square pans or three big loaf pans. Don't use a 9 x 13-inch pan unless you like really gooey brownies with no crust. Microwave in a large microwaveable bowl until melted—about a minute, but watch to be sure:

1/2 cup salted butter

Add and stir in just to mix:

2 cups brown sugar, packed
4 eggs

1/2 teaspoon salt

1 cup flour

1/2 cup cocoa

2 teaspoons baking powder

1 teaspoon vanilla

1 cup coarsely chopped walnuts, lightly toasted in the oven (maybe 5
    minutes, while preheating)

Spread the batter in the pans and bake for 10 to 15 minutes (depending on pan size) or until they look done as much as you like them. They will get all puffed up and holey looking on top, like a pancake, and then sink back down and start looking drier. The moment they sink down and start looking drier is when I like to pull them out. My daughters are brownie purists and insist I leave the nuts out, so I usually make two loaf pans for them but leave enough batter in the bowl to make at least one pan with nuts, using somewhat fewer than I call for here. Brownies, in my opinion, should have walnuts.

Peanut Butter Cookies Entirely from Scratch

Drink milk with these and you will return to some happy moment of childhood that you have forgotten.

I had no measuring cups or spoons and couldn't regulate the temperature very well, so I just eyeballed everything. Roast raw peanuts in a pan in the oven until light brown—around 10 minutes, but watch to be sure. Grind them to butter with a mortar and pestle (or food processor) to make about 1/2 to 3/4 cup. Then, using the mortar and pestle or food processor again, mix in the same amount of butter, a packed cup of brown sugar (or about one-half of a cone of brown sugar from a Mexican food store, smashed), 1/2 teaspoon salt, 1/2 teaspoon baking soda, an egg, and enough flour to make a fairly soft dough. Make balls with your hands and flatten them on an ungreased cookie sheet with a fork, first one direction, then the other, to leave a crisscross pattern. Bake until brown on the edges.

19

Rice

One of the first arguments of my early marriage—and in fact, it is an argument my husband Kris and I still have not resolved—was about the free market. We were farming full-time then and, as such, were thrown upon each other's company more than is perhaps healthy in such a young relationship. Although we had much in common—writing, a belief in responsible stewardship of natural resources, a desire to have children before it was too late—we were discovering daily that we were about as different from each other in every other way as it was possible to be. I was atheist; he was Christian. I was liberal; he was conservative. I was from a big family; he was an only child. I came from a wealthy suburb of Southern California; he was raised on a farm in the poorest county of one of the poorest states. I had lived abroad most of my adult life and was all about packing my bags and going somewhere else. Leaving was my constant temptation—especially whenever life got boring or difficult, as it does almost daily on a farm in modern times. Kris, by contrast, seemed the embodiment of inertia. He had never left the country before the day he flew to Berlin—to which I had returned during my first summer break in graduate school—to fetch me back.

He knelt at my feet in a sidewalk café and asked me to marry him.

"Get up, you idiot," I told him. "You're embarrassing me."

Imagine it: We were surrounded by contemptuous Germans—perfect English speakers every one of them—drinking an afternoon beer and not only overhearing this exchange but finding in it the confirmation of every prejudice they might have had about silly Amis. So began our unlikely alliance.

On the farm, in any case, our differences intensified, and increasingly I felt lost in a culture more foreign to me than any I had encountered abroad. Kris had grown up in a farming family, and every one of his opinions—about not only free enterprise but guns, taxes, the environment, animal rights, and government subsidization—was formed through this experience. Our neighbors were farmers, too, so most conversations I had with anyone at all in the course of a day revolved around cows and chickens, forage, and the weather. Everything these country people said or did was a mystery to me, and most of my views met with consternation. I tried to avoid open conflict, particularly with my new mother-in-law, who lived down the road from us on our farm and whom I saw every day. When I questioned her about why she did something the way she did, her answer was always the same: "That's just the way we've always done it." I not only lost the argument but felt further excluded—no less by the "we" who had always done whatever it was a certain way as by the fact that I did it differently.

With Kris, though—my companion every minute of every day—frank disagreement was unavoidable. I took to reading his farming magazines with the goal of bolstering my position from his own sources, a rhetorical tactic I was always recommending to my students. From between the slick pages of bemused-looking cattle, milking machines, and ads for hay or dairy farmers available for marriage, I secretly hoped I could make out the lay of things in my new life, see the gears turning and spot any bits of chaff choking up the works. Most importantly, though, I wanted to find my place in it all. But the more I found out, it seemed, the less I understood.

Case in point: rice. In article after article I read that the American farmer was put out because Japan wouldn't buy our rice. The United States, although a relatively small producer of rice and an even smaller consumer, was and is one of the world's major rice exporters. Since the Japanese, who haven't the space necessary to farm this land-intensive staple of their diet, could have been importing massive quantities of rice, American rice farmers were understandably frustrated. The Japanese claimed our rice was inferior, but the farm magazines argued that the Japanese were just resisting free trade. They rallied around the U. S. Secretary of Agriculture, who threatened in a letter to his counterpart in Japan: "There are over two million farmers in America. Should they band together against buying Japanese products? Or are we united in our goal of accomplishing liberalized trade?"

I was musing about this remark at the breakfast table one morning, about how the Americans were missing the point. The Japanese were talking about rice, it seemed to me, not trade, and rice was a topic about which *they* were surely the experts. People know what they like.

"The Secretary of Agriculture thinks we should band together with the rest of the world and force the Japanese to buy rice they don't want to eat," I commented to Kris, as he started in on his bacon and eggs.

To my amazement, Kris was irked, and a real argument—our first of any substance—ensued. He took the side of the Secretary of Agriculture—the side of his fellow farmers, as he saw it. The side of, as I saw it, the all-subsuming culture I had tried to leave behind me when I went abroad: the side of money, McDonald's, American consumerism. And of my parents, who had not only similarly touted the free market when I was growing up, but sat my siblings and me down at the table and forced us to eat foods that Every-Child knows are poison: deviled ham sandwiches, Chicken à la King, three bean salad. Food, in my view, was about a lot more than simply eating what was on one's plate.

"How can you know if the Japanese *want* to eat our rice, if their government won't even let them sell it?" Kris demanded from across the breakfast table. He contended that if cheap American rice were available in Japanese supermarkets, the Japanese consumer would buy it.

"But it's not about *cheap* rice," I insisted. "It's about *good* rice. The Japanese know about rice. It's about rice that tastes and smells and acts the way they want it to."

"It's about money," he told me. Grimly, I thought, but nonetheless ratifying—to my horror—an attitude that sums up what's wrong with our American way of thinking about food. It's about money more than anything else. Food is cheaper in America than anywhere else in the world, and, in my limited experience, Americans really do select food on the basis of price more often than quality. As a result, we have lost the ability to appreciate one taste as distinct from another. In the undiscriminating pot of popular American cuisine, the flavors of the individual ingredients that might go into the soup have become fused. Rice is just rice. Chicken chicken. Food is merely food: important for its capacity to fill us—or overfill us, as is so often the case in our rich country—and not for its ability to satisfy, as it has from the beginning of time, our deeper desires—our *needs*, I would say—for beauty and identity and goodness. Can the world be united to "accomplish liberalized trade" independently of gut longings? To me, the whole question smacked of a culture clash of international dimensions.

I knew something about culture clashes by then. Having lived in different cities and countries than the ones of my childhood for so long, I was a walking culture clash, always at odds with the locals, always out of place. Of all the places I had lived after leaving California and Connecticut behind me, the only address which I had kept for longer than a year was Plantagenstrasse 11, 1000 Berlin 65. To this one bedroom/no bathroom apartment, with the assistance of a friend who used it in my absence, I returned again and again. I especially liked the parquet floors and the big windows of its front room, which overlooked a pretty cemetery that contained one of the two remaining crematoria in Berlin.

From my green velvet chair by the window, I could see the crematorium's long brick chimney, no longer in use because bodies nowadays are no longer burnt up, the authorities there told me, but *braised* by some bizarre new process that eliminates smoke. The chimney was left standing as a historical monument too costly to tear down. The leafy beauty of the cemetery, the elementary school two buildings away with its little asphalt hills built into the playground for the kids to play on, the low spot I always had to skirt on Ruhestätte Strasse where oily water collected in the grid of the cobblestones, the sour frying smell of the sausage stand as I rounded the corner to enter the U-Bahn—recognition alone made me love these landmarks and dream of them from faraway cities. For the longest time, Plantagenstrasse was the only street in the only city that had the reassuring familiarity of what others I knew called *home,* and I always returned to it from the stranger cities of Asia and the United States with a noisy dropping of bags and a tight little exhalation of relief.

Still, there were times when I remembered my real home and missed it. I longed for my family, for familiar experiences untarnished by the perils of estrangement— by loneliness, insecurity, fear. I longed to be understood immediately, without explanation—not just my words but my impulses and reactions, my most mundane values and views. Secretly, I longed even for things my friends back in America mocked and despised about their country. For a comforting cup of weak black coffee, on occasion, that didn't need to be diluted with milk to be drinkable. For a cavernous refrigerator, big enough to store a turkey in. For store clerks to tell me "Have a nice day!" and cull my patronage rather than growl at me, *"Das gibt es nicht!"*— which is the German way of saying "We don't have it." Translated literally, it means, "What you're looking for does not exist."

The clerks were right. Wherever I went, what I was looking for did *not* exist. "If you don't like it here," people told me in Berlin, Hong Kong, Beijing, "go home." But it wasn't that easy. My homesickness was acute, not chronic. It came in terrible bursts of misery and then left me. And anyway, home, by then, was as difficult to locate as any other general pain. But I could press down at any spot on my body and feel it there, aching, burning.

Certain foods brought home closer, I discovered, so I treated my homesickness with foods from my childhood—sloppy Joes, grilled cheese sandwiches, French toast. I even made things I had hated as a child—sandwiches, Jell-O salads—because the ingredients were relatively easy to find and hating them was as much a connection to home as anything else. They were part of my history. I dug from deep and dark in the forgotten first years of my life the murky memory of our babysitter, who made the same dish every time she came. She called it "porcupines": balls of ground meat rolled in rice and cooked in a sweet tomatoey sauce. I tried to reconstruct it from that remembrance, always in vain, even after I finally found a recipe for it in the *Joy of Cooking* on one of my trips home to see my mother before she died.

I also longed for the "foreign foods" of America, the Mexican and Italian and Vietnamese foods I had come to think of as the cuisine of my country. The cuisines of other countries were exotic rarities in Germany in those days, and what you could find in ethnic restaurants bore no relation to what I knew. I was forever encountering dishes called "Mexican" merely because the cook had thrown in a can of corn. When I said as much to my German friends, those who had traveled in the United States pointed out that what *they* called "good food"—a huge and wonderfully crusty piece of pork like what you could get in virtually any German restaurant, say, with red cabbage, boiled potatoes, and wild mushroom gravy—couldn't be had in one of our American restaurants for less than a fortune, if at all. I had to admit they were right, as far as I knew. But in America, I assured them—dipping into theretofore untapped resources of patriotism, resources I didn't even know I had—the national cuisine is not a creation of restaurants and renowned chefs but is found only in the sacred intimacy of the family: at home.

Home. It was a pardonable lie, if a lie at all, a lie borne of longing. What did I know about home anyway? And anyway, the foreign foods I longed for were probably hardly more authentic than the German attempts. I missed them not because of their authenticity, but because they were what I knew.

Rice, for example. When I lived in Germany, I found that rice was a food associated with bad memories. In childhood, every German I met had been forced to down a monstrosity called *Milchreis* (milk rice): an overcooked mash of short-grained rice served with a tart fruit compote or simply a sprinkling of sugar. The dish had the consistency and reputation of our oatmeal, which Germans regarded with similar loathing and referred to as *Haferschleim*, oat slime. *Milchreis* was generally regarded by children as punishment food, much as Chicken à la King was in my family. All children in Germany hated *Milchreis* and grew up to be haters of rice in general, of the very word.

Order rice at an Asian restaurant in Berlin and you will get something as far removed from *Milchreis* as can be achieved with the same simple ingredient. It will arrive in a neat pile on a large plate: separate dryish little rectangles, each one split down the middle by a deep groove, fluffy and tasteless, not unlike our Uncle Ben's pre-cooked bastardization and equally as incapable of sticking together and remaining suspended, in a clump, between a pair of chopsticks—which I never saw a German use the entire time I lived there.

When I serve Chinese or Japanese or Thai food to guests in the United States, I always put chopsticks on the table for those who want to use them. It's no big deal—if you want to, you can; if you don't, you can have a fork. It's just that I like to eat certain things with sticks. It brings back memories of good times I've had with friends in other lands. I like to watch guests poke idly at the bare bones of a red-cooked fish I made for them, savoring the tiniest remnants they can still find, while they talk and drink and wait for dessert.

Back in my undergraduate years in California, I peer-tutored a group of Vietnamese students—all girls just slightly younger than I was and each prettier and more perfectly groomed than the next—and afterward we always went out to eat at a Vietnamese greasy spoon in Fullerton, where they all lived. There were many such restaurants in the tired towns surrounding Camp Pendleton, the port through which the majority of Vietnamese immigrants had entered the United States. However hopefully these restaurants attempted to encourage a broader patronage, with menus in English and reassuring-sounding offerings like chop suey, they were all strictly Vietnamese. Invariably, I was the only person there who could not murmur the sweet tones of their soft burping language or understand the words of the love songs playing in the background, which, my tutees told me, were all about sadness and home.

We always ordered the same thing: first the uncooked summer rolls to which I was addicted, then noodle soup, and for dessert canned longan fruits served with their syrup in a tall glass of ice. The noodle soup came accompanied by a platter of fresh hot peppers, lime wedges, and herbs to be used as condiments: fresh mint and cilantro and a licorice-tasting basil. Beside each bowl of soup were both chopsticks and Western cutlery. The Vietnamese girls all ate the same way. Holding the spoon steady in one hand, they used the chopsticks in the other to lift one long noodle out of the bowl and then coil it daintily in the bottom of the spoon. They then dipped their loaded spoons into the cloudy caramel-colored broth; arranged a sprig of coriander, a slice of hot pepper, and a few bits of vegetable or meat from the soup on top; and raised these delicate compositions to their glossy lips.

Rice, especially, I like to eat with sticks. Especially when I'm all alone. I fill a small bowl with rice, ladle over it a modest portion of something savory, like *mapo doufu*—

a spicy dish of soft tofu sautéed with ground pork—or else, my favorite, greens sautéed with garlic and a little salt and sugar. Then I tilt the bowl to my mouth, as the Chinese do, and ferry the rice in a steady stream the short distance to my tongue. It is a satisfying way to eat, violating all the rules of etiquette I was taught as a child: Never shovel your food into your mouth, never hold the bowl you are eating from in your hand, and always alternate each mouthful with a long interval of chewing.

Rice, eaten this way, must stick together, so I buy round grains, preferably Japanese, when I want to eat it Asian-style. Generally speaking, since I have finally left Berlin and Asia behind me and opted to settle down in the United States—in what is really my home, like it or not—I prefer to buy American. But American short grain rice is hard to come by, and even when I do find a California or Louisiana variety that looks the way it ought to—with shiny, stout, almost translucent whole grains and no broken matter between them—it seems to me it doesn't cook up right. I follow the directions on the plastic bag it comes in, and I've experimented with different proportions and washing the rice beforehand as most Asian cooks do. The result is always either mushy and thin-tasting or else dry and hard in the middle. There is no sticky and fragrant medium.

Rice, in the Asian countries where it is a staple, is usually cooked pretty much the same way. You rinse it several times to remove the chalky exterior, bring it to a boil in about one and a half times as much plain water, and then cook it slowly until, based on your experience with that particular sack of that particular rice, you know that it will be done. The time varies a good deal, as does the exact amount of water, as does rice itself, so you will have to experiment a few times every time you buy new rice. Asians generally buy their rice in large quantities, enough to last a long time, so the trial and error process of determining when the grains are cooked to perfection is an experiment that must be performed only once a year. In any event, when the rice is done, you will know it from the smell.

How to describe the perfume of good rice perfectly cooked? It is a low nose smell, more a suspicion than an identifiable fragrance, actually—an anticipation. It is like the smell of homemade bread your lover is about to make for you or the brief elusive scent of a field of forget-me-nots when you are almost, but not quite, upon them. Good rice smells like rain in the summer air, just before it pours down.

The people of Thailand grow and sell worldwide what is called "fragrant rice," a long, clear yellow grain which, although it doesn't stick together as well as the short-grained Japanese and Chinese rices unless you figure out just the right amount of water to cook it in, sure does smell nice. Even if the slim, pointed grains do remain as independent as minnows in a shallow creek, fragrant rice is really good to eat. Internationally regarded as one of the highest quality rices on the market, it is nevertheless cheaper than rices produced elsewhere. Thais eat and also export a lot of it. Even the picky Japanese buy Thai rice.

In the People's Republic of China, when I was there, good quality rice was hard to come by unless you bought it for high prices on the free market. Since it is one of the products for which citizens received ration coupons, most bought inferior rice—dull, opaque, often broken grains full of grit and husks—from the government stores and ate the more expensive good rice available in the free market only on special occasions. Chinese restaurants served the expensive rice to foreigners—and charged accordingly—and the cheap horrible kind to locals who came in with ration tickets in their hands. (Unlike American food stamps and the ration tickets given out in Berlin to asylum-seekers, Chinese ration tickets could be used back then in restaurants.) The cheap rice does not stick together and is hard to eat with chopsticks unless you hold them together and shovel. In your mouth, the government rice is much like the results of my experiments in cooking American rice Asian style: water-logged, weak in taste, and uneven in texture.

I'm not saying that American rice is not worth eating. It's just not the same as Japanese or Chinese or Thai rice. Sometimes I crave good, cheap, Louisiana long-grain rice, cooked as I learned to like it in New Orleans: exactly as directed on the package except for the addition of two or three small onions, whole, each with a single clove stuck in it. Fifteen minutes after the rice comes to a boil, the onions will have softened to a mealy slime and imparted a sharp blast of clove taste to the rice. I put lots of butter and salt and pepper on this kind of rice and eat it as a main dish. Sometimes I add a big handful of frozen peas in the last five or so minutes of cooking and mix them in when the rice is done. I have the recipe from my friend Gail. She never cooked anything else when I was at her house, which was often. Her husband Mario usually did the cooking, and when he cooked rice, it was always according to the Cajun method, which I guess might be the Indian method as well, since Mario was from Bombay. He boiled the rice in lots of salted water until, by biting into a grain or two, he judged that it was cooked just right. Then he poured the rice and water through a colander and left it to drain while he fixed everything else.

My Berlin friend Siovosch, a Persian, took Mario's method a step further. He bought Thai rice, because Iranian rice—an opaque, white, long-grain variety—wasn't available in Berlin. After cooking the rice al dente by the colander-and-too-much-water method, he layered it with melted butter back into the big pan he had cooked it in, the bottom of which was at least a centimeter deep in more melted butter and thin slices of potato. When he was done layering, an event which required at least one helper (usually me if I was there) and lots of noise and chaos and worrying about the rice being too cooked or not enough, Siovosch covered the pot tightly with a lid and a towel and cooked the contents until the pot "burned him in a certain way" when he spit on his index finger and touched it low on one side. He said he couldn't describe it any better than that. He served the rice by upending the pot onto a platter with the browned potatoes on top and then sprinkling over it sour, bright red, dried berries, which his mother sent him from Iran and which he had previously fried with sugar in more butter. Siovosch's German girlfriend told me the fruits are called *Berberitzen* in German—barberries in English, I've since learned—but I've never been able to find them for sale anywhere. In any case, this simple platter of Iranian rice may be the best home cooking I have ever eaten.

When it comes right down to it, Americans eat very little rice. For a culture so richly influenced by rice-eating cultures—the Chinese who built our railroads, the Mexicans who picked our grapes, the Japanese who built our sugar cane industry and excel in our universities and work places as in their own—we are rather strangely uninterested in this international staple. We might fork up a few bites of the rice that comes with our beans that come with the taco-enchilada combo we order at the Red Onion or savor the few thumb-sized mounds of seasoned rice buried beneath dainty slabs of raw tuna at Mishima's Sushi Lounge, but what we're really after is the meat, the sauce, the snow peas and water chestnuts, the real substance of the meal. "Where's the beef?" we joke in reference to empty rhetoric, but when it comes to food we really mean it. Beef—which we differentiate, as minutely as Alaskans do types of snow, into prime rib, filet mignon, rump roast, hamburger—*means* something to us. Rice, on the other hand, is a commodity we wish to deal in, but not eat—like soybeans.

As a graduate student in creative writing at the University of Arkansas, I participated in an arts outreach program called Writers in the Schools. Working in pairs, we taught creative writing for a couple of days at a time in schools all over Arkansas. One elementary school I visited was in the Arkansas Delta, where vast farms utilize the cheap land and labor available there to grow soybeans, cotton, and rice, all for export. A fellow writer and I were trying to get some fourth graders to write poems for us. As inspiration, we wrote on the board the names of things we had noticed in their town that we thought would be familiar and concrete enough for them to write about with authority. The Mississippi River. The cottonwood trees that lined the river. The paper mill, where many of their parents worked. Soybeans, the primary crop grown in that region. One of the kids raised his hand and pointed to the last word.

"Can you eat 'em?" he wanted to know.

I did a lot of thinking about America in the months and years after I came back and got married. I decided there were some things I liked about the country where I was born. Important things. I liked that government-initiated massacres of protesting students, like the one that happened not long after I left China in the main square of Beijing, are further in America's past. I liked that Americans seem to believe that they ought to *enjoy* their work rather than just labor for raises and longer vacations, as many of the Germans I knew did. And it pleased me that not a few of my American students were working their way through college, as I had. I liked our rich and potent melting pot of cultures, however smelly and poisonous a stew it might be at times, and I liked good, American, down home cooking: chicken-fried steak as my grandmother had taught me to make it, tacos, spaghetti. I decided that I liked all these things well enough to settle down with my American sweetheart and stay. I wanted to raise cattle and grow a big garden and bring up happy, healthy American babies who—in my father's words—would "know what's good."

I will never understand why in the world we wanted—why we still want—to force our rice on the Japanese. Although Arkansas, where I lived when I first returned to America, is the top rice-producing state in the nation, I was never once served rice in my years there. I don't even know how native Arkansans cook rice, if they cook it at all. Still, the farm magazines—in those years when I was reading them and arguing from them with my maniacally pro-American husband—went on and on about the unassailable appeal of our American rice and how the Japanese would love it if they could just get their sticks on it. They clearly expected the Japanese to *want* our rice—not just to buy it and eat it but to *like* it—merely because it was cheaper. They expected the Japanese to be like us, to *become* us, and they were amazed that they resisted our efforts to make them so. In my first years back in the United States, I found the idea amusing. And scary. And I still do.

What will happen to a country in which food is cheap and availability seems to know no limits, but where farmers struggle to survive, and matches and cars and paper bags are imported from abroad? What will become of a country, built on a mélange of races and traditions, which forgets that people are different, that a bean to one is a gold nugget to another? If our only response to foreign consumers' refusal to buy our hormone-tainted meat is to punish them with all manner of hysterical threats and boycotts and with higher tariffs on their olive oil—which we could but choose not to produce ourselves, because we can get it so cheap from abroad—how can we hope to solicit the world's help in pulling us out of the political difficulties in which we, as a superpower in the world, find ourselves again and again and again?

Surely it says something about our future, our national state of mind, that we get angry when another country, willing to pay premium prices for a specific product of pristine quality, refuses to buy a different type altogether of low-grade rice—which we ourselves do not eat and to which we add dirt up to the allowable level of foreign contaminants just to make another buck. It is someone's job description to add this dirt—I can't fathom this—and yet we insist that the quality of the American product is not the issue.

As long as I can still buy sticky and sweet-smelling Japanese rice at my local Asian market—they carry four varieties, as well as several types of Thai fragrant rice, ranging from three to six dollars a pound, as compared to a dollar or so a pound for American rice—and as long as the Korean woman who runs the store won't let me out the door without elaborating on the character and proper cooking method of the variety I have chosen, the American economy will have to suffer. If those of us Americans who *eat* rice won't buy our own American product, how can we expect anyone else to?

It worried me in those early years of my marriage, honest to God. I thought about it as I counted our heifers to make sure they were all there and broke the ice on the pond so the cattle could drink and cooked up a pot of jambalaya to share with my husband and mother-in-law. What would happen to a country that had forgotten what home meant, that ignored the taste, the smell, the essence of good rice, perfectly cooked?

SLOPPY JOES

Brown together, breaking up the meat well:

1 pound ground beef
1 onion, minced

Add and simmer for 15 to 20 minutes:

1 cup ketchup
1 tablespoon Worcestershire sauce
1 teaspoon mustard
1 teaspoon paprika
1 tablespoon vinegar

2 tablespoons brown sugar
1/2 teaspoon Tabasco sauce

Adjust seasoning to be as sweet or sour or spicy as you like it by adding more or less of the above ingredients. Serve spooned on hamburger buns.

FRENCH TOAST

Combine in a shallow bowl:

2 eggs
1/2 cup milk
1 tablespoon sugar

Soak on both sides, one at a time, in the egg mixture:

4 to 6 slices of white bread or as many as it takes to soak up the egg mixture

Sauté the soaked bread slices in a little butter until golden on both sides, sprinkling with cinnamon as they cook. Serve with butter and maple syrup.

MA PO TOFU (Mapo Doufu)

To make this dish, you will need to go to your local Asian store and buy a few special ingredients: hot chili bean sauce in a little jar; dried salted black beans, which come in a bag and you can store afterward in a jar; and, if you can find it, Sichuan pepper. You may not find this last ingredient, because the substance has been banned on and off in the U.S. for carrying citrus canker, a disease disastrous to crops in Florida, California, and Texas. You can make the dish without the Sichuan pepper—I often do—but it's worth looking for if you really like mapo doufu, *as it imparts a flavor and texture like no other hot spice you have tasted. The Chinese call it* ma la, *literally "numb and hot," but I find it not so much hot as herbal tasting. And gritty between the teeth, like bugs. It reminds me of the local flora and fauna I sampled growing up in Southern California.*

Combine and set aside:

1/2 pound ground pork
2 tablespoons cornstarch
2 tablespoons soy sauce
1 tablespoon sweet sherry

Cut in 1/2-inch cubes and blanch for a few minutes in boiling water:

1 pound firm tofu

Cut lengthwise twice into quarters and then into 1-inch lengths and set aside:

4 or 5 green onions

Grind in a mortar or spice grinder and dry-roast until fragrant in a frying pan, then set aside:

1 teaspoon Sichuan pepper (omit if you can't find it or if you think your
    family will object, as mine does, to a gritty texture)

Stir-fry the marinated meat in just enough oil to keep it from sticking—about 1 to 2 tablespoons. Add and continue stirring:

1 tablespoon dried black beans
the ground Sichuan pepper

After about a minute, add and allow to simmer for about 5 minutes:

the cut up onions
the blanched tofu
2 tablespoons chili bean paste
1/4 cup water or broth

Combine and add, stirring carefully—to keep from breaking up the delicate tofu cubes too much—until thickened:

3 tablespoons water
2 tablespoons soy sauce
2 tablespoons cornstarch

Serve with rice.

CHICKEN-FRIED STEAK

I'm going to tell the plate method, but you may use a meat mallet, if you have one.

Use one small, lean steak—the thinner and cheaper, the better—for each person. Tenderize by pounding the edge of a small (not delicate) plate into each steak until it is ridged all over. Turn the steak over and do the same to the other side. Salt and pepper the steaks, dip them in flour, and fry them in about 1/4 inch of oil until they are dark brown on both sides, turning once. Pour off most of the oil in the pan and make a milk gravy out of the remaining drippings by adding about the same amount of flour, letting it get a little brown, and then whisking in milk and stirring until thick. Season the gravy with salt and lots of pepper and serve over the meat with mashed potatoes.

20

Country Cooking

Although some part of me knows, without ever having been taught, how to cook certain foods of my maternal ancestry—biscuits and gravy, for example, and fried okra—I nevertheless feel a certain loss whenever I contemplate the plain country cooking my mother must have grown up eating. I want to know it more intimately—see it frying in my own skillet, taste it, feel its substance in my mouth. What were her favorite foods as a child? What did she look on with revulsion? She died before I thought to ask her. Is my desire to know merely the result of losing her so early in life? Do I seek to hold onto her through food, where other mourners hoard photographs and letters? Or is the urge to know exactly what my mother ate before I knew her and what *her* ancestors may have eaten before she knew *them*—to know the food not only of her past but, in some sense, of all of our pasts—part of a general longing we all share to recapture some lost essence of truth in eating, to rediscover the original fruits and vegetables, to taste the first animals killed as food, and thereby to relive those wonders, those horrors?

The country foods my mother ate, in any case, are hard to research. Most recipes—and especially the ordinary ones I'm talking about—were not written down back then. In boxes of speckled, handwritten cards inherited from country grandmas and great aunts you may find recipes for the fruitcake baked once a year but not for the hash or beans or fried squash that appeared on the table every day. It is assumed, apparently, that everyone knows how to make such common-place products of daily living.

Modern cookbooks typically "refine" the simple foods I'm looking for beyond recognition. In the cookbooks on country cooking I lug to my table in the Barnes & Noble café, I find recipes like cheddar-and-jalapeño biscuits, sweet potatoes whipped with orange juice and ginger, peanut butter pie, all foods I'm sure my mother never tasted as a child.

Older resources, though, such as the country cooking pamphlets I pick up in used book stores and flea markets, seem the least reliable of all, invariably romanticizing the hard times of the past with cutsey stories and simultaneously calling for canned soups and potato flakes and self-rising flour and marshmallows, none of which even existed in the places and times I want to know about. The directives often seem unnecessarily arduous: beating a cake batter by hand for twenty minutes—twenty minutes!—or hauling out the mortar and pestle just to ready a few sprigs of parsley for the soup.

Opening such a repository of nonsense is like accidentally entering an antique store crammed full of kountry krafts. Calicos everywhere you look. Clothespin dolls made of cheap pine pins that would never actually work for hanging heavy wet overalls. Dry-clean only aprons dangling appliquéd fruits from their bibs. Miniature butter churns painted with Holstein cows and dusty candles reeking of air freshener. Here and there in the midst of these embarrassments you might find a rusted tool that looks vaguely culinary, and you pick it up, but when you ask the emphysemic woman who runs the place what it's for, she can't tell you. Or she makes something up. Or she starts lecturing you, between bouts of wet coughing, about how hard folks had it back then and how they used to do so many things and people don't do anything like that anymore.

I have decided that what I am looking for in a country cookbook—doable recipes for real country foods eaten every day—just can't be found. What did people actually use to eat around here—in Arkansas, in eastern Oklahoma, in the tiny Ozark farm community where my mom grew up—before they got caught up in Jell-O salads and green bean casseroles sodden with Campbell's soup and topped with limp French-fried onions from a can? What did the old country people around where I live now have for breakfast and dinner as children? What did my mother's kin eat for the big Sunday meal—even the poorest had one, I'm guessing—or to celebrate a birthday? What did they eat at funerals?

When I first met my husband's mother, when I ate my first familiarly chewy biscuit at the Formica bar in the kitchen of her 1970s ranch house, I knew she contained all the information I wanted. My mother-in-law, whom we call Mamaw in my family, was born in 1922 on a 247-acre farm not five miles from where we live today. There were ten kids in Mamaw's family, one of whom died at the age of three from diphtheria and the rest of whom have died since, in adulthood, except for Mamaw, who is in perfect health. They had no car in her growing-up years. No indoor bathroom. No running water, but instead a dug well from which the kids had to carry water in buckets to the house, where they either used it cold or heated it in the ten gallon reservoir of their wood-fired, Home Comfort stove. Mamaw's dad raised everything they ate, except for sugar and coffee, and her mom did all the cooking: three sit-down meals a day for twelve people and whatever guests showed up. She began cooking at five in the morning and ended after nightfall, and all her daughters learned—actively or vicariously, depending on when they arrived in the steady progression of children—to do the same for their own future families. Mamaw remembers her childhood in detail. She is articulate. She cooks. I was certain she would be the best resource there could be for how they cooked around here in the past. All I needed to do to recreate the foods of my own mother's childhood was to watch Mamaw cook, question her, and record what I found out.

Mamaw and I were culinary rivals at first. From the day I married her only son, we fought yearly over who got to do Thanksgiving and Christmas and Easter dinners, and we still struggle weekly over how often my family should eat with her and she with us. Cooking, for her as well as for me, is a significant way of showing love, and having the people we love enjoy the food we cook is an important way we get loved back. So, we compete for opportunities.

All the same, I love Mamaw's cooking, especially what she disparages as "just a country meal." Like her brothy potato stew, flecked with beef roast and heavily seasoned with pepper and fresh sage. Or fried pork jowl with biscuits and meal gravy—a cornmeal-thickened milk gravy into which we stir mustard at the table. She only ever serves this meal to celebrate the New Year, along with the requisite black-eyed peas, although she does sometimes make the biscuits and grainy meal gravy just for me. But neither of these specimens of country cooking represent the food that she "came up with," as she says. The stew is her own invention, happened upon late in life when she had some leftover pot roast she didn't know what to do with, and the meal gravy she learned from her *husband's* mother.

Mamaw's cooking often evokes but never truly elucidates what is, for me, her genuinely foreign past, in which pork jowls were as familiar as pork chops and sage and rhubarb grew along the edge of everyone's garden and you kept down the varmint population—squirrels, raccoons, rabbits—by eating them, usually fried, with biscuits and gravy. What Mamaw ate fresh growing up was what was in season. New potatoes—scrubbed well and then simmered in milk and butter—were eaten only in spring. Lettuce and green onions—wilted with a hot dressing of bacon grease, vinegar, and sugar—only in early summer. Shelly peas—black-eyed or purple-hull peas with some of the green young peas boiled with the mature dry ones—only in late summer or early fall. Fresh meat was only available in the cold of winter, at hog-slaughtering time because, without refrigeration, all the meat that could not be eaten immediately had to be preserved.

But Mamaw, now in her mid-eighties, is a modern woman. She has not only a huge, coffin-shaped freezer for storing meat in all year long but a microwave, a dishwasher, and double wall-ovens. She no longer cooks according to the seasons but according to her desires, and over the years she has slowly abandoned most of the lingering country practices of her childhood: putting in a big garden, canning, picking berries.

She grew up in a family that killed and cleaned every chicken or guinea hen or squirrel they put on the table and left cabbage to rot in stone crocks to make sauerkraut—or, with the addition of jalapeño peppers, her sister Edna's hot jack. They scooped homemade cider vinegar out from beneath its "mother," a massive livery-looking colony of bacteria that floated at the top of the barrel. Nevertheless, over the years she has become as squeamish as most modern Americans are about the realness of food. She throws away any fruit or vegetable that shows the slightest indication of having been touched by an insect. She peels everything, even tomatoes. She's finicky about variety meats. And before using an egg, like one of those pernickety cooks of French haute cuisine, she first removes the little glibbery string—the chalaza—that anchors the yolk in its white. When I ask why, she makes a face. Nauseating!

In the stories Mamaw tells of her childhood, though, she is an entirely different person. In one account my daughters like to hear, she and her siblings routinely chased down barn mice and squashed them to death in their bare hands. In another story, whenever it was hog-killing time, Mamaw and her mother, as a special treat, shared steaming pig brains direct from the pig head simmering in the pot to make souse. They committed this act in the cold dark kitchen at night. Earlier that day, while Mamaw and her sisters were at school, her father had bashed the pig in the head with a post maul to kill it, and then he and his sons had hung it from a tree and bled it and cut the carcass apart.

Her mother's main job on hog-killing day was to cut up mountains of fat into two-inch cubes to be rendered as cooking lard. When the rendering was finally underway in every pot in the house, she cleaned the pig's head, removed the skin and eyeballs, and put it on to cook in the only vessel she had that was big enough: her iron washpot out by the well. She built a fire under it and kept it going all day long, then let it die down when it was time to get the evening meal around for her family. After supper, the head would finally be cool enough to handle. Before she settled in to pick the meat from the bones and then cook it some more in the cooking liquid with seasonings and pour it into all her big bowls to set overnight, she would call in little Texie, the third youngest of her children, to eat some of the pig's brains with her. All the other kids, even her big brothers, were disgusted. But Mamaw didn't care. Her brothers did all kinds of things *she* found disgusting, she reasoned. And anyway, she explained to me, a big part of her enjoyment of this treat was the one-on-one time with her mother, a rare pleasure in big families. When she tells of how her mother would pass her a spoon and she would reach in through the pig's broken face to retrieve bite after bite of the delicate grayish-white flesh, salt it, and then eat it, her voice thickens.

"You know that was the best-tasting meat!" she says now, her eyes wet with remembrance.

These are the sort of recipes I long for, but when I ask Mamaw for specifics on what all went into that souse, she suddenly goes blank.

"Oh, a little of this and a little of that," she tells me.

And when I sit her down to talk about the cuisine of her childhood, she is short on the kind of details I want and, like the nostalgic old-timey magazines she subscribes to, long on assertions about how lucky they were never to have had to go hungry. She stresses how hard they had to work, automatically lapsing into the voice of *Good Old Days* or *Reminisce*. She uses the word *plenty* all the time. They made *plenty* of apple pies and cream pies, ate *plenty* of homegrown popcorn and peanuts on Sunday afternoons, used *plenty* of milk and cream and butter in their cooking because they had their own cows and *plenty* of pasture, and her dad had *plenty* of work to do to keep up with the farm. They had meat with every meal, and her mother made hot bread three times a day every day. By "bread" she means not the yeast-raised breads we generally think of when we use the term without an adjective but freshly baked biscuits or cornbread. Or the fried bread that Steinbeck refers to as "fried dough" in *The Grapes of Wrath*—essentially the same bread that Native Americans call "Indian fry bread" and that Mexicans call *sopapillas* and eat with honey and that New Orleanians call *beignets* and bury in powdered sugar: that is, biscuit dough rolled thin and deep fried. Yeast bread was called "light bread" in Mamaw's family, and they rarely had it.

Mamaw repeatedly emphasizes how the neighbor kids liked to come home with her and her siblings because *they* didn't have a pig to kill—or popcorn, or melons, or pies—at their own homes. Neighbors came asking to borrow farmstuffs like vinegar and even store-bought items, like baking powder or what they called "east," dry blocks of yeast they used back before refrigeration. Mamaw's family's farm was relatively prosperous for those times. But she stresses that there was no end to the effort it took to get all this food on the table. Butchering. Threshing. Hauling the wheat off in a mule-driven cart to Cincinnati, Arkansas—twenty miles away—to be milled.

No matter how hard I try to pin Mamaw down on a recipe, she somehow slips out of my grasp and into panegyric. So blessed. So much. Such hard work. I wonder if there is an ethnographic term for this habit of subjects to escape objectivity in favor of argument. And then when I'm just about ready to give up on finding out what I want to know, she suddenly becomes super-explicit in trying to make plain to me what something is—some implement or circumstance—that is entirely unnecessary to the recipe under discussion.

A lard stand, for example, was a container in which Mamaw's family stored their lard, which was what they used for all frying. Frying was how they cooked most of their food, even what was cooked in the oven, not on the stove. *To me, that's not frying,* I think as Mamaw tells me this, but I don't say it. I don't want to get her off track from the recipe for fried bread. We return to the lard stand. It's a tall tin cylinder with handles on the sides and a lid instead of a bail, she explains.

"Or is it *b-a-l-e*?" She spells out the word, as though I had spelled it the other way in my head the first time she said it. She gets the dictionary, but the word for the wire handle of a pail or bucket is strangely missing. I suggest it might be a regional usage, but she is off looking for the bigger dictionary. Meanwhile, I try to draw the lard stand. She comes back and corrects my drawing. The handles, she says, were like ears coming out of the sides, and the lid was like the one on her old coffee cans that she still stores her meal and beans in, the cans they used to have that came with a key for removing the lid. You never see those anymore, she tells me.

"How big was it?" I ask.

"Oh, great big," she says. But she can't say what that means. First she says five pounds. Then growls, "No, that can't be right. Maybe five gallons."

Every time I question her at any length about foods from the past, she passes on to her old lady friends—each of whom calls her by habit at a certain time of day—and to Uncle Jim, her widowed brother-in-law, the interesting news that her daughter-in-law wants to know how to cook what her family used to eat in the olden days. Uncle Jim has always been interested in olden ways himself. Like Mamaw, he grew up around here and knows all about the ways of the country first-hand. As an elementary school science teacher, he invested a lot of energy and enthusiasm into reliving the past with his students—hunting, cooking, and skinning wild animals; buying old tools; researching the stories of some relatives of his who were locally famous for having robbed banks.

The next time I see Uncle Jim, he says, "I hear you've been romanticizing how we used to eat in the olden days."

I bristle, but before I can defend myself, he launches into a description of how it really was. So hard. So poor. Nothing like what I think. How they used to dig a hole in the dirt and line it with straw and bury their crop of turnips in it come fall, to eat through the winter. They would cover the turnips over with more straw and put a door on top that they could just lift up whenever they needed more turnips.

"Now those turnips," I say, when he stops for a gasp of air. "How did you cook them?"

"Just cooked them, you know, and ate them," he tells me. "Sometimes we ate 'em raw, like apples. We didn't have anything fancy back then. We came up hard."

Then, somehow, he turns the conversation to his famous uncles who robbed that bank in Eureka Springs, how they were not properly executed but just shot to death.

"When the police told him to put up his hands, he couldn't. Said, 'I can't. I got too many holes in me.'"

I try to imagine that bank robber a few hours before the crime, enjoying what would be his last meal back in the hovel where he lived and thinking about the robbery he was about to commit. He lived on a farm, perhaps. Or in a boarding house. Or maybe on the lam here and there with various people who protected and perhaps even loved him, people who listened to his complaints and fed him and laundered his clothes and raised his babies. Possibly he stole not just money but his food, too, taking what he could get from strangers' houses, like that dish of field peas with molasses I've always wondered about that Joe Christmas finds in the dark kitchen on Miss Burden's table in Faulkner's *Light in August*. What exact desire incarnated that bank robber's hunger? What, exactly, of life's good things—what bread or meat or dish of greens, what fondly remembered meal, what favorite dish of childhood, what delicacy too expensive or rare to eat more than once in life—captured the appetite of this man who pointed a gun in a teller's face and made off with other people's money?

Recently, in a memoir of Bonnie and Clyde's exploits written by Clyde's sister-in-law and sometime accomplice, I read that Clyde especially liked "English peas cooked with a lot of cream and pepper" and "ate them at almost every meal except breakfast." While Uncle Jim talks, I try to envision his uncle taking such particular pleasure in a meal. What was it? Ham from a pig someone had lovingly slaughtered, then smoked and hung in a cool dry place, protected from rats, and then scrubbed clean and sliced and fried in the oven and served up with that thin, black jus called red-eye gravy, made by pouring sugared coffee into the pan of drippings? What had Jim's uncle last eaten, with gusto, when he died? Brown beans and cornbread? Three eggs fried hard in bacon grease in a restaurant? I try to see him excited about the plate before him, hungry, raising the laden fork to his red mouth, but all I can see is the sweaty back of a man hunching up to lift that door in the dirt and fish around in the moldy straw for a raw turnip. For what delights did that hapless bank robber scheme and Mamaw's parents toil? For what specific delights did country people back then labor so endlessly?

I know more about the food storage of Mamaw's childhood than I do about the preparation of any single dish. I know her family stored and "cured" sweet potatoes in bins in a warmed potato house, where they had to keep a stove going throughout the winter, but I've never gotten her to give me any more precise a description of how to prepare sweet potatoes than this one of a favorite dish her mom used to make: sliced sweet potatoes cooked with butter in a big pan in the oven and sprinkled with sugar. How thick the slices, how much butter, what kind of sugar, and when you sprinkle it on the potatoes—these details vary each time I set out to write the recipe down. Mamaw herself has never tried to recreate this dish. She won't or can't explain why not, except to tell me, "I just never have."

Hams and sausages were hung from the rafters in the well-house. Canned goods were stored in the cellar under the house—what some people call a "base-ment," she specifies, but they just called "the cellar"—but not out in the *storm* cellar, where they all piled in if a tornado threatened, even if it was the middle of the night.

"Why not there?" I ask. She doesn't know.

Once Mamaw's dad bought a quarter beef from a neighbor who had gotten mad at his bull for acting surly and shot it, even though it was summer and that much meat was bound to spoil. Mamaw's mom had cut the entire quarter up—that's a couple hundred pounds of meat—then cooked it and preserved it in jars, topped with melted lard and stored upside down. They ate it warmed, straight from the jar—with biscuits, of course—and boy, was it good. But how it was pre-pared before it went into the jars remains a mystery.

They put the apples from their trees—Winesap and Jonathan and Ben Davis and a big flat apple called Black Twig that had yellow meat but was reddish on the outside—in a certain haybarn out in a field, away from animals. It was *not* one of those barns full of loose hay that you pick up with a fork and pulley, Mamaw specifies, but a barn for square bales. Her dad would untwist the wires on a few bales and bury the apples and also Irish potatoes between the flakes, which is what you call the layers square bales fall into when you undo them.

"Give me your mom's recipe for apple pie," I beg her.

"Well, she just peeled the apples and cooked them. She never put raw apples in the crust like I do. And then she put sugar and spices and a little butter."

"What spices?"

"Oh cinnamon and ginger and nutmeg, you know. There was a peddler that came and sold spices and flavorings and pudding mixes and the like for eggs. No one ever had any money, so we just paid with what we had. But my dad was against my mother selling her eggs to peddlers. He said you couldn't get as much."

"So, then, cinnamon, ginger, nutmeg. Is that all?"

"Well, they had cloves, too. Oh, all kinds of spices."

"She put all that in her apple pie? Cinnamon, ginger, nutmeg, and cloves?"

"Nah, just cinnamon and nutmeg, I guess."

"And what kind of crust did she make?"

"I don't know, really. I know she used lard. That was all we ever had to bake with, but we had plenty of it. Kept it in a lard stand out in the screened room."

Mamaw's Beef and Potato Stew

The stew is made with leftovers from what Mamaw calls "beef roast"—what I call pot roast—so this is really a recipe for two meals. Be sure to cook enough beef roast to have leftovers for the stew!

Beef Roast

Salt, pepper, and flour a beef roast; then brown it all over in a little oil. Put it in a large pan with a cover—or a pressure cooker, if you have one—with water to cover. Cook until tender, adding more water as needed. Remove the tender meat to a platter and slice it into slices as neat as you can manage. Season the thin, dark gravy with additional salt and pepper, if necessary—and you can thicken it, if you like, with a little flour mixed with cold water. Serve the roast and its gravy with mashed potatoes and something green and light, like green beans or cucumbers and onions in a mixture of equal parts cider vinegar and water seasoned with sugar, salt, and pepper.

Beef and Potato Stew

Combine and bring to a boil:

leftover beef pot roast, cut into bite-sized chunks
any liquid leftover from the roast (remove fat by refrigerating first and then
    lifting off what rises to the surface and hardens)
as much cold water as you want soup

Add and cook until almost tender:

2 to 3 cups potatoes, diced
1 cup onions, chopped

Add and finish cooking:

salt and pepper to taste
at least 4 to 5 leaves of sage, finely sliced (or 1 to 2 heaping teaspoons dry sage)

FRIED PORK JOWL WITH BISCUITS AND MEAL GRAVY

*The trick is to get a butcher to thinly slice unsmoked jowl meat for you. Jowl meat
is blubbery and very hard to slice. The best way to do it—if you have the sort of
relationship with the butcher that allows you to make suggestions—is to slice it
frozen. Done right, it will look like pale sliced bacon.*

Fried Pork Jowl

Salt the jowl meat lightly; then fry it in a skillet over a medium flame, turning
often. Be careful about the heat: It will pop grease if it's too hot.

Mamaw's Buttermilk Biscuits

*Mamaw's biscuits are low in fat and rather chewy, not buttery and fluffy, as most
cookbooks seem to think they should be. I like hers better than any I've had
elsewhere. They remind me of my grandmother's biscuits.*

Combine and mix well:

2 cups flour
1/2 teaspoon salt
3 to 4 teaspoons baking powder
1 teaspoon sugar

Add:

1 tablespoon oil

enough buttermilk (or regular milk or a mixture of yogurt or sour cream and milk, whatever you have) **to make a soft dough**

Knead the dough a few times; then pat or roll out to about 1/2 inch thick. Use a biscuit cutter to cut 8 to 12 biscuits. Put in a greased pan, turning them once to grease the tops lightly. Bake 12 to 15 minutes in a preheated 450° oven—until lightly browned.

Meal Gravy

When the jowl meat is fried, it makes a great deal of grease. Pour off all but 2 or 3 tablespoons, add the same amount of cornmeal, and stir until the cornmeal is slightly browned. Add 1 to 11/2 cups milk and cook, stirring, until it begins to thicken. Add some pepper and salt. Pour over hot biscuits, accompanied by fried potatoes (see page 28), mustard, and sweet onion.

HOT JACK

No, there is no cooking whatsoever involved here, and, yes, eating something preserved this way sounds dangerous. But it's not. Germans have made sauerkraut and Koreans have made kimchee this way for centuries. When I double-checked with Mamaw about whether you weren't supposed to process it in a hot-water bath, she said that some people did, but then it tasted cooked. And she made a face. Hot jack should be hot, sour, salty, and quite crunchy. Above all, it should not taste cooked.

Combine and let set until juice accumulates—about 10 minutes:

9 pounds cabbage, shredded
12 to 18 jalapeño peppers, chopped
6 to 8 medium green tomatoes, chopped
5 tablespoons salt

Pack loosely in pint jars. Fill to 1 inch from the top, screw on lids lightly, and set aside to ferment for a week to 10 days. Juice will run out of the jars as the hot jack ferments, so put the jars in a plastic receptacle of some sort. After the hot jack is ready, wipe down the jars and lids—the lids will have rusted, but that's okay— and then just tighten the lids and store the jars in a cupboard.

HOMEMADE VINEGAR

You can actually make vinegar of any fruit, except maybe bananas. I recently spent a summer learning how to make vinegars from berries. Here's what I learned.

All you do is juice or cook the fruit and let it sour somewhere for a couple of months in a plastic or glass container with a piece of gauze on top to let in air but no bugs. Bacteria from the air will collect in the juice and emit a smell, and little fruit flies called vinegar flies (*Drosophila melanogaster* or *D. simulans*) will gather around it. Both consequences are good: the bacteria (specifically acetic acid bacteria, called *acetobacter*) are what sours the juice, and the vinegar flies are reassuring proof that your juice is actually turning into vinegar. You can actually see the bacteria at work. A floating mass of livery-looking material called the "mother" will form on top of the vinegar. This allows the bacteria to stay on the surface, where they can get air. Other, less-desirable bacteria can also form, though, and to discourage this and also speed up the souring process, you can augment your acetobacter colony by adding some unpasteurized vinegar, which you can buy at a health food store, or else, even better, a piece of mother from your last batch of vinegar.

Some vinegars, like Italy's expensive balsamic vinegars, are subsequently aged in wooden casks, where they grow thicker and sweeter and take on the flavor of the wood. The most expensive balsamic vinegars are aged in a series of casks, each of a different wood and smaller than the one before it, for as long as forty or fifty years.

Although my own berry vinegars had interesting fruity flavors I liked, I often found them to be either too sour or too flat for my taste. I suspect the problem may have been that I didn't age my vinegars long enough and had no reliable way of measuring how acidic they were. Vinegar should end up between 5% and 6% acetic acid. Theoretically, when it reaches the acidity and taste that you like, you should bottle it. I just used old condiment bottles that didn't have rubber seals, and I found that if I bottled the vinegar without heating it first to kill the bacteria, they somehow found a chink of air and continued to grow in the bottle until they filled it up entirely with dark, blubbery mother. Therefore, I recommend you either use sealable bottles, which you can find in a beer-making store, or else pasteurize the vinegar before bottling it by bringing it to a boil and then straining it.

MAMAW'S COCONUT CREAM PIE

I'm not usually a fan of coconut cream pie—something about the texture—but I really like Mamaw's.

Combine:

1/3 cup flour
2/3 cup sugar
1/4 teaspoon salt

Bring just to a boil, then add gradually to flour-sugar mixture:

2 cups milk

Cook mixture in a double boiler for 10 minutes. Add and cook until thick:

3 slightly beaten egg yolks

Cool slightly, then add:

1 teaspoon vanilla

Mix in:

1 cup grated coconut

Pour into baked pie shell. (See page 29.)

Meringue Topping

Combine in a saucepan:

1 tablespoon cornstarch
2 tablespoons cold water

Add:

1/2 cup boiling water

Cook, stirring, until thick and transparent. Let stand until completely cold. Beat until foaming:

3 egg whites

Gradually add and beat until stiff:

6 tablespoons sugar

Mix with a mixer and gradually add:

1 teaspoon vanilla
pinch of salt
the cornstarch mixture

Continue beating at high speed until thick. Spread the meringue over the pie filling and sprinkle with a little more coconut. Bake at 350° for about 10 more minutes, or until browned.

21

The Turkey

Not long after I married, when the girls were still little, cattle prices dropped, and I got alternatively certified to teach high school and took a job at our local school. One day, I happened to mention to a fellow teacher and farmer how I'd always wanted to eat wild turkey. An account of roasting one in Brillat-Savarin's gastronomical writings was one of the romantic reasons I offered surprised friends for why I had gone to graduate school in Arkansas. In Arkansas, I had read, wild turkeys were still prevalent. The move had led to my meeting my husband Kris— a rancher from nearby Oklahoma who unfortunately didn't hunt—and ultimately to my spending a lot of time in just the sort of back country wilderness of which Brillat-Savarin was so enamored. My new home, I discovered, was full of the same ragged-edged, strange-talking natives that Brillat-Savarin's narrative bespoke, but it was seemingly bereft of any turkeys besides the shabby white domestic ones I saw caged six birds high on semi-trailers bound for processing plants. Such a disappointment. Some of my students at the school claimed to have shot wild turkeys, and local newspaper articles reported flocks in all counties of Oklahoma. But I never saw one.

Friends and students brought me other delicacies from our Oklahoma woods: deer meat, ducks, wild onions, a spinach-like weed called cochanny eaten by local Cherokees, big plastic bags stuffed with morel mushrooms, and, once, a brace of skinned partridges with their red-feathered heads left on them for identification. These last I simmered all day long for broth, thinking them likely too tough to roast. They filled the air of the house with an intense bird smell, like the most wonderful chicken soup you could ever imagine, and when the girls got home from school they wanted to have the broth then and there as their after-school snack. But I fought them and served the partridges up as a simple fricassee: the silky meat in a sauce of the fragrant broth thickened with flour and lightly enhanced with a little sherry. Old people will tell you chickens used to taste completely different than they do now—more flavorful, chickenier—and I think the way that partridge fricassee tasted must have been along the lines of what they mean. If someone ever brought me a wild turkey, I decided, I wouldn't roast it, as Brillat-Savarin did his. I would fricassee it just as I did those partridges.

Anyway, I don't remember how the subject of wild turkeys came up at school that day, but this fellow teacher of mine, Margaret, said, "Well, I've got a great big wild tom you can kill and eat, if you want to." Those were her words. Talk about having your fantasies put to the test.

So she brought the turkey to school the next Friday in a beat-up fiberglass dog carrier and left it in the shade by the bus barn until after school, when I could take him home. The plan was that I would slaughter and clean the bird the next day and then sometime after that roast it, and Margaret would come over and help eat it.

Roger, the school mechanic, looked after the turkey all day. He put water in its coffee can and made sure it didn't get too hot. When Margaret went to load the carrier in her pick-up, Roger reported that the turkey had drunk a lot and was feeling good. He told Margaret he wanted a bite of him when I got him cooked. Margaret followed me home, and when we got there, I got my first good glimpse of the turkey. He was pink-faced and bedraggled-looking. His enormous, bluish-pink, featherless breast almost touched the dog carrier's carpet between the turkey's wide-set, scaly grey legs. A knobbly, blood-colored wattle spilled down to one side of his grey beak, which was wide and ridged as a thumbnail. His eyes were yellow and glittered with motion.

Margaret told me he had rubbed his front feathers off on the wire of his pen because some neighbor children out by her house had taunted him. He didn't like children, she warned me.

"He'll flog your little girls if you let him out," she said.

I wasn't sure what "flog" meant but got the idea that he'd throw himself at them if he got the chance. He looked about their size. We dragged the carrier out under the dogwood at my mother-in-law's house down the road because I thought our dogs wouldn't heckle him there as they would at my house. I couldn't imagine how Margaret had gotten him loaded all by herself; he weighed at least thirty pounds. Then Margaret left.

The turkey eyed me with what seemed like rage through the wire door of the carrier as Margaret's old pick-up putted down the road. His wattle was now a violent red and sort of wet-looking. I sent Mamaw out under the dogwood to see the turkey without telling her anything beforehand, thinking it'd be a good gag, but she came back with an almost angry, set look on her face rather than surprise and barely paused to ask where it had come from before she launched into an afternoon-long narrative about all the turkeys Kris's dad used to win at shooting contests, sometimes six or eight of them at a time because he was such a good shot, and how he'd hang them from the wide lintel of the chicken house and slit their throats and let them bleed dry. Then he'd give them to her to dip in boiling water and pluck and singe the pinfeathers off of and then pressure cook because they were so tough. She called them gobblers.

"Law! I was never so glad as when they started giving out frozen birds to the winners," she told me.

Nevertheless, she offered to help me process the turkey if I could get someone else to kill it. That it was already half featherless was definitely a plus, but she wasn't enthusiastic. We discussed which old farmer neighbors—i.e. big strong men good at killing things—might help me out. She assumed my husband would help, too, but I knew better. Kris was what my high school students called a wuss when it came to messy or murderous projects. Mamaw and I discussed where we might get a pot big enough to dip the turkey in once we got it killed. We discussed paying to have it slaughtered.

When my daughters woke up from their naps, we went out to look at what they also called the gobbler. As soon as he saw them, he got really mad, stomping his foot in a strange syncopated rhythm by balancing himself on one foot for so long that it seemed as though he would fall over and then suddenly thumping his other foot down, hard, and jerking it back up again. The girls grabbed their Mamaw's legs. She commented dryly, "A gobbler'll do that when he's wanting to fight." It was a dimension of my mother-in-law with which I was not familiar: Mamaw, the gobbler expert.

Then the gobbler started making noises, not the gobblegobblegobble I expected but a loud, long garble, such as a person with Tourettes Syndrome or delirious with high fever or just about to wake up from the most terrifying part of a bad dream might make, a noise on the very verge of comprehensible, some dire communication—like war news—rendered incomprehensible and irretrievable by static. My daughters shrieked and ran off toward safety, but moments later they drew near again, and again the gobbler spoke, and again and again and again they screamed and ran.

This went on for days. I was right about Kris. He refused to have anything to do with the killing of the turkey. Neighbors who once had bragged of shooting downed cows and routinely hung dead coyotes on their fences were suddenly busy. It was the weekend, and none of the local slaughterhouses even answered their phones. I was all gung-ho to try killing the turkey myself, perhaps using the hang-it-up-and-slit-its-throat method, but I couldn't even allow myself to think about touching its red, foamy-looking neck. I tried not to think about the turkey at all.

By Sunday the girls were feeding him corn and watering him, studiously funneling water into his can with a thin-spouted plastic watering can of their Mamaw's and squealing when he banged his beak at the wire door. At dinner, Kris suggested taking the turkey to Cane Hill the next day to have him, as he put it, "worked up." At Cane Hill—off in Arkansas a ways, the site of a Civil War battle, Kris explained—was the processing outfit where our neighbors had the deer they shot made into burger meat. Evidently, Kris had been asking around. I kept imagining the Cane as Cain, as in Cain and Abel. As in, *What in the Cain Hill?!* But I was relieved to have a plan.

In class on Monday Margaret asked me about the turkey, and I said we were having him slaughtered that afternoon. I thought she'd be mad that I hadn't slaughtered him myself, as I had bragged I would, but she just seemed sad. I think she was missing that bird. When I asked her if she wanted him back, though, she said no. Emphatically.

Luckily, we called Cane Hill before we took the turkey all the way out there. They told us they didn't slaughter turkeys. They'd work up just about anything else—deer, ducks, squirrels, coons. Just not turkeys. "Specially if you got you a mad one," they said.

By then I was thinking about the turkey all the time, and at night I was dreaming about it, my hands on its thick, wet neck—trying to get a firm hold, trying to avoid its beak and claws, which looked metallic and grotesquely dangerous, like weaponry from the Middle Ages. Kris was worried about the turkey, too. He had not been in support of my project from the beginning, and now he just wanted it gone. I suggested he shoot it with the emergency shotgun we kept up in our closet—disassembled because I have a thing about guns. Then Mamaw and I would pluck it and dress it and I'd roast it. He wasn't in favor of shooting it.

"It's not like we're just going to kill it. We're going to eat it. And anyway, how's it any different from shooting a skunk?" I asked him. Although mild-mannered and peaceable by nature, reluctant to get even legitimately angry, Kris would go wild with that shotgun whenever a skunk got under our house, and once I saw him hack a snake to pieces on our kitchen floor with the edge of a shovel.

"It's different," was all he would tell me.

Finally, about two weeks later, we decided to let the bird go. We knew our dogs or maybe one of the neighbors' dogs would get him if we let him out on our farm. So, we decided to take him out to Lake Wedington, a man-made pond of warm, yellowish water in the middle of some ticky woods where we had taken the girls to swim a couple of times. Wedington is what passes for a park in these parts: It has a pay parking lot and a dirt road through it and a few picnic tables and grill pits dotting the perimeter. Supposedly, there were wild turkeys in the woods around the pond, and we thought the turkey might take up with them.

This was our plan: We would load the turkey in the back of the pickup, then drive along that dirt road until we found a remote enough looking spot to let him out. Then we'd drive off.

We hadn't reckoned with the terror the bird would cause us as we lifted the carrier up into the pickup bed. He shrieked and hammered with his feet, lurching the carrier from side to side like a cabbage in a shoebox. And all the while all I could think of were those silvery claws and that ridged beak, so near my hands. I was wearing thick leather work gloves, but still I figured he could snip off one of my fingers—as Mamaw had warned my daughters he could—if he was in the notion. And he seemed in the notion.

Finally we got him in the truck. Kris wouldn't talk, no matter how much I chitchatted to try and make him. He just stared grimly ahead of him at the road, which slowly changed from broad to narrow and finally to the dusty orange chert of Wedington Drive. I kept looking back at the turkey behind us, but all I could see was the back of his carrier.

We'll have to clean that thing somehow, I busied myself thinking. The carrier hadn't been cleaned out in two weeks, and its carpet was gooey with turkey droppings. The turkey himself was smeared with feces on his featherless breast and elbows. It was hard to imagine eating a bird as dirty as this, but I knew from having worked in the chicken houses when we were first married that birds—especially housed birds—are filthy. We grew our last flock the year I was pregnant with Charlotte, and it was a year or so after that before I could bring myself to eat chicken again.

Finally, Kris slowed the truck to a stop under the trees. I didn't know I had been crying until Kris said, "Stop." I had to breathe deeply to quit.

We climbed up in the pickup bed and dragged the carrier to the edge of the open tailgate. Then I got back in the cab and watched while, standing up in the pickup bed, Kris opened the carrier from behind to let the bird step out. I craned to see, but nothing happened. No sound. No movement. No angry thumping of the carrier. I waited five minutes or so, and then I got back out of the pickup and went around to the side to see what was wrong.

"He won't come out," Kris said. And then, when he saw I was crying again, "Stop it."

Finally we got on both sides of the carrier and lowered it to the ground and, after waiting for forever for the bird to see the trees and make a dash for it, we decided that that wasn't going to happen and we'd have to dump him through the carrier's opening to get him out. We'd drive off a ways, leaving the carrier in the road until he flew off, and then we'd turn around and come back, pick up the carrier, and go on home. Kris was in favor of just leaving the carrier there, but I was against it. I had to give it back to Margaret, I told him, but more than that I wanted to clean it out. Do some sort of penance for having taken him in the first place. I thought of Margaret seeming sad when I said I hadn't been able to slaughter him. Sad that he was gone from her. Sad that he wasn't dead. Sad that he was going to be.

Although he was now quiet, we were still wary of him. Any second I expected him to leap out and flog us both, leaving us mangled in the dust before flying off to join the other invisible turkeys in the woods. But he let us dump him and even gave us time to run back around to the cab doors and get in. As we started to drive away, he rotated slowly to watch us leave, and when he saw us slow down at the spot where we planned to watch him fly off, he came running toward us, dragging his pink breast in the dirt and flapping his wings excitedly.

Kris speeded up again, and the turkey followed us until the road curved around to where we couldn't see him anymore. I was sobbing by this time, and Kris was crying, too. We drove without saying anything for a long time, ten or fifteen minutes or longer, before we finally turned back around to go get the carrier.

As we rounded the bend, we saw him in the middle of the road, standing where we had seen him last, and when he saw us, he started running toward us again with his wings opened out as if in welcome. He ran fast, and we had to swerve out of the way to miss hitting him. Kris jumped out, grabbed the carrier, and threw it into the back of the truck. And we drove off in a burst of red dust, with me wailing and Kris yelling "Stop it!" and the turkey running after us with everything in him.

FRICASSEE OF FOWL

I learned to cook fricassees in Germany, where recipes typically include mushrooms or asparagus and recommend refining the sauce further with cream just before serving, but, except for maybe the mushrooms, I disagree. What you're after in a fricassee, in my opinion, is not refinement but the intense flavor of the bird, which can be anything from a chicken or turkey to pheasant or quail.

Cook the bird(s) whole, in water to cover, until tender. Remove to a platter—reserving the broth—and pick the meat from the bones in pieces as large as you can. Set aside. Combine and roast over medium heat until lightly golden:

3 to 4 tablespoons butter
an equal amount of flour

Add and stir with a whisk until smooth:

2–2 1/2 cups broth

Cook over medium flame, stirring occasionally, until thickened somewhat, but not too thick—about the consistency of heavy cream. You may need to add more broth to get it right. Season with salt and maybe a tablespoon—no more!—of sweet sherry. Add the meat and, if you like, sautéed mushrooms. Continue cooking until heated through. Serve with mashed or boiled potatoes.

22

Wild Fruit

I t is late summer in eastern Oklahoma: 91 degrees. 65 percent humidity. 40 percent chance of rain.

As usual during this season, I am in the middle of preserving a batch of wild fruit. Not because I am starving. Or because I am some sort of homemaking weirdo, eager to impress my friends with my culinary prowess. Or because I have nothing to do. I struggle mightily to fit the time-consuming tasks of picking and washing and preserving seasonal fruits between writing and teaching, getting my family ready for school and work, starting loads of clothes and dishes, making my romantic daughter Charlotte the bread that she told me she had dreamed about this morning, cooking dinner, and getting us all in bed by 10:00 so that my husband can get me up at 5:30 the next morning and start the whole process all over again.

I am not complaining. I do most of what I do—write, grade papers, bake my daughter's fantasies, wash the clothes, cook the dinner, and even wash up afterward—because I like to. And, although these responsibilities often pile up and become onerous, gathering and preserving fruit is not just another chore. It is my reward.

We are surrounded by fruit in this part of Oklahoma, and I pick and preserve whenever I can, all summer long and on into the fall. First the sour dewberries that grow in the ditch out by the road. Then domesticated blueberries from a farm across the state-line in Arkansas, where you pay less if you pick your own. Then blackberries from the overgrown former racetrack behind our house. Then wild plums from outside my neighbors' chicken houses. Then elderberries that I steal from a neighbor's neglected field out by the highway. Then crabapples from the ornamental trees at the university where I work. And so on as the weather turns colder and black walnuts fall from the trees in our woods and the bitter wild persimmons freeze and darken and become as sweet and soft as dates. All of these fruits accumulate in my consciousness throughout the summer and fall and winter, and it is no more of a chore to acquire them than to desire them in the first place. I gather and preserve fruit because it is the best thing I do all year long.

Berry-picking is my year's retreat—my "thin place," to use a Celtic Christian term from a book I'm reading for a place where one feels unusually aware of God's nearness. Every aspect of berry-picking has spiritual relevance for me. Nothing proves God's abundant love like the provision of huge blackberries among the brambles, arriving in such profusion that the birds and deer and June bugs and my family and friends and I combined can't begin to deplete them. Even our dogs—who, though not normally fruit-eaters, always accompany me berry-picking if they are around—hunger for the sweet black nuggets among the thorns and paw at the brambles for their share.

Nothing shows God's foresight like the shade of a tree that I share with nearby cows when I think I will faint from heat in the armor I am wearing against ticks and chiggers and thorns and sun: my jeans tucked into thick socks and boots, a long-sleeved turtleneck under a more thorn-resistant button-down shirt, tight rubber gloves, sweatband, hat. Nothing makes me as aware of the curse of toiling, or the threat of serpents at my heel, as thrusting my arm through the prickly branches for the same prize that the skinny green tree snake seeks, the same glistening berry, taut with sweetness. When I am picking berries, I am in communion with all creation and with God as at no other time. My daughters call me from the yard, their voices so far off and faint that they sound like birds, and I can't tell if it is the phone or their hunger or a visitor that is so urgent that I must be called away. Often I feign deafness and pick on until the bowl is too heavy and full to carry back home without leaving a black trail for any little animals that might scamper in my wake.

Today it is elderberries, from which I will make jelly. I picked them yesterday evening. The birds had gotten almost all the berries on the few bushes on our place, and I knew my neighbor wouldn't want the berries for himself. No one does. In his overgrown pasture, the elderberries hang in heavy, flat-bottomed bunches, bending down the slender branches to the tops of the tall grasses and thistle beneath. I waded through the high weeds, awkward in my husband's rubber boots, now and then popping a puffy, green wild apricot underfoot. They're not actually apricots, despite the name, but a local species of *Passiflora*, passion fruit—also called maypops—that grow on spiny vines and have a heady, passion-fruit flavor and smell when ripe. There are masses of wild apricots this year, more than I have ever noticed before. They, too, will go uneaten by my neighbor and anyone else who comes this way—except me, perhaps. I may try jam from them this year, since there are so many. They will be ready for harvest when they go soft and begin to shrivel up on the outside, probably in a few weeks, judging from the already powerful smell of the squashed ones.

Last night, after I got home from picking the elderberries, I rinsed them, clump by clump, in cold water and laid them out on an old sheet to dry. And this morning I spent an hour pulling the tiny black balls from their stems. If you have never seen elderberries, you need to know that they are among the most beautiful berries on earth and the most satisfying to collect. The bushes have no thorns, and each time you reach up to pick yields a satisfyingly heavy clump. Imagine a flat plate of small, black berries, each one lifted up on a tiny stem. Imagine Queen Anne's Lace with dark berries instead of little white blossoms. You will want to eat them, they are so beautiful, and you may do so, but their flavor is alarming. Not so much sour or even bitter, as they are often described, but bland and vaguely herbal. Like medicine of some sort—which, in fact, they have been used for, in times past. High in vitamins A, B6, and C as well as iron and potassium, they have been used throughout the centuries and around the world for treating everything from colds to burns and acne.

The berries are cooking now. Cooking, they gain a weirdly appealing smell of dirt and air and winy fruit, which is also how they taste if you spoon up bit of the hot juice. And the black-purple jelly I will make—once the juice has all dripped through a piece of cloth in which I will suspend the cooked berries from my pot rack and once I have added almost a whole bag of sugar and a lemon or two and cooked the mixture down until it drips in a sheet from a spoon—will taste like that, too: like earth and air and wine, only sweeter and more delectable. Like the outdoors. Like Oklahoma in late summer. Like the rain that is predicted and hangs in the air this moment and is visible in the sagging clouds but still hasn't come down.

Last week I attended a summer workshop for interested faculty at my non-denominational Christian university. We were learning about the shared doctrine of the various brands of Christianity we practice and believe in, the fundamentals our students learn in more detail in a required course called Essentials of Evangelical Christianity. As a relatively recent convert to Christianity, I take advantage of any available opportunities to learn more about my faith. Plus, we get paid to attend such faculty development workshops, which is nice. It's like being paid to gather blackberries.

Nevertheless, in class I was struggling to stay rapt. A friend's husband had dropped off a big bucket of goose plums: thumb-sized, bright red, startlingly sour fruits that make the best jelly in the world, better even than the red currant jelly the French make, if that's possible. And the elderberries, I knew, were coming ripe. What we were discussing in the workshop seemed obvious. The trinity. Creation. Redemption. And what we *didn't* discuss increasingly annoyed me. What exactly did we mean by "evangelical," I wanted to know, but no one had a clear answer. And if everything was all so obvious from the Bible or creation or any other source reputed to testify authoritatively to one benevolent God and an existence beyond the one we know now, why couldn't even those who called themselves Christians agree on what any of it meant for us in our day-to-day lives?

I have always struggled with the problem of denominational differences. We are, after all, supposed to have been created in God's own image. Shouldn't that mean we know what we're about?

The workshop leader read from Genesis:

God made the wild animals according to their kinds, the livestock according to their kinds, and all the creatures that move along the ground according to their kinds. And God saw that it was good.

Then God said, "Let us make man in our image, in our likeness, and let them rule over the fish of the sea and the birds of the air, over the livestock, over all the earth, and over all the creatures that move along the ground."

> So God created man in his own image,
> in the image of God
> he created him;
> male and female
> he created them. (Genesis 1:25-27 NIV)

Then the workshop leader listed on the whiteboard some ways in which we are like God and unlike other animals and solicited more examples.

"We like order," someone said. "We love," someone else added. Everyone had something to say. We steward. We work. We rest. We tell stories.

We ran out of room on the whiteboard before I could offer my revelation. Here it is. Just as God combined parts of his creation—lights and dark sky, dirt and breath—to make other things, we also combine things—berries and sugar and lemons and heat—to make other things and pronounce them good. We don't just graze, like cattle. We plant and till and fertilize and harvest the plants we eat, and then sort and grind and prepare them further, often in mixtures or using heat to make them taste different. We don't simply kill and devour the animals we eat, as my dogs do. We slaughter them, remove their skin or feathers, and roast or boil or sauté them. We make sauces for them from grains and liquids and combine them with vegetables. In short, we cook.

From the earliest chapters of human history, we have not only gathered and hunted but combined what we amassed of God's creation with other wonderful creations—salt, honey, fragrant greens, clean dry air, fire—and made our own, admittedly lesser, creations. We cooked before cookbooks. And before civilization as we know it now. Before we knew we were cooking but were only mindlessly mimicking the divine impulse to create something new and good. Cooking, for me, is the emulation of the deity's most essential habit: to create. As such, to cook is to worship.

Most of the cooking we do these days begins in medias res. Recipes don't start with raising and slaughtering animals or with harvesting and grinding our flour but with packaged meat, prepared grains, and fruits and vegetables that have been grown and picked and often partially or entirely cooked or preserved before we ever see them. The only part left of the creative act is the combining and pronouncing good, and more and more people leave even those opportunities for worship to restaurants and underpaid factory workers they will never meet.

Gathering and preserving wild fruit, for me, is to share, in the most elemental way, in what it means to be human, made in the image of God, guardians of earth and sea and sky, male and female, alive. God's creation—the berries themselves, the creatures that I share them with, the shade, the minute breeze I wouldn't have noticed if I were not picking berries—humbles me in comparison to my own, however heavenly the smell that wafts through the house as my elderberry jelly cooks down in its pan. To participate in the created world in this way, and to give the little jars of sweetness to the people I love, seems to me the greatest blessing I can expect in this world or the next.

JELLY

Jelly, as opposed to jam, uses only the juice of the fruit, not the fruit itself. It is transparent and seedless and can be made from any kind of fruit. All jelly is made about the same way. I never use pectin, as all fruits have their own, though in varying degrees. There's nothing wrong with using pectin, however, and it is more foolproof to do so. If you want to use it, just buy the little box of Sure-Jell and follow the directions for your type of fruit. The recipe here is for jelly made without commercial pectin. Generally speaking, the sourer a fruit is, the more pectin it has, and unripe fruit—which is sour—has more pectin than ripe fruit. If you pick some of the unripe fruit with the ripe and cook the juice with sugar long enough, it will generally jell. If a fruit is relatively low in natural pectin—as are, for example, late-season blackberries—I sometimes add lemon juice or a little bit of high-pectin fruit, such as an unpeeled sour apple. If the jelly is still liquid after it cools in the jar, either use it as pancake syrup or else dump it back in the pot, add some lemon juice (or if you're worried, a tablespoon of powdered pectin cooked with 1/4 cup each of sugar and water) and boil it again briefly—no more than a minute—then jar.

The jellies I make are blackberry, elderberry, wild plum, crabapple, apple, pear, peach, raspberry, quince, wild grapes, chokecherries, and combinations of these. Wild plum and crabapple are my favorites, either alone or together. You can add mint or jalapeños to crabapple, apple, quince, or pear to make mint or jalapeño jelly, both of which are fine creations. Mint jelly goes, of course, with roast lamb, although I prefer sweet-sour British mint sauce: vinegar boiled with some sugar and lots of chopped mint. Jalapeño jelly goes with any white cheese—Jack, farmer, Mexican white cheeses, Brie, and even cream cheese—and water biscuits as a perfect appetizer, party food, after-school snack, or dessert.

Wash and either mash slightly or cut up and remove large pits (do not core or peel) and put in a large pot:

> **any amount of fruit,** including some unripe fruit, if possible

Add:

> **just enough water to keep it from burning and cook the fruit** (For berries and other juicy fruit, this is almost none; for apples and other hard fruit, add enough to see the water through the top layer of fruit.)
>
> **the juice of a lemon**—if the fruit is very ripe or very sweet or known to be low in pectin

Bring the fruit and water to a boil, cover, and let it cook on low until the house smells good and the fruit has collapsed into a juicy mush. Strain the mixture through a thin, clean piece of cloth suspended above a big bowl for about a day. Do not squeeze. (With crabapples, apples, peaches, and plums, I run the leftover fruit mush through a food mill and sweeten it to make a filling for little baked turnovers.)

Cook the resulting juice in small batches of 4 to 6 cups in a large pot over a medium flame with the same amount of sugar until just past when the mixture drops from a spoon in two drips and begins to drop off in a clump or sheet (about 220° F). Be careful not to overcook—jelly should be soft and spreadable—or let the mixture boil over. If it threatens to do so, stir it down or, if necessary, reduce the heat slightly.

While the jelly is cooking, boil small, clean jars—enough to hold about one and a half times the total amount of juice you started with—in water to cover in a big pot and keep them at a simmer until you are ready to fill them. (I reuse pretty jars that food comes in and their lids and never have any trouble, but you can also buy small canning jars and two-part lids. I recommend small jars because it takes a while to go through a jar of jelly and smaller jars keep it fresher. Also, the jelly in the pot is easier to divvy up into smaller jars, and there are ultimately more jars to give away.)

When the jelly is ready to jar, remove a few of the jars from the hot water with tongs, shake out any water, and set them on a towel near the stove. Using a metal measuring cup and a funnel, fill the jars one by one to within 1/2 inch of the top edge. If you accidentally spill jelly on the rim, clean it with a clean towel dipped in the boiling jar water. Screw the lid on tightly and set the hot jar safely out of the way to cool. Later on, as you are filling the rest of the jars and cleaning up, you will hear the jar seal itself with a little popping noise. Repeat until you have used up the jelly in the pot. Label the jelly with its type and date when it's cool and store the jars in a dark cupboard. Don't forget to give some of it away: It makes a great Christmas gift.

JAM

Jam is the same as jelly but contains not just the juice but particles of the fruit itself. It will require that you core and slice or chop larger fruits. For berries, just rinse them lightly, put them in a pot, and crush a few to get the juice running. If you want to remove tiny seeds from fruits such as blackberries, cook them first as you would for jelly; then use a food mill of some sort or a spoon against a heavy-duty sieve. You lose the shape of the berry doing this, which my daughter Lulu objects to, but some people, especially people with dentures, are really bothered by little seeds.

When you have prepared the fruit the way you want it, bring it to a boil in a covered pot—adding the tiniest bit of water if the fruit is rather dry at first—and cook till soft. Add the same amount (measure what your pot holds and then eyeball it) of sugar, all at once. Jelling is not as critical with jam as with jelly, since the fruit itself provides some bulk. Dropping the jam off a spoon also won't work as well as it does for jelly, so use a thermometer and go for a lower jelling temperature of 217° to 219° F. Again, you want a soft, smearable jam. Jar the jam as for jelly.

You can make any fruit into jam. A New Orleans friend recently told me there was a small fruit that grew on neighborhood trees there that the kids all eat, and, when I lived there I collected it and made it into jam. I don't remember this fruit or this jam in particular, but it seems to me I have done this everywhere I have lived. If the fruit can be eaten, it can be preserved. Here are some specifics for different jams I especially like.

Apricot Jam

My favorite jam. Include some hard, barely ripe apricots. Quarter or halve the fruit. Some people would call this recipe "preserves" because the fruit is left relatively large. For an interesting, almondy back-flavor, add two or three kernels from the apricot seeds per jar as you fill them. Use a hammer or a big rock on a concrete surface, such as a porch, to get the kernels out. This recipe also works for peach jam, but you'll want to slice the fruit.

Chokecherry Jam

Chokecherries are wild tree fruits that grow all over the U.S. They are bitter and mostly seed but make an intriguingly herbaceous-tasting black jam. Cook them first and use a sturdy food mill to get the little pits out. Or make jelly and forget about the pits. This recipe also works for grapes.

Plum Jam

Most store-bought plums make luscious jam. Coarsely cut up the fruit or crush it as it cooks. Plums—both wild and domesticated—have tons of pectin, so don't even think about adding any. So pretty. Plum jam must be eaten with biscuits.

23

Lost Recipes

The other day a friend told me the story of an unmarried aunt known in the family for her plum dumplings. My friend went into a rhapsody of description here, trying in vain to recreate in my imagination a wondrous taste made from ingredients utterly unknown to her. The dumpling dough was chewy and bland, but the plums exploded with a surprising sweetness when you bit into them. When the aunt died, the women in the family went through every cupboard in her bleak kitchen searching for the recipe, but they never found it. Evidently, the aunt had made the dumplings from memory, the recipe printed there in that most indelible of inks, a dusky mixture of love and duty and dedication to what is beautiful and satisfying.

The aunt probably had the recipe from someone else—her mother or grandmother, perhaps, or an unmarried aunt of her own who, in an earlier time, likely would have been a more integral part of her household than she was in the lives of her nieces and nephews. She had watched this woman mix and roll the dough, spice the poaching water, slit and squeeze the pits from a dozen black plums, and press a sugar cube into each hollow. She took note as the wrinkled hands pinched pockets of dough around the fruit, dropped the finished dumplings into the roiling water, then scooped them back out again when they floated to the top. Finally, after a childhood of watching, my friend's aunt repeated what she had seen, taking on the rhythm of the craft herself. According to habit and her own peculiar longings, she practiced and probably changed the recipe, perfected it, made it hers. In any case, my friend's aunt never found it necessary to write the recipe down, and her special dumplings were lost forever.

Another friend remembers another aunt's cinnamon cake, how it had always sat in the same place in the front window when the family came to visit. On a certain plate. With a paper doily underneath it. All the cousins remembered this cake, but when she died, there was no recipe.

"One of the cousins thinks she has recreated it," my friend told me, "but I've never tried her recipe, the one she thinks comes close." I didn't ask her why not. I know the answer, I think.

This is, to me, the quintessential women's story. A story that I have never heard a man tell but that women tell so often that it fills regular columns in newspapers and sections of women's magazines. There are databases on the Web entirely devoted to our wistful attempts to locate lost recipes. More than that, for women, this story is burdened with significance—longing and belonging, giving and losing, and a deep consciousness of the honor due, but not often granted, to both the living and the dead. For men, I'm guessing, the story is empty. Plotless. Passionless. Trivial. A woman makes dumplings and then dies. So what?

I have lost more recipes than I can remember. Recipes my befuddled mother made back in the sixties, before I took over the cooking. Her sagey chicken and dressing. Her chipped beef on toast. Her particular take on tamale pie—a sad mixture of ground beef and cornmeal mush into which she sank tamales that came paper-wrapped in a can. Her Chicken à la King, flecked with pimiento, that my siblings and I so hated. I wonder about these specialties I lost with her. How did she come to make them? Do they represent phases of her life, as my recipes do mine? Her impoverished childhood? Her unhappy years in the Air Force. Her rise to suburban comfort and wrathful motherhood. I can find myriad versions of each of her dishes in old cookbooks and on the Internet, but I can never recreate from these recipes exactly the taste, exactly the smell, exactly the texture from those days.

I have lost the chewy biscuits my mother's mother made when my mother and sisters and I took the train to Arkansas to visit her, although I can still see in my mind the angry-looking arm-thrusts into the tough yellow dough. I have lost the porcupines that Ruthie, our occasional babysitter, made for us back in the cul-de-sac days of my childhood. She was a career babysitter, sitting for someone in our neighborhood every night of the week. I remember nothing else of Ruthie—not her last name, not her face or even whether she was nice or mean—nothing but those rice-prickled meatballs in a sweet tomatoey sauce, a certain bulk to her shadowy form—a heavy, pale upper arm. Charlotte and Lulu enjoy my attempts to recreate this child delicacy using a recipe from an older edition of the *Joy of Cooking*. (The recipe in newer editions is way off.) Nevertheless, these porcupines are not the same. The rice softens too much in the sauce to look like porcupines, and, well, they just don't taste right.

I have even lost the recipes for foods I made myself over and over again as a child from yellowed index cards that disappeared after my father remarried. A wonderfully dense, sour cream pound cake flavored with cardamom that was called Swedish Pepparkaka. The only versions I can find now have other spices, too—ginger, cinnamon, cloves—but the cake I used to make, if my memory obtains, tasted nothing like an ordinary American spice cake at all. I made those, too, and iced them with brown sugar frosting—another recipe lost. But the Pepparkaka we ate plain, in brown-edged slices, with big glasses of frothy skim milk from the blue-lidded plastic carton in which my mom mixed it.

My mother used to praise my cooking and say I needed to enter the Pillsbury Bake-Off Contest and win $50,000, and I remember paging through magazines looking at the winning recipes from previous years, trying to figure out if anything I might invent was likely to impress the judges. In one such magazine there was a recipe for cream cheese cookies made mille-feuille style. You rolled out an almond-flavored yeast dough, folded it over thick pads of cream cheese and butter, then rolled and folded it again and again until it was flaky. After I rolled in all the cheese and butter, I sliced the dough into narrow bars. They baked up blistery pale and golden around the edges, and my dad said they were the best cookies he had ever eaten. This recipe has passed from existence. Although the Bake-Off is still going strong almost forty years later and I have searched every Pillsbury recipe repository there is, it is as though I dreamed this recipe. My attempts to recreate its exact sweetness and consistency from hunches have all failed. Sometimes I dream that I dreamed these cookies, but I know they were real. I remember taking a bite from one still too hot from the oven to hold and dropping it on the vinyl floor, then snatching it up, checking to see if my mother was watching, and biting into the soft, barely sweet, flaky wafer again.

I even feel I've lost recipes I've never had, but only read about. The raisin cake that the fatherless Pepper children bake—and accidentally singe in their cracked stove—to surprise their mother in *The Five Little Peppers and How They Grew*. The sun-cooked coconut fish from the sex scene in *Hawaii*. Recently I reread my *Lost Souls* from college, an irritating shaggy dog of a novel full of irritatingly stupid characters, just to find Gogol's description, near the end, of an elaborate fish pie that one of Chichikov's many duped hosts, Petukh, orders for him:

"Make a four-cornered fish pie," he was saying, smacking his lips and sucking in his breath. "In one corner put a sturgeon's cheeks and dried spinal cord, in another put buck-wheat porridge, little mushrooms, onions, soft roes, and brains and something else—you know, something nice. . . . And see that the crust on one side is well browned and a little less done on the other. And make sure the under part is baked to a turn, so that it's all soaked in juice, so well done that the whole of it, you see, is—I mean, I don't want it to crumble but melt in the mouth like snow, so that one shouldn't even feel it—feel it melting." As he said this Petukh smacked and sucked his lips.

The pie ingredients go on and on. Beetroot cut into little stars. Turnips. Kidney beans. A monster of a pie, it must have been. A monstrosity. But in the twenty-five years of my imagination's memory it is a delicacy as much a part of my identity as if I had eaten it myself, in some far away past, when I was a traveler and alone, like Chichikov, enjoying the bounty of a stranger's hospitality.

Here is a fantasy I have. Remember when that prehistoric iceman was discovered in the Tyrolean Alps, frozen in the snow? With his five-thousand-year-old quiver and arrows and leather shoes and woven grass cape, his prehistoric hair and tattooed skin and inner organs, even the dying expression on his face, all intact? In my fantasy, the iceman has with him—in addition to the berries, mushrooms, and gnawed bones found in his birch backpack—a clay pot or a tanned pig's bladder or a leaf-lined basket full of cooked food, a stew perhaps, or wild grains boiled with herbs, to be reheated over a small fire he would make along the way. I imagine the dish was made for the journey by his wife or mother or lover, someone who told him, "God speed you on your way." Someone who intended this provision not only to warm and nourish him but to remind him that he was loved.

Scientists believe the iceman died as the result of an arrow wound, that he had fought for his life and was perhaps in flight from enemies rather than on a planned journey, so it may be there was no time for someone who loved him to make him a proper meal for the trip. By examining the dead man's teeth—the "archives of childhood," as one report I read called them—researchers posit other particulars of his life: in what valley he had lived (whether in current day Austria or Italy has been a crucial question for those laying claim to the cadaver), what he ate, and how it was prepared. Tooth enamel records for eternity the chemical makeup of the dirt one's vegetables were grown in and the water one drinks.

From the contents of the iceman's stomach, scientists know precisely what he had eaten before he left home—wheat bread, a green leafy vegetable, and ibex meat. But in my fantasy—by some miracle no less wonderful than that which preserved his flesh for over five thousand years, no less amazing than the forensic science that offers us these details of his history—an actual stew survives, frozen for 5,300 years, a mystery of forgotten spices, culinary habits of a simpler time, and animal breeds and vegetables now long extinct, all preserved into our present. And in my fantasy, I am permitted to taste that stew and experience flavors that predate not only my time and culture but the recording of history itself, the only preventative to forgetting.

What would it be? Bland? Fetid? Spicy? Familiar? Strange?

Would it call up some forgotten dish of my own childhood, a dish from the iceman's incredible future and my own irretrievable past? The answer, more than any lost recipe for some remembered delicacy, is what captivates me, captivates all of us, in looking backward, toward a beginning we can only narrate through the meager ingredients of our own experience. I crave it. That past. The past of my past. The past of my past of my past. How it formed me. Fed me. Made me who I am.

Apricot or Plum Dumplings

Once, when I was visiting my friend Susanne in Berlin, her mother was also visiting and made apricot dumplings for us all, rolling them in butter and sugar afterwards. She said they could be also be made with plums. This, then, is her recipe. Sort of. Actually, when I called to get the recipe, Susanne only wanted to give me her own version, which she said is based on her mother's recipe but better. After some wheedling, she eventually also detailed what she said was the version her mother had made that time. All this off the cuff, mind you, and the recipe I really wanted was, as I have said, extorted. Both recipes are good, but neither tastes exactly as I remember it.

Susanne's Mom's Dumplings

Wash apricots or plums and allow them to air-dry as you make the dough. Into 2 cups of boiling water seasoned with salt and a little butter, whisk enough "instant flour" that it clumps together into a dough. (Instant flour—a common American brand name is Wondra—is flour specially formulated to mix into hot sauces without making lumps. If you can't find it, use regular flour, but add it very slowly and whisk all the while.) Scoop up a bit of the warm dough and squish it around one of the whole fruits, pinching it to enclose it entirely. Do this until you use up the dough (or the fruit). Lay the dumplings on a greased plate as you work. When all the dumplings are ready to cook, drop them into boiling water. They will sink at first. When they rise to the top, they are done. Roll them around in a pan full of butter and serve, along with a sugar bowl. Those dining sprinkle lots of sugar on the buttery dumplings. This recipe for dumplings requires you to spit out the pits as you eat.

Susanne's Dumplings

Combine and knead to make a soft dough:

2 pounds potatoes, cooked in their skins and then peeled and riced or finely
  grated while still hot
1/2 cup flour
1/2 cup cream of wheat
1 egg

To prepare the fruits, remove the pits—but try not to otherwise mangle the
fruit—and replace each pit with a sugar cube. As soon as you get one apricot or
plum assembled, enclose it, as in Susanne's mom's recipe, with some of the dough
and cook the same way. Susanne roasts finely chopped hazelnuts in a pan until just
fragrant and rolls the cooked dumplings first in the hazelnuts, then in butter.
Provide a sugar bowl so diners can sugar their own dumplings at the table.

PORCUPINES

From the 1953 edition of The Joy of Cooking, *with slight alterations that get you close.*

Combine well with your hand and then form into walnut-sized balls:

1 pound ground beef
1/2 cup bread crumbs
1 egg
1/2 cup onion, minced
3/4 teaspoon salt
1 teaspoon paprika
1/4 cup green or sweet red pepper, minced

Roll balls in:

1/2 cup long-grain rice

Bring to a boil:

1 can tomato soup
21/2 cups water
1/2 onion, cut in large slivers

Lay the rice-coated meatballs on top of the onions, cover the pot, and simmer
for 30 minutes.

SWEDISH PEPPARKAKA

A guess that tastes good.

Preheat oven to 350°. Butter and flour two narrow loaf pans or a Bundt pan. Combine and set aside:

12/3 cups flour
1 tablespoon cardamom
2 teaspoons baking powder
a pinch of salt

Melt in a small container in the microwave or on the stove, then cool completely:

1/2 cup butter

Add and combine well:

11/2 cups sugar

Add, one at a time, beating the mixture afterwards until it is fluffy and light-colored and the sugar loses its grittiness against the bowl—i.e., a long time (at least five minutes):

3 eggs

Beat in, on low, in three parts:

1 cup sour cream
the flour mixture

Put the batter in cake pan(s), heaping it in the middle a little. Bake for about an hour or until brown. Ideally, the pepparkaka should have a pretty yellow crack down the highest point. Cool in the pan(s) for 5 or 10 minutes before removing and cooling entirely on a cake rack.

ALMOND-FLAVORED CREAM CHEESE MILLE-FEUILLE COOKIES

Possibly a Pillsbury Bake-Off prizewinner. If you know where I can find this recipe, contact me through my Web site—www.amateurbeliever.com—and let me know!

SUN-COOKED COCONUT FISH FROM MICHENER'S *HAWAII*

I haven't tried this, although I've always wanted to. I think you need to be in Hawaii, though. If you are in Hawaii and would like to try, read Michener's book. The directions—like the sex scene itself—are fairly explicit. Or order it in a restaurant; it's called, I believe, poke.

RUSSIAN FISH PIE *(Coulibiac)*

To make the police chief's amazing pie, read Lost Souls, *then look for a recipe for coubiliac in a Russian cookbook or on the Web and substitute the main ingredients Gogol describes. Just shopping for this pie will take days.*

24

Thou Mayest Freely Eat

If you've ever gone to hear an astronaut speak or watched a TV show about the Space Shuttle or the International Space Station or visited a space museum or any of the many Internet sites devoted to the space program, then you've probably noticed that a lot of attention is paid to the subject of food. People have questions.

"What was the food like in space?" they ask the astronaut or the FAQ section.

"How do you prepare it? How do you eat it? Where does all the trash go? What was your favorite space meal? What foods did you miss the most?"

The answers are usually cheery enough, always including humorous descriptions of how the eater manages to hang onto the food without gravity or anchor it to a plate or utensil. In movies like *Apollo 13* and those strange little videos the astronauts themselves beam back from space to eager viewers down here, we watch the astronauts fumble around with little blobs of floating Tang and "gobble" M&Ms "out of the air like a goldfish," as one Web site puts it. The more scientific sources tell of freeze-dried foods in space-age containers, with a one-way valve for adding water and then another for extracting the resulting pulp from the other end. Even shaking things up in zero gravity requires special techniques, and astronauts demonstrate the arm-flapping method of making sure the liquid and the powder in the packet actually combine. The engineers who design space food have learned to coat cubes of food in gelatin so that crumbs can't get loose and gum up the instruments, and they build trash receptacles underneath the living quarters to keep from messing up space for future space travelers. They brag that their state-of-the-art technology has led to the creation of food service machines now publicly ubiquitous.

Underneath all the merry hype, though, is a sad sad story about life up there. The food comes either canned or in horrid little plastic packets with tubes on the side for sucking through, looking for all the world like the bags used in hospitals for removing waste from sick people. Utensils have Velcro and bungee cords to keep them from floating off. One does not want to think about the smell resulting from those floating drips that end up on the walls and everyone's clothes and bodies and from the weeks, sometimes months, of inescapable trash stored beneath the astronauts' cabin.

Despite those special engineers' best and surely highly paid efforts to ensure, as a NASA site touts, the "quality of the eating experience" while attending to the "nutritional needs, mood and tone of space station crew members," the bleak truth is revealed in the pictures that accompany the text. Grown men groping to retrieve their peanut butter sandwiches. Diners sucking instead of chewing. Frighteningly inedible-looking chunks of unidentifiable, vacuum packed "dinner." When you get right down to it, good food, surely our most fundamental earthly pleasure, is dependent on gravity and solidness to the teeth, on ordinary kitchens and simple homely tools made of clay and metal and glass. Eating well depends on the very dirt from which we derive our food and make our dishes and into which we eliminate our waste. Try as we may, we will never reproduce an enjoyable eating experience in weightlessness or cramped, instrument-laden quarters or even flight. Home cooking is about, well, home: not floating and fleeing but belonging and returning. Good food is about coming to rest.

Astronaut Donald Pettit, writing about his impending return home after an overlong stay aboard the International Space Station that was extended because of the Columbia disaster, reports that he was allowed to take three small items back home with him. He rejected the things he had brought with him for just this purpose—"combination pocket tools . . . engraved with (his) boys' names" that he had used in space and his wife's favorite necklace that, he says, he took with him as a knight going into battle might take along his ladylove's handkerchief.

Instead, he writes, "I have decided to bring my spoons. I have three Russian-made spoons." He then describes his spoons in almost amorous detail, remarking that they are "unpretentiously stamped from stainless steel" and that "their gracefully long handles . . . allow one to gracefully shovel in dinner from deep plastic food pouches without getting your fingers all stickey-gooey with the stuff you are attempting to eat." The spoons have a hole in one end "for attaching a string so they won't float away"—because "in space," Mr. Pettit tells us, "it is not good to lose your spoon." Nevertheless, "eating with strings" is so awkward that the astronauts take their chances and let them float.

"They will make great camping spoons," Don Pettit goes on. And then—to conclude his brief, six paragraph Space Chronicle #19, in which he has used the word *home* no fewer than fifteen times—he pictures himself and his boys with the spoons, "sitting around the campfire, eating beans out of the fire-charred can they were cooked in. As we chat about our world, our eyes will follow the sparks as they rise in the draft of hot air. Perhaps we will look at the stars and see Space Station pass overhead."

Baked beans from a can: soft, overcooked navy beans swimming in a dark sweet sauce. My daughters favor these beans, too—even over my mother-in-law's home-made baked beans. They demand that I buy not the tangy or oniony or vegetarian variety of Bush's beans but the kind that say, with the frank enthusiasm for all things sweet that Charlotte and Lulu share, "extra brown sugar." Beans in syrup, essentially—just like those field peas with molasses that Faulkner's Joe Christmas steals from a stranger's kitchen table back in the days before the advent of refrigeration and Saran wrap and processed foods in handy packages that a starving fugitive might snatch up these days. Even the act of stealing food nowadays is hard to imagine. Someone so hungry and unloved that he has to break into a house to feed himself. Someone so fortunate that, in his hunger and loneliness, he finds good food on the table in that darkened room. Sugary peas, comfortably room temperature. In a pretty bowl in my imagination and probably covered with a tea towel to keep out flies. This delicacy, I remind myself, is what my daughters are after when they want me to buy the sweetest beans. And it is what Don Pettit, surely frightened and lonely, as far from this world as a person can be, envisions sharing with his family at fireside.

For Don Pettit, temporarily deprived of all the comforts of home—his little boys, his wife's kisses, his routine, and even, in the aftermath of his colleagues' tragic deaths, much of the glory one might expect a space traveler to enjoy—it is none of these things he craves. He craves baked beans charring over a campfire, just as Jesus, resurrected from the grave and wherever else he may have gone in that mysterious three-day interlude, upon returning to earth wants, before any-thing else, some of that broiled fish his friends are eating.

I like to imagine Jesus eating that fish. Enjoying it deeply, as my mother, near death, enjoyed the taco my sister raised to her lips. Perhaps thinking to himself—with relief, with a lingering hunger for all that is good in this world, with the pure happy pleasure of recognition—the very words my mother said aloud on that day, "Good food, finally."

Remembering that moment or reflecting on the sketchy details of Jesus' bodily return to our world or reading Don Pettit's fantasy about eating campfire beans with his boys fills me with gratitude and hunger for what I have every day. It fills me with, if you will allow me that overused word, awe. Good plain food, lovingly prepared, it seems to me, is God's most essential gift to us. Minus love and the earth itself, we can never reproduce anything like the pleasure of a pot of chicken and dumplings bubbling on the stove. Or a salad of arugula and sweet onion dressed with a few drops of sesame oil and seasoned rice vinegar. Or a jagged slice of sourdough bread still warm from the oven and a little saucer of good green olive oil with coarse salt and pepper.

Good food is an essence connected more completely with who we are than any relationship or product of our own devising. Some of God's first words to his human children are about this truth. He made the waters and the dry land and the grasses and trees and animals, pronounced them very good, and, like an excited cook, presented them to the man and the woman as though they were his most esteemed guests.

"Behold," he said in the big generous language of the King James, "I have given you every herb bearing seed, which is upon the face of all the earth, and every tree, in which is the fruit of a tree yielding seed; to you it shall be for meat" (Genesis 1:29 KJV). Of all this, he told them—he tells us—"thou mayest freely eat" (Genesis 2:16 KJV). But, like Eve, we lose sight of that message and become preoccupied with the one poisonous item we are told we may *not* eat, and the best foods we could ever know become things of the past, sharp childhood memories of dishes for which the recipe is lost or forgotten or the loving preparer no longer living. Artifacts of grief and longing, of fantasy and despair, of barely remembered gratitude, of loss, of hope.

"Behold, I stand at the door and knock," God's son tells us (Revelation 3:20 KJV). And those of us who hear his voice and open the door will sup with him. What wine, what chewy bread, what sauced dishes and bright salads, await us on that table? Delicious and satisfying, all of it. I am sure of that. Good food. Finally.

MAMAW'S HOMEMADE BAKED BEANS

Mamaw's beans are from a recipe given to her by her sister Edna, who died long before I ever met Kris. Edna was, I think, Mamaw's favorite sister: not picky, never judgmental of others, and, as Mamaw says, "just one of the nicest and most understanding people" and "the best sister anyone could have." Edna had had polio in her childhood and walked with a limp. She was a fabulous cook and often rooted up recipes for Mamaw to try out. Her recipes often came, as this one, with tacked-on explanations of how she had changed the recipe she began with. The originally East Coast recipe Edna began with has evolved further in Mamaw's Oklahoma kitchen. The beans that appear on Mamaw's table on wintry days are spicier and drier and much less sweet than any baked beans I have tasted. Although they bake for six hours, they never taste cooked enough to me. I think it may be because she cooks them in an immense, flat casserole dish instead of a smaller, deeper bean pot. I have never told Mamaw this, for fear of offending her. And also because I like her beans just as she makes them, somehow: spicy, dry, and slightly hard.

Combine, laying pork on top:

1 pound small white beans, dry, unsoaked

6 cups water

1/2 cup ketchup

1/2 cup brown sugar

2 teaspoons salt

1 teaspoon dry mustard

1/4 teaspoon pepper

1 pound lean salt pork

1 onion, chopped

1 tablespoon Worcestershire sauce

Put in a heavy, covered baking dish. Bake 300° for 8 hours.

Edna's amendments:

1. *I use 1/3 lb. bacon instead of salt pork.*
2. *2 rather large onions*
3. *I also soak beans overnight and cook 6 hours.*
4. *5 hours if to freeze.*
5. *Then thaw and heat at 350° until bubbly.*
6. *May need to add more water.*
7. *I put bacon (or salt pork) in beans. Not on top.*

References

Chapter One: Good Food, Finally

Arjun Appadurai. "How to Make a National Cuisine: Cookbooks in Contemporary India." *Comparative Studies in Society and History* 30 (1): 3-24. 1988.

The Bible: Genesis 1 (creation story) and Numbers 11:4-6 (Israelites longing for cucumbers and onions).

In Memory's Kitchen: A Legacy from the Women of Terezin. Ed. Cara de Silva. Tr. by Bianca Steiner Brown. NY: Jason Aronson, 1996.

Chapter Two: Sucking on Steak

"Bless Us, Oh Lord." In Latin, "*Benedic, Domine.*" Traditional Catholic prayer. Circa 8th century.

Benjamin Spock. *The Common Sense Book of Baby and Child Care.* 1946.

Chapter Five: The History of California

The Bible: Genesis 29 (Jacob's years of toil in exchange for his wives).

Mary B. Ballou. Letter to son Selden, October 30, 1852. *"I Hear the Hogs in My Kitchen": A Woman's View of the Gold Rush.* Ed. Archibald Hanna. New Haven: Yale UP, 1962. Reprinted in *Let Them Speak For Themselves: Women in the American West, 1849–1900.* Christiane Fischer, ed. New York: Dutton, 1977. 42–46.

Mrs. James Caples. "Overland Journey to California [in 1848]." 1911. California State Library, Sacramento.

Harry Kelsey. *Juan Rodriguez Cabrillo*. San Marino: Huntington Library, 1986.

Jo Ann Levy. *They Saw the Elephant: Women in the California Gold Rush*. U Oklahoma P, 1992. 95.

Hideyuki Oka. *How to Wrap Five Eggs: Traditional Japanese Packaging*. NY: Weatherhill, 1975.

Margaret Sidney. *The Five Little Peppers and How They Grew*. 1881.

Johanna Spyri. *Heidi*. 1880.

Dr. Suess. *Green Eggs and Ham*. NY: Random, 1960.

J. R. R. Tolkien. *The Hobbit*. 1937. *The Lord of the Rings*. 1954-55.

Jade Snow Wong. *Fifth Chinese Daughter*. NY: Harper Collins, 1950.

Chapter Seven: Working Girls

All in the Family. TV series on CBS. 1971-1979.

Charlotte Brontë. *Jane Eyre*. 1847. *Villette*. 1853.

Charlotte Brontë. Letter to Emily Brontë. 1 December 1843. Elizabeth Gaskell. *The Life of Charlotte Brontë*. Volume 1, Chapter 13. London: Smith, Elder, 1896. 204-205.

Charlotte Brontë. Deathbed note to Ellen Nussey. Elizabeth Gaskell. *The Life of Charlotte Brontë*. Volume 2, Chapter 13. London: Smith, Elder, 1896. 265.

Emily Brontë. *Wuthering Heights*. 1847.

Daniel Defoe. *Robinson Crusoe*. 1719.

Daphne du Maurier. (1907-1989). British author of 15 novels from 1931 to 1973.

Thomas Hardy. (1840-1928). British author of 18 novels, published 1867 to 1881.

Victoria Holt. (1906-1993). Pen name of British novelist Eleanor Hibbert, author of approx. 200 pseudonymous Gothic romances published from 1948 to 1993.

"Mean to Me." Roy Turk, music. Fred E. Ahlert, lyrics. Sung by Ruth Etting. NY: Columbia Records, 1929.

"Nothing Does-Does Like It Used to Do, Do, Do." Vic Berton and the Redheads. Circa 1920.

Rowan & Martin's Laugh-In. TV series on NBC. 1968-1973.

Chapter Eight: Food Fantasies

Rachel Baron. "The Stomach Ache." *Childcraft: The How and Why Library.* Volume 13: People to Know. Chicago: Field Enterprises, 1965. 170-177.

Daniel Defoe. *Robinson Crusoe.* 1719.

Dr. Suess. *Green Eggs and Ham.* 1960.

Jacob and Wilhelm Grimm. "Hansel and Gretel," "Red Ridinghood," and "The Two Brothers." *Household Tales.* 1812.

H. A. Rey. *Curious George.* 1941.

Irma S. Rombauer and Marion Rombauer Becker. *The Joy of Cooking.* Indianapolis: Bobbs-Merrill, 1964. 380.

Maurice Sendak. *Chicken Soup with Rice. The Nutshell Library.* 1962. *Where the Wild Things Are.* 1963.

Johanna Spyri. *Heidi.* 1880. Trans. Charles Tritten.

Margaret Sidney. *The Five Little Peppers and How They Grew.* 1881.

Chapter Nine: In Which I Consider Zeal, Restraint, Sandwiches, and What It Means to Be Holy

The Bible: Genesis 22 (Abraham's sacrifice of Isaac), Genesis 38 (Onan spilling his seed), Judges 3 (Ehud plunging the knife), and Judges 4-5 (Jael killing Sisera).

William Peter Blatty. *The Exorcist.* 1971.

Evarestus. "The Martyrdom of Saint Polycarp, Bishop of Smyrna, as Told in the Letter of the Church of Smyrna to the Church of Philomelium." Early Christian Fathers. Cyril C. Richardson, ed. Philadelphia: Westminster, 1953.

The Golden Children's Bible. NY: Golden, 1965.

The New American Bible. United States Conference of Catholic Bishops. 1970.

Fulton Oursler. *The Greatest Story Ever Told.* 1949

The Sailor Who Fell from Grace with the Sea. Dir. Lewis John Carlino. Performers Sarah Miles and Kris Kristofferson. AVCO Embassy Pictures, 1976.

John Gilmary Shea. *Little Pictorial Lives of Saints.* 1878.

Teresa of Avila. *The Life of St. Teresa of Avila.* Circa 1567.

David Wilkerson. *The Cross and the Switchblade.* 1963.

Chapter Ten: The Abalone Story
William Shakespeare. *The Tempest*. Circa 1611.

Chapter Eleven: Salmagundi
The Bible: Revelation 21:5 (making everything new).

Chapter Twelve: The Summer Before the Jubilee
"Hadrian." *World Book Encyclopedia*. 1958.

Chapter Thirteen: Hand Cheese
Theodor Fontana. *Effi Briest*. 1895.

Chapter Fourteen: Bitter Sweet
Brian Wansink and Cynthia Sangerman. "The Taste of Comfort: Food for
    Thought on How Americans Eat to Feel Better." *American Demographics*.
    Ithaca: Jul 2000. Vol. 22, Issue 7.

**Chapter Fifteen: Shame, Part 1: "Whatever You Do, Don't Become a
Dishwasher."**
The Bible: Hebrews 11:13-16 (believers are aliens in this world).

Scott MacLeod. "A Jihadist's Tale." *Time* (4 April 2005, p. 38–9).

Julie Sahni. *Classic Indian Cooking*. NY: William Morrow, 1980.

Chapter Sixteen: Shame, Part 2: Abfallfresser
Jacob and Wilhelm Grimm. "Cinderella" and "The Robber Bridegroom."
    Household Tales. 1812. Margaret Hunt, trans. 1884.

Robert Herrick. "Her Legs." *Hesperides*. 1648.

Chapter Seventeen: The Hunger Voyages
Pearl S. Buck. *The Good Earth*. 1931.

Charles Dickens. *A Christmas Carol*. 1843.

In Memory's Kitchen: A Legacy from the Women of Terezin. Ed. Cara de Silva.
    trans. by Bianca Steiner Brown. NY: Jason Aronson, 1996.

Chapter Eighteen: The Oven

Buwei Yang Chao. *How to Cook and Eat in Chinese.* 1945.

Marion Cunningham, ed. *The Fannie Farmer Cookbook.* 12th edition. Knopf: NY, 1979.

"Fitcher's Bird." Jacob and Wilhelm Grimm. *Household Tales.* 1812. Trans. Margaret Hunt. 1884.

Chapter Nineteen: Rice

Edward Madigan. Letter to Motoji Kondo. Quoted here from "Japan Chided for Threat." *New York Times.* 26 March 1991.

Chapter Twenty: Country Cooking

Blanche Caldwell Barrow and John Neal Phillips. *My Life With Bonnie & Clyde.* University of Oklahoma Press, 2004. 40–41.

William Faulkner. *Light in August.* 1932.

Good Old Days. Berne Indiana: House of White Birches. 1964-present.

Reminisce. Greendale, Wisconsin: Reiman Publications. 1991-present.

John Steinbeck. *The Grapes of Wrath.* 1939.

Chapter Twenty-one: The Turkey

Brillat-Savarin. *Physiologie du Goût, ou Méditations de Gastronomie Transcendante; Ouvrage Théorique, Historique et à l'Ordre du Jour, Dédié aux Gastronomes Parisiens, par un Professeur, Membre de Plusieurs Sociétés Littéraires et Savantes.* 1825. *The Physiology of Taste: Or, Meditations on Transcendental Gastronomy.* M. F. K. Fisher, trans. 1949.

Chapter Twenty-two: Wild Fruit

The Bible: Genesis 1 (creation overview), Genesis 1:25-27 (humans made in God's image), and Romans 1:20 (creation is evidence of God).

Tracy Balzer. *Thin Places: An Evangelical Journey into Celtic Christianity.* Leafwood: Abilene, 2007.

Chapter Twenty-three: Lost Recipes

The Bible: Psalm 139 (God formed us in the womb).

Nikolai Gogol. *Lost Souls*. 1842. David Magarshack translation. London: Penguin, 1961. 311.

Johanna Spyri. *Heidi*. 1880. Trans. Charles Tritten.

Wolfgang Müller, Henry Fricke, Alex N. Halliday, Malcolm T. McCulloch, and Jo-Anne Wartho. "Origin and Migration of the Alpine Iceman." *Science* Vol. 302, Issue 5646, 10/31/2003.

Margaret Sidney. *The Five Little Peppers and How They Grew*. 1881.

Irma S. Rombauer and Marion Rombauer Becker. *The Joy of Cooking*. Indianapolis: Bobbs-Merrill, 1953.

Chapter Twenty-four: Thou Mayst Freely Eat

Apollo 13. Directed by Ron Howard. 1995.

The Bible: Genesis 1 and 2 (God's provision of food), Luke 24:36-40 (Jesus asks for broiled fish after his resurrection), and Revelation 3:20 (Jesus at the door inviting us to dinner).

William Faulkner. *Light in August*. 1932.

Don Pettit. Expedition Six. Space Chronicles. 14 May 2003. NASA Johnson Space Center. <http://spaceflight.nasa.gov/station/crew/exp6/spacechronicles1>.

"Space Food." National Aeronautics and Space Administration videos. <http://spaceflight.nasa.gov/living/spacefood/index>.

Acknowledgments

Recently I made the acquaintance of my daughter Charlotte's fifteen-year-old friend, Nicole Reardon, who, in her culinary aptitude and enthusiasm, reminded me of myself at her age. She spent a week and a half at our house and never stopped cooking the whole time. Her mother is Irish, and one morning, out of that influence, Nicole cooked up an Ulster fry for us. Now she and I are exchanging recipes and cooking experiences via email. Through her cooking stories—of Ireland, of the little marinated and grilled sausages that her family was enjoying (and she was missing out on) to celebrate the visit of an uncle in her absence, of the banana bread and other delights she is perpetually making from her Delia Smith cookbooks—she expanded my culinary excitement to include her parents, whom I barely know; her friends, whom I've never met; her relatives, in a country I've never visited; and a British writer of cookbooks, whose opus was previously unknown to me. That's how it is with cooking. Every new dish enlarges not merely one's cooking repertoire but one's connection to humanity at large.

I wish I could list here all the relatives, friends, friends and relatives of friends, and even strangers who have influenced, through our shared experience of God's provision of life and love and good food, how I think and who I am. I can't. Suffice it to say I value them all. A few are acknowledged by inclusion—often pseudonymously—in the stories I tell here, others in the recipes. Many more are not featured prominently or at all in the book. Of the countless fellow cooks—some included, others left out—who highlight important moments of awakening I have experienced in the kitchen, the following come immediately to mind: my father, my mother-in-law, Jeanette Anderson, Ali Arant, Geoff Bellah, Johanna

265

Bomster, Carla Boyer, Mark Harris, Chen Kaige, Jacques Meunier, Monaray Noah, Ines Ragghianti, Susanne Röh, Valerie Sattler-Kuboth, Liping Tan-Blume, Susanne Teichmann, Mario and Gail Vaz, Susan Vila, and Donald West.

About the Author

Patty Kirk is the author of a spiritual memoir entitled *Confessions of an Amateur Believer* (Thomas Nelson 2007). She is Writer in Residence and an associate professor of English at John Brown University in Siloam Springs, Arkansas. She and her family live on a farm in eastern Oklahoma.

For additional information about Patty Kirk and her books, go to www.amateurbeliever.com.

Index of Recipes